The Freedom Writers Diary

The Freedom Writers Diary

How a Teacher and 150 Teens Used Writing to Change Themselves and the World Around Them

The Freedom Writers with Erin Gruwell

Foreword by Zlata Filipovic

Main Street Books · Doubleday

New York · London · Toronto · Sydney · Auckland

A MAIN STREET BOOK
PUBLISHED BY DOUBLEDAY
a division of Random House, Inc.
1540 Broadway, New York, New York 10036

MAIN STREET BOOKS, DOUBLEDAY, and the portrayal of a building with a tree
are trademarks of Doubleday, a division of Random House, Inc.

Library of Congress Cataloging-in-Publication Data

Freedom Writers.
The Freedom Writers diary: how a teacher and 150 teens used writing to
change themselves and the world around them / the Freedom Writers with
Erin Gruwell. — 1st ed.
p.   cm.
1. Teenagers—United States Diaries.   2. Toleration—United States.
I. Gruwell, Erin.

HQ796.F76355   1999
305.235—dc21   99-30342
CIP

ISBN 0-385-49422-x

10 9 8 7 6 5 4 3 2 1

To our incredible teacher Ms. Gruwell,
  Who taught us to believe in ourselves

To Anne Frank,
  Who inspired us to write

To Zlata, our friend,
  Who passed us the torch

To our beloved Miep,
  Who recognized the hero in each of us

To the Freedom Riders,
  Who paved the way

And,
To kids everywhere,
  Whose lives were lost to senseless violence but whose spirits
  live on.

Contents

Foreword

Zlata Filipovic

When I was asked to write the foreword to *The Freedom Writers Diary*, I must say I was extremely honored and proud, but at the same time amazed by how many wonderful things can happen in such a short time.

I met the students of Wilson High School in March 1996, when thanks to their dedication, effort and will, they invited my parents, Mirna (my best friend from Bosnia, who was living with me at the time) and myself to come to the city of Long Beach, California. When I met them, I was touched by their warmth and kindness. They were teenagers just like me, and like all young people all over the world, they have an amazing potential to grow into truly great people, leaders, ones who will inspire others.

These students and their teacher, Erin Gruwell, chose to read *Anne Frank: The Diary of a Young Girl*, my own book, *Zlata's Diary: A Child's Life in Sarajevo* (and many other books), and were inspired to start writing their own diaries. They had organized themselves and chose to do something different, something memorable, something powerful and humane. They chose to rid themselves of doing things the easy way, the way they've always been done, and chose to write, to create, to fight stereotypes and live up to the name of true Freedom Writers. I am immensely proud and happy to have had a chance to meet them and to play some role in their "growth" as human beings.

I started writing my own diary before the war in Bosnia because I wanted to have a place to record my childhood and create something that I could look back on and laugh, cry and reminisce. I wanted to see myself grow through my writing. Some of my older girlfriends had their own diaries, and having read the diaries of Anne Frank and Adrian Mole, I was absolutely certain that writing a diary was the right thing to do. I never imagined that my diary would be published, and certainly didn't expect it to become a war diary. I also never dreamed that my childhood would be cut short. These things seemed too impossible to think about, because it's human nature to always believe that "bad" things happen to other people, not us. But when misfortune comes our way, we find ourselves surprised, confused, scared, angry and sad.

When the Bosnian war started with all its horrors and disrupted my happy and carefree childhood, my diary became more than a place to record daily events. It became a friend, the paper that it was made of was ready and willing to accept anything and everything I had to say; it could handle my fear, my questions, my sadness. I discovered the beauty of writing—when one can pour oneself onto a great white emptiness and fill it with emotions and thoughts and leave them there forever. And I kept on writing during almost two years of war; it became a type of therapy for dealing with everything that was going on.

I see a parallel between the Freedom Writers and myself because we've all been subjected to things in our surroundings that could have made us feel like victims. Life brings good things and bad things, it makes people sad and happy in their own homes, within their families, in school and on the street. Sometimes we suffer because of many things over which we have no control: the color of our skin, poverty, our religion, our family situation, war. It would be easy to become a victim of our circumstances and continue feeling sad, scared or angry; or instead, we could choose to deal with injustice humanely and break the chains of negative thoughts and energies, and not let ourselves sink into it. Writing about the things that happen to us allows us to look objectively at what's going on around us and turn a negative experience into something positive and useful. This process requires a lot of work, effort and greatness, but it is possible, and the Freedom Writers have proved it—they've chosen a difficult, but powerful, path.

After I left Bosnia, the war continued, and as we've recently seen, a similar thing happened in Kosovo. People have asked me what I think about this, and all I can say is that it makes me terribly sad. Now, almost all of the young former Yugoslavians know what a bomb sounds like, what a cellar is and what the absence of water, electricity or home feels like. And again, these children and young people had nothing to do with the situation they found themselves in. I just hope that the anger, hate and sadness they have experienced will not remain inside them, and that they will be able to rise above their experiences. Because if they grow up holding on to such terrible feelings, it could lead to another war sometime in the future when the fate of the country is in their hands. This is why I believe that everything the Freedom Writers have overcome and accomplished is very important and must be respected. If they had chosen to stay encapsulated in the anger and hate that surrounded them in their neighborhoods, the seeds of hatred and fear would have grown with them and history would repeat itself with their children in the future. The Freedom Writers chose to break this cycle and make their positive experiences a lesson for generations to come.

And, of course, I will always very highly respect and admire the Freedom Writers' mentor, their friend and teacher, Erin Gruwell, who is also my friend. She never wants to be congratulated or held responsible for the great things that came out of Room 203 at Wilson High School, but she must be. She was (and still is) much more than a teacher to the Freedom Writers. She was a parent to those who did not have, or could not communicate with, their own; she was an older friend who was fun to be around; but she was also very loyal, someone who cared and fought for each one of her "kids." She shared her education, tenacity and love with them and made a huge difference in her students' lives. They could have remained the "underachievers" they'd been labeled before they arrived in her classroom. But in just several years, she made a tremendous difference and created a safe place for them to grow and blossom into amazing people. She made authors and, I dare say, historical figures out of them. Many teachers consider their after-school time to be precious, but Erin gave herself over to her work. She was dedicated to helping her students learn, opening their eyes to injustice and guiding them to the weapons (in this case a pen, knowledge, a measure of faith, and an unyielding determination) with which to fight intolerance. Finally, she taught them how to assume their rightful place in the world. I know her students will remember her the rest of their lives, as well they should. I wish that teachers everywhere were like her—because the world would be a much better place. I always say that the young people are the future of the world, and if we start with them first, if we educate and develop a sense of tolerance among them, our future, the future of this world, will be in good hands for generations to come.

How many good things can come out of a bad situation? I'm a perfect example. I was a small happy Sarajevan girl whose country was struck by war. Suddenly I was put in the position of having some say and possible influence in the world. I did not want that responsibility, and I wish that my diary had never been published; if not for the war, there would have been no reason to share it with the world. But nonetheless, some good has come out of it.

Anne Frank's diary inspired the world, and good has come out of her tragedy. Her strength kept her going for as long as it could, and subsequently has been recognized by millions of people, young and old. The greatness of those who are no longer with us fortunately remains to lead and inspire those left behind.

My diary partially inspired the Freedom Writers and maybe some other people to start writing their own diaries, and do something about the situations they found themselves in. I have heard people say that it is not what happens to us that matters, but how we deal with it—and the Freedom Writers are a perfect example. They could have chosen to fight racism with racism, hate with hate, pain with pain. But they did not. If we all do what the Freedom Writers have done, and choose to deal with inhumane situations in a humane way, we can turn the world around and create positive lessons for ourselves and for others.

Unfortunately, I have realized that we cannot completely erase all the evil from the world, but we can change the way we deal with it, we can rise above it and stay strong and true to ourselves. And most important, we can inspire others—this is what makes us human beings, this is what can make us immortal. I hope this book will inspire people to write their own diaries, stories, poems, books, to fight prejudice and to choose to deal with what happens to them in a positive way, to learn new lessons and share them with other people. This is for you, the reader, to consider, and I wish you good luck.

Dublin, July 1999

The Freedom Writers Diary

Freshman Year
Fall 1994

Entry 1 · Ms. Gruwell

Dear Diary,

Tomorrow morning, my journey as an English teacher officially begins. Since first impressions are so important, I wonder what my students will think about me. Will they think I'm out of touch or too preppy? Or worse yet, that I'm too young to be taken seriously? Maybe I'll have them write a journal entry describing what their expectations are of me and the class.

Even though I spent last year as a student teacher at Wilson High School, I'm still learning my way around the city. Long Beach is so different than the gated community I grew up in. Thanks to MTV dubbing Long Beach as the "gangsta-rap capital" with its depiction of guns and graffiti, my friends have a warped perception of the city, or L B C as the rappers refer to it. They think I should wear a bulletproof vest rather than pearls. Where I live in Newport Beach is a utopia compared to some of neighborhoods seen in a Snoop Doggy Dogg video. Still, TV tends to blow things out of proportion.

The school is actually located in a safe neighborhood, just a few miles from the ocean. Its location and reputation make it desirable. So much so that a lot of the students that live in what they call the "'hood" take two or three buses just to get to school every day. Students come in from every corner of the city: Rich kids from the shore sit next to poor kids from the projects . . . there's every race, religion, and culture within the confines of the quad. But since the Rodney King riots, racial tension has spilled over into the school.

Due to busing and an outbreak in gang activity, Wilson's traditional white, upper-class demographics have changed radically. African Americans, Latinos, and Asians now make up the majority of the student body.

As a student teacher last year, I was pretty naïve. I wanted to see past color and culture, but I was immediately confronted by it when the first bell rang and a student named Sharaud sauntered in bouncing a basketball. He was a junior, a disciplinary transfer from Wilson's crosstown rival, and his reputation preceded him. Word was that he had threatened his previous English teacher with a gun (which I later found out was only a plastic water gun, but it had all the makings of a dramatic showdown). In those first few minutes, he made it brutally clear that he hated Wilson, he hated English, and he hated me. His sole purpose was to make his "preppy" student teacher cry. Little did he know that within a month, he'd be the one crying.

Sharaud became the butt of a bad joke. A classmate got tired of Sharaud's antics and drew a racial caricature of him with huge, exaggerated lips. As the drawing made its way around the class, the other students laughed hysterically. When Sharaud saw it, he looked as if he was going to cry. For the first time, his tough façade began to crack.

When I got a hold of the picture, I went ballistic. "This is the type of propaganda that the Nazis used during the Holocaust," I yelled. When a student timidly asked me, "What's the Holocaust?" I was shocked.

I asked, "How many of you have heard of the Holocaust?" Not a single person raised his hand. Then I asked, "How many of you have been shot at?" Nearly every hand went up.

I immediately decided to throw out my meticulously planned lessons and make tolerance the core of my curriculum.

From that moment on, I would try to bring history to life by using new books, inviting guest speakers, and going on field trips. Since I was just a student teacher, I had no budget for my schemes. So, I moonlighted as a concierge at the Marriott Hotel and sold lingerie at Nordstrom. My dad even asked me, "Why can't you just be a normal teacher?"

Actually, normalcy didn't seem so bad after my first snafu. I took my students to see *Schindler's List* in Newport Beach, at a predominately white, upper-class theater. I was shocked to see women grab their pearls and clutch their purses in fear. A local paper ran a front-page article about the incident, describing how poorly my students were treated, after which I received death threats. One of my disgruntled neighbors had the audacity to say, "If you love black people so much, why don't you just marry a monkey?"

All this drama and I didn't even have my teaching credentials yet. Luckily, some of my professors from University of California–Irvine read the article and invited my class to a seminar by the author of *Schindler's List*, Thomas Keneally. Keneally was so impressed by my students that a few days later we got an invitation to meet Steven Spielberg at Universal Studios. I couldn't believe it! The famous director wanted to meet the class that I had dubbed "as colorful as a box of Crayola crayons" and their "rookie teacher who was causing waves." He marveled at how far these "unteachable" students had come as a junior class and what a close group they had become. He even asked Sharaud what "we" were planning to do next year as an encore. After all, if a film does well, you make a sequel—if a class surpasses everyone's expectations, you . . .

. . . dismantle it! Yep, that's exactly what happened. Upon my return from Universal, the head of the English department told me, "You're making us look bad." Talk about bursting my bubble! How was I making them look bad? After all, these were the same kids that "wouldn't last a month" or "were too stupid" to read advanced placement books.

She went on to say, "Things are based on seniority around here." So, in other words, I was lucky to have a job, and keeping Sharaud and his posse another year would be pushing the envelope. Instead, I'd be teaching freshmen—"at risk" freshmen. Hmm . . . not exactly the assignment I was hoping for.

So, starting tomorrow, it's back to the drawing board. But I'm convinced that if Sharaud could change, then anyone can. So basically, I should prepare myself for a roomful of Sharauds. If it took a month to win Sharaud over . . . I wonder how long it's gonna take a bunch of feisty fourteen-year-olds to come around?

FREEDOM WRITERS' NOTE
Each teenager played an integral role in developing the diary entries—reading, editing, and encouraging one another. To protect their anonymity and illustrate the universality of their experiences, we decided to number each diary entry rather than attach a name.

The students have shared their life experiences freely, without inhibition.

Diary 1

Dear Diary,

I always thought that "odd" was a three-letter word; but today I found out it has seven, and they spell G-r-u-w-e-l-l. My freshman English teacher is way out there. I wonder how she got this job. The administrators should have known better than to give her this class, but I guess she didn't know any better than to take it. How is *she* going to handle four classes full of this school's rejects? Most people at this school doubt that we can even read or write.

She probably drives a new car, lives in a three-story house, and owns like five hundred pairs of shoes. It seems to me that she belongs across the hall with the Distinguished Scholars. Yeah, she would fit in nicely there; she and those supposedly gifted white kids who think they're better than everybody else. She walked in here on "I'm sweet and I care about you" mode. It's not going to work. We all know she's going to treat us like everyone else has. The worst part is, I'm pretty sure she thinks she's the one who's going to change us. She alone, the "too young and too white to be working here" teacher is going to reform a group of helpless "sure to drop out" kids from the 'hood.

I can't deny the fact that this class does seem like a bad rerun of *Cops*, though, and she has the records to prove it. She'll probably sit us in alphabetical order to try to stop any fights. Right now she's probably deciding who she's going to transfer out. To her, I'm sure we're the "below average" kids no one told her about when she was getting her credentials. I have to admit, though, some of these fools need an attitude adjustment.

Most of these niggas come strapped and ready to bust a cap. It's not like they can't get away with it, with their big-ass pants; they could fit me and six of my friends. They could hide a bazooka and no one would notice.

I don't even think everyone in this class is supposed to be in here, because there's a white boy in the corner looking down at his schedule, hoping that he's in the wrong room. For his entire life he's always been part of the majority, but as soon as he stepped into this room, he became the minority. Being white in this class is not going to give him the same status that he gets in society. In here, he gets stared down by most of us, and the other people just think that's he's either stupid or must have ditched the day he was supposed to take the assessment test.

Then, there are the other ones, like me, who are in the middle. Not a bad-ass, but definitely not wearing a pocket protector. I wonder how I ended up in this class. I'm not a disciplinary transfer, and even though English is not my first language, I know I don't belong here.

I can already see it: We're going to be stuck with some fat-ass, second-grade English book that will put us to sleep before we can even flip a page. With this class, though, she's probably going to have a fatter stack of referrals. I wonder how long she's going to put up with these punks; even I want to get out of this classroom. I'm sure one of these days she's going to go to principal and ask for her leave, but then again, what else is new?

"These kids are going to make this lady quit the first week," my friends were saying. Someone else said, "She'll only last a day."

I give her a month.

Diary 2

Dear Diary,

What the hell am I doing in *here*? I'm the only white person in this English class! I'm sitting in the corner of this classroom (if that's what you want to call this chaos), looking at my schedule and thinking, "Is this really where I'm supposed to be?" Okay, I know in high school I'm supposed to meet all kinds of different people, but this isn't exactly what I had in mind. Just my luck, I'm stuck in a classroom full of troubled kids who are bused in from bad neighborhoods. I feel really uncomfortable in here with all these rejects. There aren't even enough seats. My teacher, Ms. Gruwell, is young and determined, but this class is out of control and I bet she won't last very long.

This school is just asking for trouble when they put all these kids in the same class. It's a disaster waiting to happen.

I had lunch before class in the high school quad and noticed that, like everywhere else, it was really separated by race. Each race has its own section and nobody mixes. Everyone, including me, eats lunch with their own kind, and that's that. There is a section known as "Beverly Hills" or "Disneyland" where all of the rich white kids hang out. Then there's "China Town" where the Asians hang. The Hispanic section is referred to as either "Tijuana Town" or "Run to the Border." The Black section is known as "Da Ghetto." Then there's the freak show in the middle of the quad that's reserved for the druggies, also called "Tweakers," and the kids who are into the Goth scene. From what's going on around me, it's obvious that the divisions in the quad carry into the classroom.

All my friends are across the hall in the Distinguished Scholars class. It's almost all white. The only people I'd have to worry about in that class are the really cool and popular people who

think that they're better than everyone else is. Other than that, I'd be safe with my own kind. In here, I already know it's going to be survival of the fittest. I'm just waiting to get jumped.

As soon as possible, I need to get out of this class and into the class across the hall with my friends. Right after the bell rings, I'm going to talk to my counselor and make her move me out of here. I'll lie and insist that there's been a computer error and that I am supposed to be in the Distinguished Scholars class, even though I suck in English and have a learning disability. I know she'll believe me 'cause I'm white.

I can't believe all this noise. I just want out of here. I hope the bell rings soon. I don't want to spend another minute in this room. If I stay in here, one of two things will happen: I'll get jacked or I'll die of boredom.

Diary 3

Dear Diary,

"Fuck!" was the first word that came to mind when I saw those stupid motherfuckers coming toward me today after school. I knew I was going to get my ass kicked because there were three guys and two girls against me. I wasn't afraid or anything. Its not like it was the first time, and I know it sure as hell won't be the last. But why today? It's the first day of school and I don't feel like dealing with this shit!

I knew I didn't wanna come to this school. My probation officer thinks he's slick; he swears he's an expert on gangs. That dumb-ass actually thinks that the problems going on in Long Beach aren't going to affect me at Wilson. If it was up to me, I wouldn't even be in school, but he threatened me, telling me that it was either Wilson or boot camp. I figure it's less painful to go back to school.

My P.O. hasn't realized yet that schools are just like the city and the city is just like prison. All of them are divided into separate sections, depending on race. On the streets, you kick it in different 'hoods, depending on your race, or where you're from. And at school, we separate ourselves from people who are different from us. That's just the way it is, and we all respect that. So when the Asians started trying to claim parts of the 'hood, we had to set them straight. We had to let them know who the true OGs (Original Gangsters) were. We're the real O.G.'s And like I said before, everything penetrates through. Soon enough you have little wanna-bes trying to hit you up at school, demanding respect they haven't even earned.

That's why they got pissed when they hit me up, 'cause I refused to bow down to them. I looked at them up and down, laughed, paused, and then said, *"Mi barrio es primero."* As I stood in the middle of the quad, I thought of how much they looked like the people they hated. They dress just like us, they act just like us, and they want the territory we own. For that reason, I have no respect for them or the so-called barrio they're willing to die for. I don't even know why they tried to come up to me, asking me where I was from. Those fools should know what happens when we get hit up—we get pissed off and all hell breaks loose, and the consequences can be deadly.

Latinos killing Asians. Asians killing Latinos. They declared war on the wrong people. Now it all comes down to what you look like. If you look Asian or Latino, you're gonna get blasted on or at least jumped. The war has been declared, now it's a fight for power, money, and territory; we are killing each other over race, pride, and respect. They started the war in our Aztlán, a land that belongs to us by nature, and by nature we will bury them.

They might think they're winning by jumping me now, but soon enough, they're all going down!

Diary 4

Dear Diary,

Damn! It's the second week of school and I'm already getting busted up because of the people I hang with. A fight broke out today. I don't know how it started, it happened so quickly. Rumor has it that a little freshman got punked a couple of days ago and her gang was planning to retaliate. I heard people were even planning to bring bats to school with them. I was hanging out with a couple of friends when the fight broke out, and like every other kid on campus, I wanted to see it up close. I moved closer and closer until I got too close. Before I could move away, I felt a fist hit me straight in the face. What are you supposed to do when someone swings at you? Swing back.

After what seemed like hours (but I'm sure were only a few minutes), the fight continued to grow. By this point, my nose was bleeding, but other than a few bruises, I was OK, seeing as how I wasn't on the floor getting the shit beat out of me. Then I heard someone say, "Watch out!" Everything from that point on was in slow motion, like a low-budget kung-fu movie with bad voice-overs. A football helmet had nailed me and I blacked out. When I came to, everybody was shouting, "Run, run!" Run? Why? Then I saw half of the school staff running toward the scene of the fight. I wasn't about to stick around and get blamed for starting the fight, so I pulled myself up and ran.

It's kind of sad when you have to run away from something that isn't your fault. Since I'm Mexican and Mexicans were involved in this stupid race war, I figured no one would have listened to what I had to say anyway. I'm not a bad person, but because of my friends, I sometimes get blamed for shit I have nothing to do with.

I really don't know how I made it through the rest of the

schoolday; hell, I don't even know how I made it to my next class. I couldn't see straight, couldn't walk straight. All I know is that after the fight today, the shit's really gonna hit the fan on the streets of Long Beach.

Diary 5

Dear Diary,

For many, it's the start of a new day, but for me, it's the continuation of a nightmare. Every day before I leave my mom *me percina* with the sign of the cross, praying that I come home safely.

Going to school is less of a problem, 'cause that's when the city sleeps, but on my way home, it's a whole other story. I'm fourteen, and people think I should be scared because I'm surrounded by violence, but around here it's an everyday thing. The first thing I see when I get off the bus is graffiti on walls, beer bottles filling trashcans, empty cigarette packs, and syringes.

On the way home, I get chased mostly by older fools with bats and knives. I try going different ways, but they always notice me and chase me anyway. At first I didn't know the reason why they always hunt me down, but then I figured it out, it was simply because I was of a different race.

I figured I had to find a way to protect myself from these fools, and the only way was to get a gun. At school, some of my friends have been talking about a homie being strapped. I asked them where he got it from, and they told me that some guy sold it to him. With memories of my homies getting smoked and all my problems on the way home, I decided to get one. It's so damn easy to get a gun; it's like getting bubble gum from the corner liquor store. All you need is $25. All I had to do was ask my parents for money to buy school supplies. It was easy, 'cause in the 'hood, for the price of a backpack, you can get a gun, a couple of rounds, and probably even have some money left over. The next day, I met my friends in the bathroom and I bought a .22 caliber with a clip. I quickly stashed it into my backpack and left.

The whole day at school, I couldn't keep my mind off my new gun. I felt like a little boy with a shining new toy. When school was out, I began my journey home. As I got closer to my stop, I looked out the window and saw the guys were waiting for me. Then I thought to myself, "Damn, here we go again." I got nervous and my hands began to sweat. I opened my backpack, took the gun out, and put it in my waist, then I slowly walked to the back and waited for the door to open.

As I walked off the bus, they began to call me names. "What's up, *ése?*" "Wait up, fool." Fuck them niggas. I kept on walking. I checked out of the corner of my eye, and I saw that one of them was eager to catch up to me. Usually, I would have run, but this time I had a gun. I knew they were getting closer, so I turned around, reached for my gun, took it out, and pointed the gun at his head. Luckily, he ducked and ran, 'cause I didn't want to smoke him. The others were still after me, but once they saw I had a gun, they also ran. I put the gun back in my waist, and went home. No big deal, just another day in the 'hood.

The next afternoon, when I got off the bus, the guys weren't waiting for me. I didn't see them for the next few days. I didn't know if I had scared them off or not, but I hoped I had.

But my hopes were cut short, when one day, as I was walking home, I saw a guy mad-dogging me from across the street. We locked eyes, reached for our strap, pulled it out, and began shooting at the same time. The only thing between us was a major street and some parked cars. It was just like a movie, except in this movie when the characters bleed, the blood is *real*. I don't remember when I actually pulled the trigger; all I remember is shooting and waiting until I was sure the other guy was out of bullets. After the last shot rang through the air, he disappeared. We both ran, and have never met eye to eye again.

I'm not afraid of anyone anymore. Now I'm my own gang. I protect myself. I got my own back. I still carry my gun with me just in case I run into some trouble, and now I'm not afraid to use it. Running with gangs and carrying a gun can create some problems, but being of a different race can get you into trouble, too, so I figure I might as well be prepared. Lately, a lot of shit's been going down. All I know is that I'm not gonna be the next one to get killed.

Diary 6

Dear Diary,

A couple of days ago one of my friends was laid to rest.

His funeral was just like any other. Family members were crying. Someone said, "Not another one," while his friends were swearing that they would get revenge. "An eye for an eye . . . payback's a bitch."

There were not a lot of people at the funeral, but the friends and family who showed up were very proud of him. We're all going to miss him, but what could we have done to prevent his death? After he was lowered into the ground, our lives went on. His friends didn't talk about him anymore. It was as if he had never existed. When his birthday comes, presents will no longer be given to him. They will be replaced by flowers, which will be put on his grave. That's just the way it is.

I still remember exactly what happened the night my friend died. I was in the liquor store buying some candy. I was having trouble deciding what kind of candy I wanted. Then I heard gunshots. I turned to the door and saw that two of my friends were running into the store. When the first one came in, he dove to the floor; the other one simply fell. I looked down and saw that one of my friends had blood coming out of his back and mouth.

In a matter of minutes, his sister and mother ran into the

store. I stood in front of the candy rack and watched his sister drop to her knees and gather him into her arms. She was crying and calling out his name. His mother stood behind her, watching with her eyes wide open with shock. Tears were rolling down her cheeks, but she didn't bother to wipe them off. She stood there and didn't make a sound. It was as if she was paralyzed with pain. It broke my heart to see his mother standing there, unable to help her baby.

After the last police car left, the people in my neighborhood were still standing against the yellow police tape, staring at the trace of white chalk. Nobody moved, but everyone was talking about "the young boy," who had been taken away by the paramedics, but there was a lot they didn't know. They didn't know that he was my friend and that he had his whole life ahead of him. He was gunned down for being in the wrong place at the wrong time. I didn't pay attention to what they were saying. I just stood there, looking at my friend's blood on the floor. He had never harmed anyone in his entire life. What were his parents going to do? What was *I* going to do?

It was late and I had to go to school the next day. I wasn't sure how the neighborhood was going to handle the death of a kid who was raised in front of everyone's eyes. I know that that night many of my neighbors, like me, went to sleep, thinking, "Another one . . ." Knowing that it would happen again, probably another drive-by, but when? Anytime, it could happen to me, it happens to everyone.

The next day, I pulled up my shirt and got strapped with a gun that I found in an alley by my house. I hate the cold feeling of the metal next to my body. It makes me shiver, and the shivers remind me of all the lives this gun has claimed, but sometimes it's the only way. I hurried to catch the bus, hoping the gun wouldn't fall out of my waist. I didn't worry about getting caught with the gun, because the only time the school's staff searched the students was the day after the race riot. Now the staff only check every fifteenth student. All I had to do was pay attention and wait for the right time.

At school, I didn't say anything to anyone. I heard people talking about the shooting, but they didn't know the person who had been blasted. They didn't know the whole story. I walked into class just in time to beat the tardy bell. I went straight to my chair and sat down. I couldn't stop reliving the nightmare of my friend's death. I went through the rest of the day just sitting, not saying a word. I didn't even write down my homework. I kept closing my eyes, and I would see his face. I know he is watching me from wherever he is. And when it's my time to go, I know I'll see him when I get there. All I have to do is wait.

My friend shouldn't have died that night. He should still be here having fun and enjoying life with the rest of us. He's not the first nor will he be the last friend that I lose. I've lost many friends, friends who have died in an undeclared war. A war that has been here for years, but has never been recognized. A war between color and race. A war that will never end. A war that has left family and friends crying for loved ones who have perished. To society, they're just another dead person on the street corner; just another statistic. But to the mothers of all those other statistics, they're more than simple numbers. They represent more lives cut short, more cut flowers. Like the ones once placed on their graves.

Diary 7

Dear Diary,

Once again, flowers on another grave and cigarettes to another friend. These days, with so many of my soldiers either dying or going to prison, it looks like we're gonna have to start recruiting. We have to be real picky, though. The people have to be down, they have to be willing to take a bullet or pull the trigger, but it's worth it. Life is easily given up to protect and respect the homies and the barrio we claim . . . the same barrio that we were born in, raised in, and hopefully, will be buried in. After we put *los tres puntos* on your wrist, it becomes survival of the fittest, kill or be killed. No wonder they call it *mi vida loca*. It's true, it is a crazy-ass life. Once you're in, there's no getting out. Sometimes I wonder if they know what they're getting into.

Every time I jump somebody in and make someone a part of our gang, it's another baptism: They give us their life and we give them a new one. All they have to do is prove they're down. It doesn't matter if you're a guy or a girl, you get your ass kicked, you can't show weakness, and you gotta pass either way. And we don't give a damn if you end up in hospital, 'cause as soon as you come out, you're considered a working soldier.

I remember when I got jumped in and became a member of the gang; I was in the hospital for over three weeks. I only had a broken arm and a broken leg, even though I could've sworn everything was busted. I had scratches and bruises all over my body. My eyes were so swollen, I couldn't even open them all the way, but it was worth it. To the soldiers and me it's all worth it. Risking life, dodging or taking bullets, and pulling triggers.

It's *all* worth it.

Diary 8

Dear Diary,

I told my friends I was going to pledge a sorority because it "looked like fun." I told my mom I was doing it because it was a "community service" sorority, but I don't think she bought it. I tried to justify it to myself by saying that it was only because my friends were pledging, and I didn't really care that much about the stupid club. However, I soon realized I was denying the obvious. I wanted to fit in just like every other high school freshman. Who wouldn't want to be in a prime club like Kappa Zeta? It's a predominantly white sorority, made up of mostly cheerleaders, rich kids, and the occasional Distinguished Scholar. All of the Kappa Zeta girls dress like they just stepped out of a Gap ad, their nails are perfectly manicured, their hair perfectly curled under at the tips. All of the upper classmen in Kappa Zeta are so elite that when they ask someone to do something, they do it. Even if it means doing something extremely degrading. So, when I received a flyer to attend a Kappa Zeta pledge meeting, I went without hesitation.

At first, pledging was really fun. All of the members were really friendly, and they gave us gifts and sweatshirts with the sorority symbol on it, like they were trying to lure us in. But after the novelty wore off, things started getting hard. The members held a traditional interview called "Questioning." They'd take us into a room in twos and ask the most embarrassing questions imaginable. As my partner, Sarah, and I waited to go in, we saw previous couples come out crying. We soon found out why. Fortunately, I am practically sinless. Everybody knows that I'm the girl who's really shy and practically faints at the *sight* of a boy. So when the members started asking about our sexual experiences, I had nothing shameful to say. But Sarah's boyfriend is a senior, and all of the members knew the kind of things the "senior men" did with freshman girls. The second they brought up Josh, Sarah started crying . . . bawling, because she knew what they were going to ask her. You'd think the members would have tried to comfort her, or at least stopped asking about him, but they just ignored her tears. I guess the point of questioning is to see how strong (or weak) the pledges were, so they just kept probing her with personal questions and rude comments. They couldn't have cared less that they were really hurting her. They had even prepared a baseball cap with "slut" painted on the front, that the girls who had boyfriends had to wear at school. After "Questioning" a lot of the pledges dropped out, including Sarah. They blamed it on their parents or the club being stupid. Maybe it was, but after Sarah quit, things were different. We weren't really friends with her anymore. It wasn't intentional. I guess it was just because we were all going to be in Kappa Zeta, and she wasn't.

The rest of the pledges and myself thought the worst was over. Little did we know the worst was yet to come. Pledge night was the scariest part because the guys got involved. Technically, they weren't allowed to tell us what to do, but they did anyway. We had to listen. If we didn't, it meant dismissal from pledging. I was really scared to go to one particular pledge night, because they told us to wear clothes that could get messed up. That night we met at the fountain in the park at eight o'clock. As soon as everyone arrived they made us lie down on the ground and "sizzle like bacon." I thought, "I can live with this, it might even be fun." I was perfectly content with sizzling like bacon, but as I looked to the right I could see my friend Shannon. I presumed she must have been given specific instructions because while we sizzled, she kneeled in front of David O'Neal, a popular junior boy. I couldn't make out exactly what was happening, but he was holding something in front of him that looked like a bottle, and I think she was crying. Then her head started moving back and forth, and as a crowd of rowdy boys gathered around them she started to cry really hard and they started yelling at her. Just as I started to go help her I was pushed back to the ground as a voice screamed, "Where do you think you're going, whore? Did I say you could get up?" It was one of the members. I realized then that it was going to be a long night. I hoped I wouldn't have to pretend to do something to a boy, like Shannon.

When I came home that night my mother almost cried when she saw me. I reeked of beer that had been poured on me multiple times. The combination of beer and the raw eggs smashed on

my head were a putrid mixture. There was a retched taste in my
mouth from food coloring the members used to make us remember their names, and my clothes and face were stained green.
They made us run a mile from the park to the beach, so I was covered in sand and still gasping for air. Then I started to cry. Not because of the smell or my stained clothes, but because there was no
way out. I had gone through so much already that it would have
been pointless to quit now. Besides, I didn't want to end up with
no friends, like Sarah. I reminded myself that soon it would be
over, and that I wasn't even treated as badly as some girls. I heard
that one girl had to lie on the ground as Matt Thompson, a senior
I used to think was cute, peed on her.

Now that I've been initiated, and I'm officially *in*, my only
concern is parties and stuff. All of the older girls drink and really
"party." And like I said, I'm practically sinless. I've never done
that stuff before. I guess everybody in high school drinks, though,
so it's not too bad. I'll get used to it. I hope. I guess now that I
look back, it was worth it. All the humiliation, the shame and embarrassment . . . yeah, it was worth it. The members are nice
now that it's all over, and I get into Kappa Zeta parties free. We all
get to wear our Kappa sweatshirts to school, and go to meetings
and everything. Maybe if I would have had to do something *really*
bad I would have dropped out, but I doubt it. It's just a matter of
how far you'll go to be accepted.

Diary 9

Dear Diary,

Ms. Gruwell just asked us to write or draw a picture describing our neighborhood. I can't believe she's allowing me to draw. I
wonder if she knows how much I hate writing.

I hate my neighborhood. It's surrounded by gangsters and
drug dealers. There are too many opportunities that seem out of

my reach. What goals do I aim for? I don't aim, because I don't have any goals; instead, I deal with what comes. Raised in a shitty neighborhood, I have had to adapt to what is happening around me. During the day racial tensions rule the streets, at night gunshots are heard from drive-by shootings, and twenty-four hours a day, the gangs and drug dealers control the block, trying to hold down their territory. I can never ignore it because if I do, I will only become part of the problem, or I will become the next victim in this undeclared war going on in our streets.

I got into tagging, because bangin' and dealing drugs or kickin' it with gangsters was not my thing. I started to hit up on walls with markers or cans. Kickin' back with the homies, smoking bud, and fuckin' shit up. I went to school, but I never really hit the books. My teachers always said, "I'm here to help," but when the time came to start helping they were never dependable, so what I do at school is what I do out on the streets. Every day I bring my markers to school. I ditch my classes, hide from the staff, and go to the restroom to kill it (write all over the walls). Who cares if I get caught? My mom won't do anything and my father is always too tired to give me a lecture.

Tagging is what gives me a thrill. The chance to express my talent. To hear people talk about my art gives me the "ganas" (strength) to continue what I do. I never do any of my classwork, so I spend my time in class sketching on my notebook, handouts, backpack, or on anything in sight. I'm an artist and I love what I do. I know it sucks for the people's property, but getting away with it is a part of the thrill. Getting smoked out with my homies, then going out and canning walls is what I call a day.

Diary 10

Dear Diary,

Everybody was talking about Proposition 187 and the planned walkout in school today. I heard a lot of people yelling, "No on Prop 187!" I even saw trashcans fly across the quad and fights broke out between passing periods. All this was building up toward a walkout.

Latinos and African Americans began to walk out. The police were everywhere. It was as if we were committing a crime, and it was necessary for them to stand outside school grounds. Some students were arrested while others left school and united as one in a nearby park with all of the other high schools.

I decided not to walk out. Instead, I was able to express my own feelings in a place where people heard my voice and my opinions were never judged. Ms. Gruwell's class was where I could express my feelings about how this event was affecting me. Discussing the situation in class helped. She wrote "Prop 187" on the blackboard, and then we got to talk about how this proposition would affect certain nationalities.

If it passes, the government can take away health care benefits and any other public program, like school, to all illegal immigrants. I'm scared because it will personally affect my family, since my mom came here illegally. She came to America in search of the American dream. Immigrants, like my mom, came to this land looking for endless possibilities, but now those possibilities seem limited.

Someone in Ms. G's class reminded us that "187" is the police code for murder. If this proposition passes, it may murder the opportunities for immigrants like me to succeed.

Diary 11

Dear Diary,

"yM enam si noraA." To a 13-year-old toe-head, those words look completely normal, but what my eyes saw was "My name is Aaron." I could always read backward and just assumed everyone else could, too. I even spelled backward. The word "cat," in my perspective, would be spelled "tac," and I could not tell the difference. My school papers were filled with red marks. Was I stupid or lazy? I felt stupid and alienated from everyone.

In the fifth grade, I had a teacher who always called me lazy in front of the whole class. She would always pick on me to read in front of the class. She knew I didn't know how to read or spell very well and when I did read, I had to do it very slow. Everyone would laugh at me and call me stupid. I hated school. Ever since that year, I have never been able to read out loud because I am still afraid people will laugh at me and call me stupid.

I found out what my problem is. I'm dyslexic, which means I have a learning disorder. My brain sees things differently and words don't look the way they do to others. My mom knew how upset I was about school and was able to find a school for dyslexic kids. Finally I had met kids like myself and I'd learned that I wasn't so different after all. The school helped me so much because they taught me how to read and take notes on what I read. I learned how to figure out how to sound out big words and work out math problems, too. I was excited because I finally understood and was able to learn. I could read, but it was dyslexic-style.

The dyslexic school was only for one year, so I didn't know what would happen when I got to high school. I knew I wasn't stupid but kids might still laugh at me and I didn't want to have to go through that again.

Kids didn't seem to laugh as much if you were good at sports.

Baseball made me feel good. I couldn't recite Shakespeare, but I could hit a baseball thrown at 75 to 85 mph. I even got the chance to play as first baseman in the Little League World Series Championship. I couldn't believe that the same kids who laughed at me and called me stupid were now cheering for me as I hit a grand slam in the Little League World Series. Imagine my surprise when I found out that my hero, Nolan Ryan, is dyslexic, too.

On my first day of high school, I met Ms. Gruwell. She's my English and reading teacher. I've learned a lot from her. She doesn't call me lazy or stupid. I have learned that reading can be fun. It is still difficult at times, but I don't get that knot in my stomach when I read out loud.

Ms. Gruwell has also encouraged me in my one true love—sports. She told me that a lot of dyslexic people do really well in sports to overcompensate for people laughing at them in the classroom. Now I know if I work hard in school and in sports, I can succeed in both.

Diary 12

Dear Diary,

The past couple of days in Ms. Gruwell's class we have been reading a book called *Durango Street*. *Durango Street* is about an African American teenager named Rufus, who was just released from juvenile hall. Before he left, he promised his probation officer he would stay out of trouble.

Most of the people in class can relate to Rufus. If they haven't been in jail, they have a cousin, brother, or friend who has. Before reading this book I was ashamed of having gone to jail. I was afraid Ms. Gruwell would hold it against me. Rufus had problems with a gang called the Gassers. They were always picking on him. I had a similar problem when I was in junior high.

I was waiting for the bus after school when three wanna-be gangsters approached me. They started trying to make me angry, calling me names. It wasn't what they were saying that made me mad. I was angry that they chose to pick on me because they thought I would just take it. As far as I was concerned, the fact that they were all bigger than me was not important. I had to prove to them that they did not have the right to pick on me because I was smaller than they were.

One of them swung at me, and missed—that was "his bad." When I felt the rush of air from his fist whizzing past my face, I went crazy! I started kicking him in the head! The only thing that made me stop was when I saw his eyes roll back in his head as though he was dead. I didn't realize I had done something really wrong until I saw the flashing lights of the police and the paramedics coming.

The police took me to the vice principal's office to make a report. The vice principal called my parents to come to the school and pick me up, but no one was home. The police officer asked if there was any one else that could pick me up. There was no one. Then they asked the vice principal, "Do you want us to take him down to juvenile hall?" The vice principal answered, "Since his parents aren't home, that would probably be the best thing to do."

When I arrived at juvenile hall it was scary. They treated me like a criminal. They even took a mug shot. This was my first experience setting foot into a caged place. I was unlike any of the people surrounding me. Caged like beasts were murderers, rapists, gangsters, and robbers. The first night was the scariest. I heard sounds I had never heard before. Inmates banging on walls, throwing up their gang signs, yelling out who they are and where they are from. I cried on my first night.

I didn't get in contact with my parents until my third day in jail. Every day I worried about when I would be free. I stayed in juvenile hall for five long and stressful days. It's true what they say; being in jail is no way to live.

When I got out, I was paranoid. I didn't want to go out and have fun with my friends. I still felt like a caged animal. Two weeks after my release from jail, I had to appear in court. The judge told me that I would be on probation for three years and have to do community service for a month and two weeks. I also had to pay the restitution of $1,500 to the boy I had beaten up. I haven't gotten into any trouble since that day. Like Rufus, I turned my life around.

Diary 13

Dear Diary,

Ms. Gruwell has some pretty amazing teaching methods. Our class just read a book called *Durango Street*, and now we are making a movie of it. The book is about a young African American teenager named Rufus, who gets out of juvenile hall, lives in the projects, and tries to find his biological father.

When we found out that we were going to make a movie, both my friend and I wanted to play the part of Rufus. I wanted to play the part of Rufus because I live in the projects, too, and like him, I've never known my father. I couldn't for the life of me fathom why my friend, this clean-cut guy who seemed to have no problems in the world, wanted to play the part of Rufus. At first I thought it was because he could act. After a while I finally asked him why he wanted to play Rufus so badly. He told me there was no specific reason. I didn't accept such a neutral answer. I felt he was hiding something from me.

I ended up playing Rufus because Ms. Gruwell thought that Rufus and I have a lot of the similarities. Even though my friend pretended he wasn't upset, I knew something was wrong. The next day I asked him why he really wanted to play Rufus. At first he was hesitant to answer. We walked in silence for a while before he told me about the first time he met his father. He was only four years old. His father walked toward him wearing an orange jumpsuit with his prisoner number across the chest. Behind him, he dragged the burden of heavy shackles. They didn't even have a chance to speak; the police took him away.

I felt sorry for him. I knew how hard it was to grow up without a father. Finally, I understood his need to play Rufus. He wanted to express his pain through this character. Ironically, Ms. Gruwell chose him to play Rufus's probation officer.

Not only did this movie give us a better understanding of *Durango Street*, we also learned a lot about one another. We began to understand the true meaning of not judging a book by its cover. When we showed our movie to other English classes, lots of the students who had made fun of us for being in a remedial English class began asking how they could get into the class.

After we made our movie, Ms. Gruwell took us to see *Hoop Dreams*. It's a documentary about two boys from the Chicago projects who had a passion for basketball. The characters were a lot like the characters in the book—but more important, they were a lot like us. Like Rufus, most people didn't expect them to do well. They proved everyone wrong. I guess it just goes to show that if your passion is deep enough, you can do anything.

Diary 14

Dear Diary,

We started reading a short story in my English class called "The Last Spin." This story is a trip. I've never read something in school that related to something that happened in my life. In the story, the main characters, Tigo and Dave, were rival gang members. One of the gangs shot up a candy store in the other gang's territory. Instead of having a war in the city, the gang leaders decided that Tigo and Dave were going to settle it one on one.

Tigo and Dave settled the war by playing a game of Russian roulette. As they were playing they began to talk, and they realized they had many things in common and that playing Russian roulette to settle a beef between their gangs was stupid. They decided to take their last turn and end the game because neither one of them wanted to die. Dave took his last turn and then he passed the gun to Tigo. What was supposed to be the end of the game ended up being the last game of Tigo's life. The fact that Tigo died because of a senseless act reminded me of the way a guy in my neighborhood had died.

Four guys from my neighborhood were chilling in the living room of an apartment; one of the guys had just bought a gun off the streets. Two of the younger guys had never touched a gun before but wanted to see it anyway. The owner of the gun took the clip out and handed the gun to them. Unfortunately, he forgot that he had cocked the gun back and he didn't check to see if there was a bullet lodged in the chamber.

One of the guys who had never seen a gun before grabbed it. He and the other guy started to fight for the gun. The gun accidentally went off and hit one of them in the forehead. He died instantly. Everyone started to panic. One of the guys picked up the gun and cleaned off all the fingerprints. He then made sure that the fingerprints of the dead boy were all over the gun. They left the room without touching anything.

When the police arrived, they found a dead body, a puddle of blood, and the gun. There were no witnesses, so they called it a suicide. The boy's parents didn't believe their son would commit suicide; they didn't believe the story the police had told them. They knew their son wouldn't do something so drastic; they were positive that he didn't kill himself. The boy who was holding the gun when it went off has not been seen in the neighborhood since that day.

I knew all of the guys who were there the day the boy died. The dead boy was a bit older than I was. I didn't talk to him much because he was a bully and he intimidated me. He would pick fights with the younger kids in the neighborhood. I almost got into a fight with him myself, but luckily, he walked away. Even though he was a bully, he didn't deserve to die, especially because he was just playing around.

Freshman Year
Spring 1995

Entry 2 · Ms. Gruwell

Dear Diary,

Ahh, I'm so frustrated! This entire semester has been one ordeal after another, from race riots to walkouts. But I don't know if I'm more frustrated with the students or the system. Although they're a pain, they're just kids. But adults created the system. The system separates them and then they're stereotyped as "basic," but in reality, they're anything but basic. In many ways they're extraordinary. But even though the labels have changed over the years—from "bonehead," to "remedial," to "basic"—the effects are still the same. It's almost like these kids are scarred from the get-go. It doesn't take a rocket scientist to figure out that if you tell kids they're stupid—directly or indirectly—sooner or later they start to believe it.

It's almost comical how stubborn they are. But so am I. So I guess what goes around comes around, right? My karma is coming back to haunt me. Even Sharaud, who's now a cocky senior, says, "That freshman class of yours is bad, Ms. G." They're testing me every step of the way. They hate reading, and getting them to write is out of the question. And homework? Please! It's totally unacceptable to be a "schoolboy." So to avoid the stigma, one kid even turns in his homework wadded in a ball because he'd get beat up for carrying a folder.

It's amazing how different I was as a freshman. Looking back, I guess I would be considered a kiss-ass. But these kids would rather kick my ass than kiss it. Believe me, there are no apples on my desk, and even if there were, they'd probably have razor blades in them.

Even though a lot of people have given up on them, I refuse to believe they're a lost cause. Judging by the turnout at "Back to School Night," it makes me wonder if some of the parents have thrown up their hands as well.

Even though their reading scores don't indicate that they're "smart" in the conventional sense, it's amazing how savvy they are. They're a walking encyclopedia when it comes to pop culture, quoting the lines from their favorite movies verbatim or reciting every lyric from the latest rap CD. But when I ask them what a dangling modifier is, they say, "Dangle this." Actually, even *I* hate dangling modifiers.

I think the key is to build on what they already know. I've been trying to pick stories they can relate to and then challenge them to bring the story to life. We just finished reading a story about a kid living in the projects who had to deal with peer pressure and gangs. Some of them admitted that this was the first novel they'd ever read from cover to cover. They loved the book so much, I suggested we make a little movie. Since *Boys 'n the Hood* is a realistic portrayal of their environment, I thought making a movie would give them the opportunity to emulate John Singleton. When I gave them creative license, they surpassed my expectations. They wrote a script, made scenery, brought in props, and even held the camera. The kids said it was "Da bomb!" As a reward, I took a handful of them to see the documentary *Hoop Dreams*, because both the book and the movie deal with what it's like to grow up in an urban community.

I read that John Singleton has a new film coming out examining racial issues. If I can hang in there until June, maybe I'll take the whole class to see it. They're out of control in my class-room, so I can just imagine them in a movie theater. I don't know if I would be able to handle them all by myself. But maybe I won't have to. Someone actually offered to help me take the kids on a field trip. His name is John Tu, and he's a self-made million-aire. He heard about the racist reaction when I took the kids to the theater last year to see *Schindler's List* and thinks we're a pretty worthy cause to support.

So, to whip them into shape, I'm gonna have to get down and dirty. I'll have to burst their "Beverly Hills 90210" stereotype of me by getting in the trenches with them. Since I'm tackling Shakespeare soon, I need to convince them that this guy in tights who talks funny "has it going on." I need to show them Shake-speare's got a little "something something" for everyone. So what I'm going to do is make the Montagues and Capulets into a mod-ern-day posse. They were the true "OGs," as the kids say, the original gangsters, and although the language, colors, and turf have changed dramatically over the last four hundred years, the theme is universal.

Diary 15

Dear Diary,

Ms. Gruwell's always trying to give meaning to everything. Like today, we were supposed to read this play, *Romeo and Juliet*, by some guy who talks funny—"thou" this, and "thee" that—and out of nowhere, she busts out with, "The Capulets are like the Latino gang, and the Montagues are like the Asian gang." What? One minute, we're reading about a guy named Mercutio getting killed, and she sets us up with the question "Do you think this family feud is stupid?" Like a dumb-ass, I took the bait and said, "Hell, yeah!" After all, they were biting their thumbs and waving their wanna-be swords. Then she couldn't leave it alone. The next thing I know, she's comparing these two families to rival gangs in this city. At first I was thinking, "What the hell does this bitch know about gangs?" But the real trip was when she actually named them.

I didn't think she knew about all the shit that happened up in Long Beach. I just thought she left school and drove home to her perfect life. After all, what's it to her? All of a sudden she questioned things that had never crossed our minds before. Did we think it was stupid that the Latino gang and the Asian gang are killing each other? I immediately said "No!"

"Why?"

"Because it's different."

"How?" This woman just wouldn't give up!

"It just *is*!" I didn't want to look stupid in front of everybody. But the more I thought about it, I realized it *is* stupid.

It's stupid because I don't even remember why we're rivals. That's just the way it is. Why is she always fucking questioning everything? She always tries to corner you into accepting that there's another side, when there really isn't. I don't even remember how the whole thing got started, but it's obvious that if you're from one family, you need to be loyal and try to get some payback. Just like it's obvious that if you're from a Latino gang you don't get along with the Asian gang, and if you're from the Asian gang, you don't get along with the Latino gang. All this rivalry is more of a tradition. Who cares about the history behind it? Who cares about any kind of history? It's just two sides who tripped on each other way back when and to this day make other people suffer because of their problems. Then I realized she was right, it's exactly like that stupid play. So our reasons might be stupid, but it's still going on, and who am I to try to change things?

Diary 16

Dear Diary,

We just finished reading *Romeo and Juliet;* I couldn't believe that Juliet stabbed herself over a guy that she only knew for a few days. I guess I wasn't as in love as I thought I was, because I'd never do something that crazy for my boyfriend.

At first when we started reading this story, I compared myself with Juliet. We are both young and in love with a guy that we couldn't last a day without seeing, only Juliet fell in love at first sight and it took me two months to supposedly be in love. Running away seemed like an easy way for us to rebel against my parents' disapproval of my boyfriend. Yet it didn't come out the way we had planned.

Juliet's parents found her dead next to her boyfriend. Unfortunately, my parents found me alive next to my boyfriend. Lucky for Juliet, she died and she didn't see the reaction of her parents, nor did she have to go through punishments. I survived, and unlike Juliet's parents, my parents didn't welcome me with tears falling down from their faces. Instead, when my parents arrived at my boyfriend's house, my mother was the first to get out of the car. As she looked into my eyes, I felt the shame I had caused her. She headed toward my boyfriend and started screaming and lecturing him. My dad came toward me, cussing and screaming. Unexpectedly, he punched me in the eye. Then, he switched places with my mom. She grabbed my hair and pulled me toward the car while he yelled at my boyfriend. I fell because I was wearing high heels and my mom was moving too fast. She screamed, *"Levántate!"* (get up). "My shoe, my shoe fell off!" I cried. She picked up my platform shoes and I got up. She pushed me into the car and started hitting me with my platform shoes. I held my hands up to my face and felt the heel of my shoe bruising my hands. She stopped when my dad got into the car.

When we arrived home, my mother kept screaming at me, *"Eres tan estúpida por irte con un muchacho que ni siquieras conoces!"* (You are so stupid for running away with a guy that you don't even know). I wonder how Juliet's parents would have reacted to their daughter's actions and how Juliet would have responded. I just went into my room, not saying a word. My parents followed me. They kept telling me that I couldn't see my boyfriend ever again. They put me on restriction. I wasn't allowed to use the phone, have any company, or go out with anybody. That's why I'm here in Ms. G's class right now.

My mother thought it would be best for me to attend a school near her work and in a different school district that was at least one hour away from home. She thought that driving me to and picking me up from school would prevent me from contacting my boyfriend and that I'd forget about him. It didn't work.

Just like Juliet, I found a way to see my boyfriend. I ditched my classes and would call him from the public phones on campus. My mother didn't have an idea of what was going on until I got caught by one of my relatives. My aunt was on the same bus that my boyfriend and I were riding.

My mom was ashamed to hear that her own relative saw me kissing my boyfriend on a bus. She didn't know what to do. Finally, my parents decided that I could be with my boyfriend under one condition. That my boyfriend and I waited until I turned fifteen (this is a tradition from my culture, indicating that when a girl turns fifteen, she is a woman and mature enough to take serious responsibilities). Since I thought I was so in love and would do anything to be with my boyfriend without sneaking behind my parents' back, we both agreed to wait. So, we stopped seeing each other, just before my class got to the end of the story.

I hate to admit that my parents were right all along. How can we both believe that we were so in love with each other if we didn't even take the time to really know each other? I was too young and stupid, like Juliet, to fall in love. Luckily, I didn't kill myself and have a tragic ending like Romeo and Juliet did. I guess I wasn't that desperate.

Diary 17

Dear Diary,

In Ms. Gruwell's class today, we played the "Peanut Game." The rules of the game included one piece of paper and a description of a peanut inside and out. I wrote about the peanut and said it was small, round, and dirty. On the other side of the paper I stated that even though it looked terrible, it tasted fantastic! We categorized all of the peanuts by mentioning their different exteriors. I soon realized the "Peanut Game" was similar to the situation I had about my weight.

One day in junior high, I was getting off the school bus from a seat in the back. It is a seat where no one likes to sit and is always empty. I heard people shouting, "Hey, Fatso!" "You big buffalo!" A group of obnoxious girls screamed such awful comments that I, an "obese" twelve-year-old girl, will sadly remember for the rest of my life.

"Oh no, not again! Please not again!" I thought to myself as I stood up to get off the bus. I had tried to ignore the girls' name-calling the entire ride home. Now that we were at my stop, I knew I had to face them before getting off. In order to leave the bus I had to walk through a long crowded aisle and face the obnoxious girls. As I stood up, the girls followed. They crowded together, and approached me as if they were ready to strike at me. Why did they want to take their anger out on me? What did I do to them? All of the sudden, the girls began to kick and sock me repeatedly. I could feel the pain all over my body but felt defenseless. I did not fight back.

They continued to hurt me as if there was nothing more important to them than to see me in pain. The last few kicks were the hardest; all I wanted to do was to get off the bus alive. My friends were staring at me, hoping that I would do something to make the girls stop. Why? Why didn't my friends help me? Finally, after what seemed like an eternity, I was able to release myself from their torture. I got off the bus alive. Imagining that the worst had already passed, I began to walk away from the bus and the girls stuck their heads out the window and spit on me. I could not believe it! They spit on my face!

The feeling of their spit striking me, running down my neck, and their germs accumulating on my face, felt disgusting. I heard paper crumbling in their hands, and then they threw it at me. I began to walk faster as the bus was on its way. While I was cleaning my face with a napkin, I could still hear the girls laughing. When they waved good-bye, my nightmare was over.

Today in Ms. Gruwell's classroom, I realized that a peanut is still a peanut even if the shell is different. Some taste better, others look fresher, but in the end they're all peanuts. Ms. G's analogy, "Don't judge a peanut by its shell, judge it by what's inside of it," made perfect sense to me. As long as I know that I am a human being, I don't need to worry about what other people say. In the end, we all are the same!

Diary 18

Dear Diary,

This game is stupid; I'm not a peanut! And what the hell does world peace have to do with peanuts? All these thoughts rolled though my mind as I tried to piece together a puzzle consisting of people and Planters. What was the message? Today Ms. Gruwell and I were not on the same continent, let alone the same page. At first I just sat there trying to glue together any two thoughts that seemed to even break surface, but still I found nothing.

There I stood with both feet out the door, on the brink of tears, and quickly closing in on insanity, when something played out in my mind. I remembered a saying that I had heard: "It's not the messenger, but the message." Slowly my peanuts began to take form. I wasn't afraid because they weren't accompanied by a tophat, tap shoes, and a corny jingle. Instead they began to have purpose, they began to set goals, dreams, and ambitions. My peanuts, before my very eyes, changed into human beings. Short, long, fat, thin, and otherwise odd, but nevertheless peanuts. Brown, black, white, yellow, and all in between, nevertheless human. So why is it we don't care about the contour of a peanut, but would kill over the color of a man?

The more I thought about this, the more the concept over-whelmed me. I began to analyze and reflect on my life, my many encounters with injustice and discrimination. It sounds strange, somewhat on the line between irony and absurdity, to think that people would rather label and judge something as significant as each other but completely bypass a peanut. I think this is one of the most important realizations I've ever had. World peace is only a dream because people won't allow themselves and others around them to simply be peanuts. We won't allow the color of a man's heart to be the color of his skin, the premise of his beliefs, and his self-worth. We won't allow him to be a peanut, therefore we won't allow ourselves to come to live in harmony.

Diary 19 1992 *April*

Dear Diary,

I can't believe what happened in Oklahoma City. 168 inno-cent men, women, and children had their lives cut short by one man who was angry with the government. Out of anger, Timothy McVeigh decided he would take his frustration out on others to give the country a wake-up call. Unfortunately, it was a deadly one.

Ms. Gruwell made us write a report about what occurred in Oklahoma. Writing about it made me realize how susceptible we are to violence. Unfortunately, not all the students at Wilson got this message. Fights still break out at lunch, during passing peri-ods, and in other classes for stupid reasons like somebody walked through a group of people who were different than them. Fights based on race or the way someone dresses are just ignorant. Fights don't solve matters, they just make things worse.

There are many Timothy McVeighs around us every day, and it is very surprising to find out that it is the person you least expect. They are just like walking time bombs waiting to go off, and when they do, the consequences can be deadly. The ticking often begins with a derogatory comment, which can spark an explosion.

No matter what race we are, what ethnic background, sexual orientation, or what views we may have, we are all human. Unfortunately, not all humans see it that way.

Diary 20

Dear Diary,

I went on a field trip to the Museum of Tolerance, for a private screening of a movie called *Higher Learning*. The movie was about hypocrisy in our society and people's prejudice. Ms. Gruwell thought it would tie in to what we had been learning in class. After the movie, we listened to a panel of successful people who had overcome adversities.

The panelist that stood out to me the most was a Japanese man named Mas Okui. His family came to America to follow the American dream, but when the Japanese bombed Pearl Harbor, they were forced into internment camps. Suddenly, as a teenage boy, he and his family became the "enemy." Mas was sent to a camp called Manzanar, the same camp we had read about in the book *Farewell to Manzanar*.

Mas lived in a barrack that was close to the author of that book, Jeanne Wakatski, so he was able to answer all our questions about it. Even though they were interned, the Japanese created a community in the camp, so Mas was able to bring everything Jeanne had written to life.

I was so excited because this was the first time I had read a book that actually related to my life, since I'm Asian and was forced to go to a camp during the war in Cambodia.

Like Jeanne Wakatski, my family was also stripped of everything we owned and placed in an internment camp. Although our camps were really different, there were a lot of similarities. For example, Jeanne lived in a small cabin in the middle of the desert, while I lived in a small hut built of straws and pine tree leaves. Besides the living conditions being really bad, health tended to be a big problem. We both got sick from the food. Jeanne described how everyone had the "Manzanar runs." Unlike me, she didn't have to worry if she would go a day without food. Even though the food may not have tasted very good, at least they were fed. Unfortunately, we constantly had to worry about how our family would survive because there was never enough. Oftentimes we would go a day without food. It seemed like we were always in search of food.

In both cases, war tore our fathers apart as well as our families. The camps stripped away our fathers' dignity, and our once loving parents were suddenly in a rage over the littlest things. Both our fathers were separated from their families, and when they came back, they had physically, emotionally, and mentally changed. They became abusive and didn't care if they hurt their family

The war brought so much damage to us. It killed our souls and tried to take away our lives. That's the result of prejudice and war; it creates enemies. But like Mas said, "I was only ten years old. How could I be an enemy?"

Diary 21

Dear Diary,

I'm still swallowing the facts and information from our panel on diversity. All the panelists came from different backgrounds, but each had faced discrimination because of their race, class, religion, or gender. Despite their background or their past, all of them went on to become very successful.

Danny Haro, a Latino from East L.A., left his barrio and be-

came a lawyer. Now he's one of Edward James Olmos's best
friends and was in the documentary we watched called *Lives in
Hazard*. Lisa Ramirez is one of the first Latina women to win an
Emmy as a television producer and director. Both she and Danny
come from poor backgrounds and were the first in their families to
go to college and accomplish their dreams. Bob Gentry used to be
picked on because he was gay, but ended up becoming one of the
first gay mayors in California and was a dean at Ms. Gruwell's college. Mas Okui, who was forced to leave his school and go live in a
Japanese internment camp, ended up becoming a teacher. And
the last speaker was Renee Firestone, who lost everything, including her family, in the Holocaust, but still came to America
and became a successful clothing designer.

Of all the panelists, Renee's story affected me the most. She
talked about her life and the lessons she had learned from being
in a concentration camp. She talked about how hardworking her
parents were before the war hit Czechoslovakia. Eventually her
family was forced into a Hungarian ghetto and then off to Auschwitz. She and her younger sister were separated from their parents when they arrived at the death camp. When Renee asked a
Gestapo agent if she would see her family again, he pointed to a
chimney with smoke coming out and said that that's where she
would reunite with her family.

When Renee was liberated from the camp, she had nowhere
to go. She needed to start over and that's why she came to America, even though she could not speak any English. She said she
left Europe with about $20 and her new baby, Klara—who she
named after her sister who died at Auschwitz—and when she got
to Ellis Island they took about $16 for a head tax. So with four dol-
lars to her name, she set out to make a better life.

Her daughter, Klara, came to the event and told us what it
was like to be the daughter of two parents who had been in a

camp. Surprisingly, after everything that happened to her parents, she said they raised her "not to have a prejudiced bone in her body." Renee interrupted her and told us never to judge people collectively—it's so easy to lump people in a group and label them, but that's how the Holocaust started.

After the panel, we had the opportunity to have dinner with the panelists at the Century City Marriott. Since Ms. Gruwell works at a Marriott on the weekends, the hotel let us have a big dinner there. When we got to the hotel, we were able to walk up to the panelists and shake their hands. During dinner, Renee came to speak with us at my table. She showed us the tattoo on her arm from Auschwitz. The tattoo looked like little numbers from a barcode. She told us how some of the needles they used were infected and that some people got skin diseases. She told us how one person sucked out the ink from her skin because the doctor who gave her the tattoo quietly told her to. If she had not sucked the ink out, she would have been sent to the gas chamber the next day, because her number was called.

Everything from today related to something we have read or watched in class. It's amazing how Ms. Gruwell went out of her way to contact all these people to come to speak to us. By meeting these people, it made the books we've been reading more meaningful. It also made me realize that anything is possible!

Diary 22

Dear Diary,

It's almost midnight and I feel like Cinderella when she was racing home from the ball, knowing that her chariot is about to turn into a pumpkin. I guess you could call what I just got home from a "ball"—we all dressed up, I got to eat dinner with more silverware than I probably own, and I met Prince Charming. This prince isn't gonna carry me off on his white horse, or anything. That's OK, 'cause I don't like horses anyway, ever since I busted my ass on one! But for this fairy tale, he'll do.

The prince is John Tu and the castle was this enormous hotel up in L.A.—the Century City Marriott. I wonder if the hotel Ms. Gruwell works at is as nice? There was crystal everywhere and the bathrooms even had real towels. There was no paper wads on the ceiling or ashes on the floor, and there was no stall doors missing like the bathrooms at school. Even the toilet paper felt good, unlike the sandpaper that could send students to the school nurse. I never knew going to the bathroom could be such an enjoyable experience!

But the bathroom was nothing compared to the dinner. There were more courses than O.J. has alibis. My napkin looked like a centerpiece and my food was too damn perfect to touch. The biggest treat of all was when John Tu sat at my table. Here was this man who had so much to say, but wanted us to do all the talking.

When I introduced myself to him, I was really nervous. Why would he pay attention to me? After all, no one, including my dad, ever has. Since my dad left, I've always felt shunned and that it was my fault. I've always felt like I don't have anything important to say. But here was this man who actually paid attention to me. He wanted to know what *I* thought about the movie *Higher Learning*. Who was *my* favorite panelist? Which part did *I* like best about *Farewell to Manzanar*?

How could someone who doesn't even know me be so interested in me? Here's this gazillionaire treating me as if I'm belle of the ball, when my own dad is treating me like I don't exist. John Tu gave me more attention in seven minutes than my dad has given in seven years.

As wonderful as everything was, when I got home, I realized I'm missing out on a lot—not the material stuff like the fancy chandeliers and the full-course meals, but bonding with a dad. In a weird way, I'm envious of his kids. They can keep the money, if I could have him as a dad. I hope they don't take for granted all the little things he does, like say "Good morning" and "good night." Or just asking about what they did in school that day. That would be the perfect Cinderella story for me—no glass slipper, just a "how was school today?"

Diary 23

Dear Diary,

I have learned so much my freshman year, and one important lesson I've learned is that people do change, because I did. It all started in the beginning of this year. I came back to school from my own little "three-week vacation" when Ms. Gruwell asked me, "Why have you been absent so much?" I didn't know what to say. How could I answer? Should I lie and tell her I was sick or should I tell her I hate school and I was ditching? Ditching gave me power. When I ditched I was my own person. I could do anything I wanted to and not have to answer to anyone. Besides, when I *was* at school, nobody paid attention to me.

I told Ms. Gruwell, "Nobody cares about what I do, so why should I bother to come to school? Why should I waste my time when I have better things to do?" When I told her this, I could see the hurt in her eyes. "What 'better things' do you have to do?" she asked. This question was even harder to answer than the first. I didn't do much except sit at my homie's pad and smoke. That was all I did when I ditched—chilled and smoked. I told her, "I have family problems and I have to stay home and help out." I chickened out. I couldn't tell her what I really did. Then she asked me, "Is there anything I can do to help you? Should I call your house and talk to your parents?" I immediately said, "NO! They will get mad at me." My mom obviously thought I was going to school. She had no idea that I had been ditching since the first day of class.

My mom has always pushed me to get an education because everyone else in my family has dropped out—everyone except her. The only reason why she graduated was because her mother pressured her. Now my mom is pressuring me to be like her. If Ms. Gruwell called my house and talked to my mom, she would freak. My mom would definitely think I'm a loser if she knew. Being a loser was the least of my problems.

My problems only got worse when I got caught. I remember I was smoking out with my homies when the cops rolled up. Boy, did I take off. I took off running so fast that I didn't even stop to see if my friends were with me. I just wanted to get away. When I got around the corner I noticed that I was alone. That's when I went back and got caught myself. They took me to juvenile hall. That was the worst night of my life. I was in a cell with other girls who wanted to kick my ass. The officer told me I could make a phone call. When I called my mom I lied to her. Of course, if I could lie to my mom, then I could lie to Ms. Gruwell.

So one day when Ms. Gruwell pointed out my 0.5 GPA, but said that I had potential, I felt guilty. Then before I left class, Ms. Gruwell told me something that would change my life forever. She told me she believed in me. I have never heard those words from anyone . . . especially a teacher.

Now you can understand why I am so excited to stay in Ms. Gruwell's class for another year. Since Ms. Gruwell cares about me, I started caring about myself. I even stopped ditching. I hate to admit it, but I'm actually starting to like school. I can't wait till next year to have Ms. Gruwell all over again. You never know what exciting things will happen.

Sophomore Year
Fall 1995

Entry 3 · Ms. Gruwell

Dear Diary,

Ever since I started student teaching at Wilson High, it seemed like some teachers had it in for me. According to them, I was too enthusiastic, too preppy, and my teaching style was too unorthodox. The students they criticized in the teachers' lounge were the same students celebrated in a local newspaper article. And to top it off, when my students received an invitation to meet Steven Spielberg, it put some teachers right over the edge.

After enduring all the rumors during my student teaching, I had been pretty hesitant to return to Wilson last fall. When I was assigned to teach freshmen with below-par reading skills, the head of the English department challenged me, saying, "Let's see what you can do with these kids, hotshot!"

Hotshot? If she only knew how nervous and overwhelmed I really was as a first-year teacher. She never even took the time to get to know me—and yet she was labeling me. Just like the students I defended, I was being stereotyped. Teachers called me a prima donna because I wore suits; I made the other teachers "look bad" because I took my students on field trips; and some had the audacity to say that John Tu was my "sugar daddy." At that moment, I understood why almost half of new teachers leave the profession within the first few years.

I contemplated leaving Wilson after a teacher printed and then distributed a letter I'd written to Spielberg's secretary thanking her for helping with my spring field trip to the Museum of Tolerance. When another teacher brought me a copy of my letter—with certain sections highlighted—I lost it. Why would a teacher, someone who was supposed to be my colleague, access my computer file and print a private letter? And then why would she make copies of it? In my opinion, she invaded my privacy, and that's where I drew the line. All my suppressed animosity came to the surface, and I decided it was time for me to leave Wilson.

I interviewed at another high school and was offered a job. I was inches away from a clean getaway, until I made the mistake of telling my principal that I was planning to leave. He was shocked and asked me why.

"All of the teachers are out to get me!" I blurted out.

"But what about your students?" he asked. "Didn't they sign up for your sophomore English class? Won't they be disappointed if you're not here on the first day of school?"

Then my hypocrisy hit me. All year long I had encouraged my students to avoid using labels like "all" and other gross generalizations. I even had people who were the victims of stereotyping describe the dangers of labeling groups of people. Holocaust survivor Renee Firestone reiterated my point by telling my students, "Don't let the actions of a few determine the way you feel about an entire group. Remember, not *all* Germans were Nazis." Now I was stereotyping by saying "all" teachers, when in reality it was only a handful who disliked me. There were actually several teachers who were supportive.

If I let a few other teachers chase me away from Wilson, the kids would be the ultimate losers. They would think that I, like so many others, had bailed on them. I realized I needed to finish what I had started. Besides, I didn't become a teacher to win any congeniality contests. So I decided to stay at Wilson and devote my energy to teaching literature, rather than perpetuating petty rivalries.

By staying, I'll have the majority of the students I had last year. In addition to them, I'll be getting a whole new crop—the kids nobody else wants! My class has become a dumping ground for disciplinary transfers, kids in rehab or those on probation. But if Sharaud, who graduated in June, could turn his life around, there is hope for these new students yet. Ironically, "hope" is one of the few four-letter words not in their vocabulary.

When I asked one of my freshmen if he thought he'd graduate, he said. "Graduate? Hell, I don't even know if I'll make it to my sixteenth birthday!" To some of these kids, death seems more real than a diploma.

Their fatalistic attitude influenced my literature choices for this year. Since the incident with the racist note segued into a unit on tolerance, I'm going to revisit and expand on that theme. I've ordered four books about teens in crisis: *The Wave* by Todd Strasser; *Night* by Elie Wiesel; *Anne Frank: The Diary of a Young Girl*, and *Zlata's Diary: A Child's Life in Sarajevo*. The last two will be the focal point of the curriculum.

It's uncanny how many similarities my students have with Anne and Zlata. Since many of my students are fifteen, and Zlata is fifteen and Anne Frank was fifteen when she died, I think the parallels between age, alienation, and teenage angst will really hit home for them.

Anne Frank's book was a natural choice, but I was really excited to discover the book by the young Bosnian writer, who critics are hailing as a "modern-day Anne Frank." *Scope* magazine's cover story about Zlata Filipovic last spring inspired me to read her diary about war-torn Bosnia. Zlata began keeping a diary when she was ten. She called it "Mimmy"—similar to how Anne Frank called her diary "Kitty." Just as Anne's life changed dramatically under the Nazi occupation, so did Zlata's during the war in Sarajevo. Suddenly, Zlata's focus switched from her studies and watching MTV to the closing of her school and the destruction of the national library. As the war progressed, she experienced and chronicled food shortages, artillery shelling, and the death of children.

In 1991, at the age of eleven, as Zlata watched her once peaceful city erupt in war, my students witnessed Los Angeles literally burn in the wake of the Rodney King verdict; as Zlata dodged sniper fire in the streets where she once played, my students dodged stray bullets from drive-by shootings; as Zlata watched her friends killed by the senseless violence of war, my students watched friends get killed by senseless gang violence. In Sarajevo, Zlata described how soldiers used a "black crayon of war" to put an "S" on Serbs, a "C" on Croats, and an "M" on Muslims. I think my students could argue that they, too, have experienced a "black crayon" of sorts, labeling them with a "W" for white, a "B" for black, an "L" for Latino, and an "A" for Asian.

I think my students will be able to identify with the teen protagonists in all of the books I've selected. But since the books won't arrive for a while, I'm going to have them read short stories and plays that they'll be able to relate to. I think they'll be surprised how life mirrors art.

Diary 24

Dear Diary,

5:00 A.M.—The sound of my alarm clock woke me to a dark room this morning. The sun wasn't out yet, so I decided not to get up. My clock saw things differently and kept beeping.

So I thanked my clock by throwing it on the floor. The beeping stopped. As I looked over to see where the clock had landed, I realized I, too, was lying on the floor. Why? Because I don't have a bed. I turned on the lights so I could get started on my day. I walked past the closet mirror in the room to get my clothes. The mirror showed my sleeping space—a thick blanket and a pillow.

The mirror's reflection also revealed that the room does not belong to me. It made me feel sad. Almost at the point of crying. I grabbed my clothes from the closet and walked down the long hallway to the bathroom. During my shower, I cried. Tears mixed with the water streaming down my face. I welcomed the pain that came with the tears. It's the only way I can deal with my current situation. The room, hallway, and bathroom don't belong to me. This is not my home. My mom is down the hall sleeping in a room, but this is still not my home. I don't have a home anymore.

5:30 A.M.—I'm out of the bathroom, done with my shower, and ready to go. I have to remind myself that today is the first day of my tenth-grade year at Wilson High School. I should be happy that I get a chance to see my friends after not seeing them all summer. But, I wonder if my friends' summer was as bad as mine. That summer was the worst in my short fourteen years of life. It all started with a phone call that I will never forget.

My mom was crying, begging, and pleading; asking for more time as if she were gasping for a last breath of air. Though I never paid attention to "adult matters," this time I was all ears. I never wanted to see my mom cry.

As she hung up the phone, she turned around to see me standing there confused and scared. I didn't know what was wrong. She quickly held me as tight as she could, hugged me, and said that she was sorry. She began to cry again, this time more so than when I walked in. Her tears hit my shirt like bullets. She told me that we were going to be evicted. She kept apologizing to me, saying she failed me as a mother and provider. She was a month behind on the rent. The landlord was already money hungry, so it made the situation worse. I was only fourteen and too young to get a job. The only job I could get in my neighborhood was selling drugs—so I decided to pass.

While kids were having fun enjoying the summer, I was packing my clothes and belongings into boxes and wondering where we were going to end up. My mom didn't know what to do or where to go. We had no family to lean on. No money was coming in. Without a job, my mom didn't have enough money to get another place. What to do? No father to help out, just a single mom and her son.

The night before the sheriff was supposed to pay us a unwelcome visit, I prayed to God for a way out of this madness. Sad and depressed, I attempted to get some sleep that night in the hope something would happen.

The morning of our eviction, a hard knock on the door woke me. The sheriff was here to do his job. We were moving all our stuff out as fast as we could. I started to look up to the sky, waiting for something to happen. I looked at my mom to see if she was all right because she was silent moving the stuff out.

Our pastor had a friend who had a nice, big house where he lived by himself. The pastor's friend, who was informed of our situation, welcomed us with open arms. The arms of a stranger were a lot more comfortable than the arms of the sheriff.

6:00 A.M.—I'm waiting for the bus. Flashbacks of this summer pass through my mind like a song repeating itself over and over again. I try to tell myself it could have been worse. Nothing like this has ever happened to me. I started to think the situation was my fault because I always asked for the top video games every Christmas and birthday. I should have asked for something less expensive; something we could afford.

6:45 A.M.—I've ridden one bus to catch another bus that will now take me directly to school. School . . . why bother going to school? What's the use of going if I don't have a place to live? When friends ask how my summer was, what am I going to say? I was evicted from my apartment? I don't think so. I'm not going to tell a soul what happened. I knew everyone would be wearing new clothes, new shoes, and have new haircuts. Me? With outfits from last year, some old shoes, and no new haircut. I feel like it's hopeless to try to feel good and make good grades. There's no point to it.

7:10 A.M.—The bus stops in front of the school. My stomach feels like it's tightening into a tiny little ball. I feel like throwing up. I keep thinking that I'll get laughed at the minute I step off the bus. Instead, I'm greeted by a couple of my friends who were in my English class last year. At that point, it hits me. Ms. Gruwell, my crazy English teacher from last year, is really the only person that made me think of hope for my future. Talking with my friends about our English class and the adventures we had the year before, I began to feel better.

7:45 A.M.—I receive my class schedule and the first teacher on the list is Ms. Gruwell in Room 203. I walk in the room and I feel as though all the problems in my life are not important anymore. I am home.

Diary 25

Dear Diary,

Damn! School just started and I have to go to the hospital again. This time I have to have sinus surgery. The doctors say I will be out of school for a week or two. I hope they are right.

I am frequently hospitalized for a lung disease called cystic fibrosis. CF has been a constant part of my life. My breathing sucks! I have coughing attacks every five to fifteen minutes that last about five minutes each. I lose my concentration and I can't even breathe. The lack of oxygen gives me a migraine. My weight is also a problem. Since I can't digest what I eat, I can't gain weight. I have to take pills to help digest my food and perform breathing treatments. If I don't, I get severe stomachaches. Most of the time I end up losing weight.

I have been on a transplant list for over six months, and I probably only have a few years left to live unless I receive new lungs. It makes me wonder if I will survive this. I know I will, but it's a tough, scary road ahead for me. Anything can happen to me, and hopefully I will be prepared.

I'm sure going to miss school and my friends. I'm really going to miss Ms. G and her class. Last year when I was in the hospital she bought like a two-foot card and everyone in her class signed it. She even came to the hospital to visit me.

I don't know what kind of assignments I'll miss, but I hope it isn't much. I hope the surgery won't keep me out for more than two weeks. I would hate to be out of school longer than that, because school is one of the only things that I love doing.

Diary 26

Dear Diary,

Today I walked into my fifth-period English class and all of the desks were lined up against the wall. On the chalkboard read *Twelve Angry Men* and under it listed the characters in the play. It looks like she wants us to role-play. With my luck I'm probably going to be the first person she picks. Why did I have to be transferred into this class?

Everyone in here seems to know everyone else; just like that TV show *Cheers*, where everybody knows your name. Well, I don't really talk to people and I'm sure nobody knows my name. I would like to keep it that way.

"Oh my God . . . she's going to pick me to be a character, I know she is . . . great, just great, she's looking at me." Now everybody will know my name. I immediately stick my head into my backpack to search for something, anything, to look like I'm distracted. I can't take this; I don't need this kind of stress. Phew, she passed me up, I guess I got lucky this time. I hate talking in front of people, and all this teacher does is talk. She calls on people to answer questions; like they could give a smart answer right off the top of their head. Why can't she talk monotonously through the whole class period? Why couldn't she just be boring like my other teachers?

Diary 27

Dear Diary,

Murder, taking a life, stealing a soul, the one thing you can never repay or apologize for. Lately the word murder has been a shadow hovering over my life. Everywhere I turn, I see the O. J. Simpson trial all over television. Ms. G is having our class read

Twelve Angry Men. And at 2:00 P.M. today my brother will be given a verdict in his own murder trial. I often think of "twelve angry men," in a hostile room, all trying to decide the fate of my brother.

I think of how there is no million-dollar defense, no dream team with briefcases filled with credentials. There is just a state-appointed attorney who probably believes that my brother is guilty, too.

I watched the O.J. trial on television. It seemed just when the prosecution began to present a strong case against him, his dream team displayed something else to weaken their evidence, and softened the hearts of the jury. Then I reflected on my brother and how his only hope was a confession statement from the person he was with, the real killer. The court stated:

> "The defendant confessed his actions to a person who was not an officer of the court. Therefore his statement is null and void, and it cannot be used as admissible evidence in court."

His lawyer came and advised him to plead the fifth amendment— no statement, no conviction. Once again, they proved that justice doesn't mean the bad guys go to jail, it just means someone pays for the crime.

I remember images from *Twelve Angry Men,* and how one optimistic juror turned the hearts of eleven jurors. As soon as I started to become hopeful, I realized it was only a book, nothing more.

Today at two o'clock my brother was without a dream team or a guardian angel on the jury. He was sentenced to serve fifteen years to life in prison.

Diary 28

Dear Diary,

Ever since elementary school I've been in accelerated classes. I had thought I was lucky getting the best education and the top-notch teachers. I was on the road to the brightest of the bright.

When I reached junior high, I started to realize that since I was in the accelerated program, I only knew the other accelerated kids. We didn't talk to anyone else. It was like an unspoken law. We weren't allowed to talk to the kids who weren't in the gifted program, or maybe they weren't allowed to talk to us. I knew it wasn't right, but it was all I knew. Going into high school, I was accepted into the highest academic program in my district. I thought it was a good thing, until the middle of my first semester. The work was piled over my head and I felt like I couldn't think straight. I didn't have time for anything but homework. It was hard to pay attention because my teachers talked like robots. I'm sure they were teaching me important information, but by the time I got home, I couldn't remember a thing. We were assigned too many pages to read in one night and too many tests in one week. I didn't have time to actually learn. I found my way out of this program and found my way into another one at Wilson High School. I crossed my fingers, hoping this one would be better.

This new program was called Distinguished Scholars. I was given a list of qualifications that had to be met. We had to have a good grade point average, good attendance, and take more classes than the average student. It seemed tough, but I felt it was a more reachable goal. I walked into this open-minded, but it just wasn't the right program for me. All of my teachers held their noses in the air, as if they were above the rest of the school. Looking around, I realized I was uncomfortable. The class was made up of all white, wealthy kids who couldn't have more stress than planning what they were going to wear the next day. They made it clear that their race, economic state, and the classes they were taking made them popular and better then anyone else. Even though I'm white, live in the same neighborhood, and had all of the same classes, I wanted out.

When I complained to a friend of mine, she told me about her English class. My friend raved about the things they did. While they were reading about Camelot, their teacher dressed up as Queen Guinevere to add an extra oomph. They also put on plays to make the stories come to life. I had never done that. We were lucky if we were able to read out loud. I begged to meet Ms. Gruwell. When I finally did, I was in absolute awe.

Within the next week, she has managed to fit me into her class. She plays reading and vocabulary games to help us learn, and she listens to our questions. She actually cares. She talks to us on a level I can understand. It's wonderful to feel like a real person and not just someone for my teachers to belittle.

Diary 29

Dear Diary,

Recently in Ms. G's class we've been studying the legend of Camelot and King Arthur. At first, many of us in the class were not too interested in the legends that occurred in medieval times. I think Ms. G saw our initial lack of interest, so she decided to add a little incentive in order to get the class to participate a little more. She announced that once our lesson was finished and the class took "the test," all the students who passed the exam would be eligible to attend a field trip to the Medieval Times restaurant. We had an opportunity to relive the medieval era and enjoy a nice dinner while being entertained by knights participating in hand-to-hand combat. There is no better way to teach than to provide some firsthand experience and a little fun.

Needless to say, the announcement of a field trip to Medieval Times perked up everyone's interest. Soon, everyone in class was determined to know everything about King Arthur and his adventures. The more I participated in class, the more I realized that I was no longer interested in the lesson plan because of the possible reward, but because I genuinely found the lesson captivating. Of course, the idea that we as a class would have the opportunity to go out to dinner together and enjoy ourselves was not bad.

As time went on and I became very familiar with the lesson material, I felt a great sense of accomplishment. Go figure. I could now understand and was able to participate in discussions that were related to great literature. I understood because I had to actually read it, not because I had seen one or two movies.

Test day came. I could feel knots in my stomach on my way to class. I passed the test with flying colors and so did everyone else. This only made the prize even sweeter, because I had worked very hard and enjoyed myself doing it. However, something ended up raining on my parade. The day before our long awaited field trip, another teacher told me and a friend in my class that we were not going to be able to go unless we dressed in slacks and a tie and not like gangsters. Gangsters? Since when do gangsters wear GUESS? shirts with Levi pants at the waist? I always thought gangsters liked to dress in pants three times their actual waist size with white T-shirts. Maybe he felt this way because of my race. I didn't know, and I was confused.

Funny that he was creating rules of his own. After all, he was only tagging along as a chaperone. He shouldn't have been pushing his weight around. "No problem," we thought. Even though neither one of us owned a tie, we were going to dress our best without one. The next day, as my friend and I stood in line to board the bus, we were asked to step out of the line and let others aboard. We were actually being denied the right to participate in the field trip because we were not wearing ties by that same teacher that had talked to us a day earlier. I was in complete shock. I had worked so hard to get to the awaited moment only to be told that I could not participate because of my appearance.

Confused and disappointed, my friend and I went home. The next day was very hard, as everyone asked why I didn't attend the field trip. Actually, what really bothered me was how everyone was bragging about how fun it was. A little while after the incident, I met with Ms. Gruwell and the other teacher who prevented me from participating in the event. Ms. G put up a hell of a fight! Apparently she felt that I had the right to go, too, just like everyone else, and that I was wrongfully discriminated against because of the way I was dressed. Even though the teacher eventually apologized to me for his blatant discrimination, I forgave him but didn't forget. To think that I was denied something because of the fact that I was not wearing a tie but was still following the dress code disgusts me. From now on, I will walk with my head in the clouds and dream of when people will stop judging books by their cover.

Diary 30

Dear Diary,

"Four eyes," "Blind as a bat," or worse yet, "Coke bottle bitch" were the mean comments I heard all through my childhood. I would come home from elementary and middle school in tears every day because my classmates or even strangers would harass me. I even begged my mother to let me change schools because people made fun of me too much. Their ruthless comments shaped my personality and turned me into a shy, insecure, quiet girl. I was always alone because I was afraid of making friends and then finding out that they made fun of me behind my back.

Just recently, I was sitting in my science class, when I heard the girl sitting next to me making rude comments about my bad eyesight. I am very sensitive when it comes to my eyesight and somehow she sensed it. I tried to ignore her, but she started writing on my jacket. I got up and I said, "You know what, I'm fucking tired of this." I couldn't believe I said that, because I used to just brush off what people said. She said, "Shut up, you blind bitch." When I heard her call me that name, I lost it. I slapped her! It was as if she represented all the kids throughout the years who had made fun of me. All of the anger that had built up in my heart throughout my childhood years was released at that moment. I was so furious that I blacked out. Literally! My mind went blank. My science teacher separated us and I was shaking uncontrollably. I don't know what happened to me next.

When I told Ms. G about the fight, she told me about one of her students named Sharuad, who was teased because he had big lips. She said she found a mean drawing of his lips and it made her lose her cool. After yelling and screaming at the class, she said the incident woke her up and made her become a better teacher. Maybe this incident could make me a better person, too.

Diary 31

Dear Diary,

The bell rang and everybody walked into class. All the desks were up against the wall. There was a table full of plastic champagne glasses and bottles of apple cider all around the room. I thought, "What the hell is going on? Are we having a party?" I saw Ms. Gruwell waving her arms around like a crazy lady, but no one was reacting to her caffeine high. We all knew the effect caffeine had on Ms. Gruwell.

Throughout the class period, things began to change drastically. Ms. Gruwell stood on the desk and began to talk about "change." I thought, "What is this lady trying to do?" What does she mean by "change"? Then people started crying. I thought to myself, "Why is everyone crying?" I didn't understand.

Ms. Gruwell passed out books and bags from Barnes & Noble. When I saw the look on people's faces, I felt like jumping up for joy. I wanted to start reading them at that very moment. I was so occupied with one of my new books that I missed the whole idea of what we were supposed to do with them. The book had never been opened and the pages smelled like a new car. I started reading *Night* by Elie Wiesel, and I can't wait to get started on *The Wave* by Todd Strasser, Anne Frank's diary, and last but not least *Zlata's Diary*. At first I thought we were going to have to do a lot of book reports. Then she told us about the "Read-a-thon for Tolerance." What the heck is Ms. Gruwell talking about? She said we'd have fun because the stories are about kids in similar situations. We were all teenagers who were going through a difficult time in our lives. Some of us succeed and others don't. That is just how it is, and all I wanted to do was be one of the people who make it.

I have always been one of the kids that needed to change—I can't even try to deny it. My mom is no help because I can't do anything wrong in her eyes. I am "Mommy's little girl" no matter how badly I am doing in school or what type of drugs I've tried. My dad is just the opposite. He's never cared about how bad I'm doing—or how good, for that matter.

Everyone changes as they get older, no matter if it's good or bad. So I guess I was offered an opportunity that not many people have. I got a second chance to change my life for the better. I thank God that he sent an angel to give me that chance to change.

I was always known as the person that was going to be a druggie, or get pregnant before I turned fourteen and drop out. Now I have the chance to prove them wrong.

Diary 32

Dear Diary,

A year has passed since two of my friends died. Man, every-one respected those two. Those guys were the most loved *cholos* of the barrio. That's how I wanted to be when I grew up. All I wanted to do was impress them. While I was in school one day, they were killed while trying to commit a robbery. To think I could have been with them.

After this incident, I started to see life from a whole new per-spective. I had been taking the wrong path all along. Now my best friend and I are the oldest cholos in the barrio. It was pitiful that all the older guys were either six feet under or living behind bars. As the weeks went by, I slowly changed my ways. I didn't want the younger ones to look up to me when I was a loser. I had done so much to hurt my community and now it was time to do something to help it.

Now the young ones are looking up to me as a role model, so I try my hardest to give a straight image on how things should be, and make them see right from wrong. My neighbors adore me. I have a warm feeling deep down inside, as if I am the "chosen one" in the barrio. But it hurts me to know that it took the lives of two dear friends for me to turn my life around.

I guess it's never too late to change in life. If I did it, others should be able to as well. It really all depends on how badly one wants to change. I'm lucky to have another opportunity at a clean start.

It's just too bad the two cholos were never given the same opportunity.

Diary 33

Dear Diary,

"You can't go against your own people, your own blood!"

Those words kept ringing in my mind as I walked down the courtroom aisle to sit in a cold, empty chair next to the judge. I kept telling myself, "Get your shit together, you don't want to contradict yourself on the witness stand, your homie's future lies in your hands." I was convinced that I had to lie to protect my own, the way I was always taught to do. As I walked through the courtroom, I kept my eyes focused straight ahead, afraid to make eye contact with anyone. It was so quiet that the only things I could hear were the steps I took walking across the marble floor and my heart.

As I sat in the chair, I felt as if I was exposed to different eyes. Those eyes, in some strange way, were touching a part of me that was deep inside, everyone was waiting for my reaction.

When I sat down, I noticed that the courtroom was divided. On one side, there was my family and my friends. Most of them are from one of the most notorious gangs in California. They had all come because they were worried about what the other side might do to me after the verdict. Even though they were there to protect me, I didn't feel safe. I guess it was because they couldn't protect me from the one thing I was actually afraid of, the guilt I had inside. But all I had to do was look in the eyes of my people for them to reassure me that I had no choice but to take care of my own. I had to protect Paco no matter what went down. We all knew, that no matter what, I wasn't going to rat on my homeboy. He would give his life for me, without hesitation, the same way I would give mine for his. All I had to do was sit there and lie about what had happened that night. The night when Paco was only proving, once again, that he would do anything for his main girl.

He was only protecting me, and sending out a warning not to mess with me again.

On the other side of the courtroom were the family members of the guy who was being falsely accused of murder. Those people, his family and his friends, of course, were looking at me with rage. I knew why, but I didn't care. I wasn't afraid of them. They were our rivals and they had it coming. They had already killed one of our friends, and they had jumped me a couple of weeks before. Then one person on his side caught my eye. Her look wasn't filled with rage, there was strength and sadness, which made it painfully familiar. She looked at me, tears rolling down her cheeks, and hugged the little girl on her lap.

When I saw her tears, a little voice inside of me whispered very quietly, "Doesn't she remind you of someone you love more than anyone else in the world?" I tried to ignore the little voice, but then the voice spoke louder. It told me that this woman was my mother, and that little girl was me. I couldn't help but stare back, imagining how life would be for that little girl without her father. I pictured her waiting for her father to come home, knowing he wasn't. I pictured her visiting him, and not being able to touch him because of an unbreakable window, and I imagined her wanting to unlock his cage, knowing she couldn't. The same memories I have of my father in prison. The woman looked at me again, and I could see that she was suffering the same way my mother suffered when my dad and brother went to prison. I wondered how they could be so different. My mother is Mexican and this woman black, yet the emotions that made them cry came from a heart that was tearing apart the same way.

Throughout my life I've always heard the same thing: "You can't go against your own people, your own blood." It got so engraved in my head that even as I sat on the witness stand, I kept thinking of those same words. "You can't go against your own . . ." Yet, my so-called *familia*, my so-called people, had put me in the worst position of my life. My feelings were starting to change, I began to have second thoughts. I was convinced that I was going to lie before I entered the courtroom, before I saw the woman, before I saw the little girl, but now I wasn't so sure.

Suddenly, his lawyer interrupted my thoughts by busting out with questions. Who shot the guy? Then I looked at my friend. He was just staring at me with a smug look on his face. He wasn't worried about anything even though he was guilty, even though he knew I had witnessed everything. When he shot the guy he looked at me and said, "This is for you." He knew I was going to lie, he knew that I had always had his back before, so I had no reason to turn on him now. I turned to look at him, and my eyes stared getting watery. He was surprised, as if it wasn't a big deal, but this time it was a big deal.

Then I glanced at my mom, she shook her head, and it was as if she knew that I wanted to say the truth. I never told her what actually happened that night, but she knew my friend had done it. When she had asked me what I was going to say, I told her, "I'm going to protect my own . . . you know how it is. You have to know, you and every other person in my family taught me about my own."

"I know how it is, but why does it always have to be that way?" She never spoke that way to me before, after all, my father is in prison and most of my family is in a gang. I always figured that my mom accepted how things were. That's just the ways things go when you're in a gang. Then she asked me, "How does it feel to be sending an innocent person to prison? You probably feel like that man that sent your father to prison knowing he was innocent, you know, he was only protecting his own, too." And for the first time in my life, the image of my mother made me believe that I could change the way things were. Because at that moment I locked eyes with Paco and said, "Paco did it. Paco shot the guy!"

Diary 34

Dear Diary,

You're going to be so disappointed in me. Actually I'm more disappointed in myself for the way I'm tricking people into believing that I'm something I'm not. Since I've been in Ms. Gruwell's class, everyone thinks I am "Little Miss Goodie Goodie." It never fails; she always uses me as the "good" example. I'm seen as the kind of student that is quiet, has good grades, and is the teacher's pet. The strange thing is that while everyone around me is changing because of our "toast for change," I seem to be the only one who's not going anywere. It's hard for me, because I have a lot of people who always tell me that I am smart, and that I seem to have it all together, and they sometimes wish they were like me. If they only knew that on the inside I am just barely keeping it together.

I am living a lie. I am struggling with a deep secret—being a "closet drinker." I walk around with my water bottle pretending to be better than what I am. Deep down inside it hurts me that I can't bring myself to tell anyone about my problem. I do want to change, but it's so hard. It's so hard for me to change because I fear that people will not like the sober me. I've been doing it for so long, it's just a daily routine like getting up in the morning, going to the bathroom, and brushing your teeth.

I can't keep on hiding the fact that I'm an alcoholic. I'm hiding it from my mom, Ms. G, and all of my friends. I know I need help, but how do I go about getting it? It has got to be hereditary because not only do I have this problem, but my grandfather, my dad, and his mom had this problem also. I guess I was going to end up with it myself sooner or later.

Let me tell you about my day. I woke up craving orange juice with a little hint of vodka. Guess what I did? As usual, I went to my secret stash, and poured my favorite drink, vodka and orange juice. I started wondering how I am going to achieve anything in life, if I can't even start the day without alcohol.

Of course my mom was already at work, so I walked out the door with my water bottle filled with O.J. and vodka and went to school like it was an everyday thing. The thing that really got me was when I got to school, no one, I mean not even Ms. G or even my best friend, had any idea that I was drunk. I talked to my friends and teachers and they didn't know. You know why? Because I have a trick: I stop off at the donut shop and buy a pack of gum after I get off the bus. Smart, huh?

During P.E. I almost drowned because my legs gave out on me while I was in the pool. Everyone thought it was because I was feeling fatigued, but I knew it was because I was drunk. At lunch I could hardly stand. I ran to the bathroom and puked all over the stall. I tried to convince myself that it was because of the flu or something. By dinnertime I was back to the way people always saw me; sweet, smart, and innocent.

My drinking never really bothered me before we started reading all these books about people changing and wanting to make a difference. It makes me feel like such a hypocrite. The story that sticks with me the most is how the Nazis deliberately hurt innocent people like Anne Frank, and in my case, I'm the one who's hurting myself. I'm the one choosing to hide. Unfortunately, Anne Frank was never free. It makes me wonder if I'll ever be.

Diary 35

Dear Diary,

Tonight I just finished one of the books for our read-a-thon, called *The Wave*. This story is about a school experiment that shows how peer pressure can get out of hand. One of the main characters was a guy by the name of Robert Billing. He pressured and bullied other teenagers into acting like modern-day Nazis. The teenagers were like sheep blindly following a leader. After reading this book, I realized how teens are very gullible; getting tricked into doing things against their will because they want to fit in and be popular. That must be why Hitler preyed on children. It's amazing how he controlled thousands of teenagers called the "Brown Shirts." I can't believe how peer pressure can take charge of a person's life and change who they are. I know that stories like this are true because I've experienced peer pressure myself. I wanted to hang out with the so-called "cool" crowd so badly that I was talked into doing things I knew were wrong.

I came to school one time and found my usual friends, and someone was telling the others about how they just got away with shoplifting. I wondered how they did it without getting caught. I listened to them because I never had any stories to tell about stealing. They always said that I'm such a "goodie two shoes." On this particular day, I felt like I should prove them wrong. Later that night, my family and I went shopping, and that's when my nightmare started.

I jacked some makeup and thought to myself as I slowly walked toward the door, "I can just walk out that door, it will all be over. Please, don't let anyone see me . . ."

"Yes, I'm out the door. I did it, I got away . . ." I thought as I passed the two automatic doors.

"Excuse me, Miss, I'm a security officer here, can you please step inside the store with me? We have evidence that you took some makeup . . ."

My parents froze in their steps.

Shit, I got caught, I can't believe this. All the blood drained from my face. My parents were shocked. All they could do was stare at me in disbelief. My dad looked like he was going to slap me. My mom looked like she could kill me. All they said was,

"What a disgrace. How can you do this to us? Do you know how humiliating this is?"

I could feel my body shaking. I had never done anything like this in my entire life. I knew my parents were going to kill me. "This can't be happening, it's just a dream, just a dream, wake up, hurry," I kept telling myself as I stepped back into the store. They took me to a small weird room in the corner. It might have been a well-lit room, but it felt cold and dark.

They told me to have a seat while my parents stood by the door, glaring down at me. They told me to pull out the makeup I had put in my pocket. They totaled up the cost, which came up to $15. Then they brought out the wrappers that I had tried to hide between other things in the store. They had also taken snapshots of me. I felt like a big-time criminal.

As they were taking the pictures, they told me to lighten up for the camera. Why the hell were they telling me this when I just got myself into such a mess?

I kept asking myself, "Why am I so stupid that I stooped this low to impress my so-called friends? They're not even here with me to help me out of this mess. My parents will probably never forgive me, or ever trust me ever again. How could I do this to them? They've always given me everything I've ever wanted." After I finished signing some papers, they finally let me out. I didn't want to face my parents. When we headed toward the car, I walked behind my parents as slow as possible.

When we got home they gave me a really long lecture that made me cry the whole night. That night before I went to bed, I made a promise to myself that I will never steal anything else or do anything stupid like that ever again. Not only did I cause my parents pain, but I also threw away my own pride and good judgment trying to be someone I'm not.

Diary 36

Dear Diary,

At first I asked Ms. G, "Why should I read books about people that don't look like me? People that I don't even know and that I am not going to understand because they don't understand me!" I thought I was a smart-ass for asking her this question. I thought to myself, "She's not going to give me an answer because this time I am right." She looked up and said very calmly, "How can you say that? You haven't even bothered to open the front cover. Try it, you never know. The book may come to life before your eyes." So I started to read this book called *Anne Frank: The Diary of a Young Girl* because I wanted to prove Ms. G wrong. I wanted to show her that what she said was bullshit, and that her little technique was not going to work for me. I hate reading, and I hate her, for that matter.

To my surprise, I proved myself wrong because the book indeed came to life. At the end of the book, I was so mad that Anne died, because as she was dying, a part of me was dying with her. I cried when she cried, and just like her I wanted to know why the Germans were killing her people. Just like her, I knew the feeling of discrimination and to be looked down upon based on the way you look. Just like her, "I sometimes feel like a bird in a cage and just want to fly away." The first thing that came to my mind when I finished reading the book was the fact that Ms. G was right. I did find myself within the pages of the book, like she said I would.

Diary 37

Dear Diary,

I'm beginning to realize that Anne Frank, Zlata Filipovic, and I have a lot in common. We all seem to be trapped in some sort of a cage. Anne's cage was the secret annex she and her family hid in, and the attic where she spent most of her time. Zlata's cage was the basement she had to use for shelter, away from bombs. My cage is my own house.

Like Anne and Zlata, I have an enemy who is gung-ho for dictatorship: my father. He doesn't truly fit the role of a father in my perspective, so I refer to him as my sperm donor. James doesn't allow us to call him "dad" or "father" or any of those other sentimental, lovey-dovey names. He says the titles aren't his name so we can't call him that.

Unfortunately, I can't relate with Anne Frank and Zlata Filipovic on the subject of their fathers. From what I've read, their fathers seemed to really love them. I can, however, commiserate with them on the situations they were forced to endure. For example, I can easily put James in Hitler's shoes, and our family in the roles of the Jews. Although not quite like the war Hitler started, the war in my house was also created by ignorance and stupidity. Like all wars, there is an enemy. There are innocent victims, destruction, senseless violence, displacement, and a winner and a loser.

I've read about the monstrous things that were done in the concentration camps in WWII. I've read about how they would torture, starve, and mutilate people's bodies to something that was not recognizable as a human being. I watched my mother being beaten half to death by James and watched as blood and tears streamed down her face, which was also unrecognizable. I felt useless and scared, furious at the same time knowing that I could do nothing to help her. I watched him steal money from my mother's purse and sell our belongings for drugs.

I'm sad to say he is the person I'm supposed to look up to for good solid fatherly advice. I can still feel the sting from the belt on my back and legs as he violently lashed me in his usual drunken state of mind. It's not likely that I'll be asking him for advice any time soon.

I can relate to Anne and Zlata. Like them, I have a diary, I write about how it feels to have disgust and hatred centered directly on you because of who you are. All I can do is wait for my mother to get rid of him. I'm surprised she hasn't already. She can be a strong woman if she puts her mind to it. I know that I will never let a man put his hands on me, won't ever tolerate that kind of abuse from anyone. I guess I'll have to wait for the war to end like Anne and Zlata did, except I won't die or get taken advantage of. I'm going to be strong.

Diary 38

Dear Diary,

We've been talking about the war in Bosnia and how similar some of the events are to the Holocaust. We have been reading about a young girl named Zlata, who many call the modern-day Anne Frank. Zlata and I seem to have a lot in common because while Zlata was living though a war in Sarajevo, I was living through a different kind of war—the L.A. riots. Ironically, Zlata and I were both eleven years old when our city was under siege. I can understand how afraid and scared she was to see her city go up in flames, because my city was on fire, too.

The problem in Sarajevo began when a sniper fired a gun into a crowd at a peace rally. People panicked and war broke out. In Los Angeles, several policemen beat on a man named Rodney King and had to go to trial. The "not guilty" verdict caused people to go crazy. People started looting, fighting, and crashing cars into one another.

Zlata and I both had to hide for our safety. This made us very frightened. Zlata was trapped in her basement while she heard bombs going off and people screaming. I was trapped inside my church while people were shooting, breaking windows, and screaming for their lives.

Zlata and I lost our childhood innocence because we were denied the right to do childlike things, like go to school, talk on the phone, and just play outside. The buildings were burning and people got beaten up just because of the color of their skin, their religion, or ethnicity. Unfortunately, we both had to suffer because of other people's ignorance and destruction.

Finally, the United Nations walked the streets of Bosnia trying to keep the peace. After days of chaos, the National Guard became the peacekeepers in L.A. Even though the United Nations and the National Guard were very successful at stopping the violence, the intolerance is still there.

I can't believe that someone I don't even know, who lives thousands of miles away, could have so much in common with me.

Diary 39

Dear Diary,

I don't understand! I mean, it's not right, yet it's still happening as we speak. I just can't believe it. How sick can it get?

Why is it that women get molested? Why is it that people in general get molested?

Peter Maass's article about Bosnia that we read today in *Vanity Fair* was like a gun that triggered the lost memory in my mind. Here are these women in Bosnia, getting molested, raped, harassed, and even impregnated by soldiers that want to feel powerful by depriving them of their womanhood, pride, and self-esteem.

Why?

After reading the article about the atrocities in Bosnia, my memory returned and made everything seem like it happened yesterday. I was only six when a friend of my father's molested me in his home. Yet to this day, I haven't told my parents. Keeping this secret inside was very hard for me. There were times when I felt that I had to tell someone, but I didn't know who. Reading the article makes me feel like I'm not the only one who felt alone. Although I'm so many miles away from Bosnia, I wish there was something I could do.

When I think about this, I think of how grateful Zlata and her whole family are because they have escaped from all of this. This very same thing could have happened to Zlata or any other person that would have remained behind.

The mere fact that the story revived the lost memory within my mind gave me goose bumps. On the way home from school, I felt like reaching out to any one that had a similar story. Even standing at the bus stop, I realized that the women and girls standing next to me may have been, molested, harassed, or even impregnated at one point in their lives.

Then there was the bus ride home. My mind was working like a shotgun with every bullet acting as a question. Round one—What if the elderly woman sitting across from me was sexually molested by her uncle when she was young? Round two— How about that man standing in the back? Had he ever harassed a little girl?

All of these questions ran through my mind at the thought of the story and of all the traumatizing things that women faced. I was glad in a way that Peter Maass had uncovered an issue that I believe we should all be aware of, and also to realize that we are not alone.

His story was written to expose the war in Bosnia and its similarity to the Holocaust. Knowing that people are getting murdered and that thousands of women were being raped is shocking. It makes me both sad and angry because history is indeed repeating itself.

Diary 40

Dear Diary,

I joined Ms. Gruwell's class a few days ago. I don't know if I should have joined in the middle of the year. Oh well, I'll just have to try to keep up with whatever they'll be discussing in the class. So far, all I've heard about is a girl named Zlata. I was clueless about who she was when I started this class, so I asked my friend Ana who Zlata was.

"Wait here," she told me. Ana searched through a box located behind Ms. Gruwell's desk. She quickly brought back a book entitled *Zlata's Diary: A Child's Life in Sarajevo*. She handed the book to me to read.

I still tried to keep up with the class discussions that were usually concentrated on Zlata. The class talked about her like they knew her, like they knew what she went through while she was in the middle of the war. But how could they know, they've *never* been in the middle of a war . . . or so I thought. I learned a lot in the first few days that I was enrolled in the class. Some of my classmates are going through a war . . . an undeclared war, waged on innocent kids just trying to grow up. Society just doesn't care about young people anymore, even if we are the future.

Now that I finished the book, I began to understand the class discussions. As one of our assignments, the class had to write letters inviting Zlata to come to Long Beach. Many of the students, including myself, did the assignment thinking it was just an assignment, but when one student asked Ms. Gruwell if Zlata was really going to come, Ms. Gruwell had a gleam in her eye. I don't think that it was her intention to actually send the letters to Zlata, but now that the idea was brought up, why not?

For the first time, I heard a teacher take a question seriously. She really wanted to fly Zlata over to the United States to meet our class! Where were we going to get the money? Where in the world would she stay? There was no way we could do this! But Ms. Gruwell asked, "When have I let you down?"

I began to write a warm invitation and jazzed it up with graphics. I still wasn't sure if Ms. Gruwell was serious. After the phrase "When have I let you down?" ran through my mind several times, I began to hope that Zlata really would come to meet us, but for now, all I and the rest of our classmates could do was keep writing and keep our fingers crossed.

Sophomore Year
Spring 1996

Dear Zlata,

They say America is the "Land of the Free and Home of the Brave," but what's so free about a land where people get *killed*? My name is Thomas (Tommy) Jefferson from Wilson High School in Long Beach, California. I am a fifteen-year-old teenage boy whose life seems to be similar to yours. In your diary you said you watched out for snipers and gunshots. I watch out for gangsters and gunshots. Your friends died of gunshots and my friend Richard, who was fifteen, and my cousin Matthew, who was nineteen, also died of gunshots. The strange thing is . . . my country is not in a war. (Or is it?)

My close friend Richard was shot in the heart by a carjacker who was trying to steal his mom's car. He died in his mom's arms. His final words were "I love you." He died on December 8, 1995, just a couple weeks before Christmas. When I saw her at Christmas, I didn't even know what to say. What could I say to a mother whose son just died?

My cousin Matthew was shot five times in the head by a Mexican gang on February 8, 1996. Matthew was simply walking home when a van full of gangsters pulled him into their car, drove him down to the railroad tracks, beat him up and then shot him repeatedly in the head. *I hurt!* It's painful when I think about his death.

Two people who I cared about died a senseless death exactly two months apart. Neither of their deaths was recognized in the papers. Why? Doesn't anyone care? I care! Their families care also, but now their mothers are scarred for life because they'll never hear or see their sons again. Sometimes I want to take a gun and get revenge, but what would that prove? Would it prove how much I cared about them? Would it prove that I stuck up for them? NO! The only thing it would prove is how dumb I am. And I am not dumb . . .

The main reason I'm writing this letter to you, Zlata, is because I know you've been in this kind of situation. Your experience moved me and made this big football player cry. (And I usually don't cry.) So please tell me, Zlata, how should I handle a tragedy like this?

Now that I've read your book, I am educated on what is happening in Bosnia. I would like the opportunity now to educate people on what is happening in my "America" because until this "undeclared war" has ended, I am not free!

Your Friend,
Timmy Jefferson

Entry 4 · Ms. Gruwell

Dear Diary,

After our "toast for change," my students experienced an epiphany. My once apathetic students seemed to transform themselves into scholars with a conscience. They were so motivated that it's awe-inspiring. And when Tommy told me he was done with all the books in our Read-a-thon for Tolerance, I almost spit out my morning coffee.

"Tommy, you're done already?" I asked.

"Yeah, well, I've been grounded for the last two weeks, so all I did was read."

Read? Wait a minute, is this the same Tommy who used to hate reading? Tommy was a disciplinary transfer like Sharaud. He had been transferred into my class mid-semester as a favor to our vice principal. Apparently, his last English teacher was afraid of him. Actually, I was, too, at first, but when he asked for more books, I couldn't help but give him a hug. Then I called his father.

It was the first time I called a parent to report good news. Obviously, it was the first time Tommy's father ever received such a call because he began the conversation with, "OK, what did Tommy do this time?" He was pretty surprised to hear that Tommy was my star pupil.

And Tommy's not alone. Grounded or not, they've all become voracious readers. They even carry around the plastic Barnes & Noble bags to show off their new books. They call it "flossing." I call it a miracle.

Their excitement has motivated me even more. I wanted to put a face on the genocide in Bosnia. Without really thinking about the logistics, I foolishly suggested that we write letters to Zlata and invite her to our class. It was a ploy to get them to write letters, but I didn't think they'd take me so seriously. I underestimated the power of suggestion. Some of them truly believed that if they wrote to her, she would come, as if it were a self-fulfilling prophecy.

Their letters were so compelling that I took them to the school's computer lab to type. Then I had them bound into a book at Kinkos. I put Tommy's letter near the top because he drew parallels between the war in Bosnia and senseless gang violence. His letter began: "They say America is the 'Land of the Free and Home of the Brave,' but what's so free about a land where people get *killed*?"

Despite being on the other side of the world, he pointed out similarities between their lives: in Sarajevo, innocent kids get shot by snipers; in Long Beach they get shot in drive-bys. Zlata's friend Nina was killed by shrapnel; Tommy's best friend was murdered. He ended his letter by stating, "Now that I've read your book, I am educated on what is happening in Bosnia. I would like the opportunity now to educate people on what is happening in my 'America' because until this 'undeclared war' has ended, I am not free!"

War? In America? It was sad to think that kids like Tommy feel like they live in the middle of a war zone. War is not something I think of as a domestic problem. I read about wars in the newspaper and watch reports on the evening news. I näively assumed that war occurred in far-off places with hard to pronounce names, not in Long Beach.

Whether it's declared or not, there is a war being fought on the street corners and alleyways of Long Beach. And even though there aren't tanks rolling down the streets, there are uzis, semi-automatics, and other weapons of war. One student even said, "Gangs don't die, Ms. G, they multiply," as if there was no solution in sight.

A casualty of war—be it at the hands of a Nazi soldier, a sniper in Sarajevo, or a gang-banger on the streets of America—is a universal tragedy. After one student hopelessly said, "Zlata survived her war, but I'm afraid I may not survive mine," I was convinced that Zlata *must* read their letters. Once that realization sunk in, I began to panic. I had no idea where to send the letters. In fact, I had no idea where Zlata lived, if she spoke English, or how much it would cost to bring her here. There was so much I didn't know. Would we have to bring her parents, a translator, or an entourage?

In a feeble attempt to squelch the idea of inviting her, I put the onus back on them. "If you want her to come, then *you* have to raise the money to get her here." Nice try, but that didn't stop them.

The next day, a student brought in an empty Sparklet's water jug and set it in the middle of the classroom. He announced, "We need to start collecting money for Zlata," and then he dropped in a few coins. He was so serious that I didn't have the heart to tell him that we probably needed to fill a couple of those jugs just to pay for one airline ticket.

A couple of days later when the bottom of the jug was filled with coins and a few loose dollar bills, he asked, "Ms. Gruwell, what happens if we raise all this money and Zlata doesn't come?" I'm used to them putting me on the spot, but I wasn't prepared for this one. Trying to be fast on my feet, I said, "If she doesn't come, we can buy more books or go on another field trip. But if she does come, your lives will never be the same!"

And then it hit me . . . I better find her and at least send her the letters. If she doesn't respond, at least we tried.

So I spent the entire Christmas vacation trying to track Zlata down. I had no idea where to start. All I knew was that she was a refugee somewhere in Europe.

I started at the Museum of Tolerance. They thought she might be living in France. Then Renee Firestone told me she thought she had moved to Ireland. To play it safe, I sent a package to both countries. Then I put my concierge skills to the test. I got quotes on airline tickets, solicited local restaurants to donate gift certificates, and my hotel even offered two rooms if she accepted our invitation. With all the provisions in order, all we had to do now was wait.

While anxiously awaiting a response from Zlata, a wonderful woman named Gerda Seifer, a Holocaust survivor from Poland, called to tell me that Miep Gies was actually coming to California to help commemorate the fiftieth anniversary of Anne Frank's diary. Miep was Otto Frank's secretary and the person responsible for finding Anne's diary. She's eighty-seven years old and will be flying in from Amsterdam. The director of the event happened to live near me. We met and hit it off. He offered to change Miep's itinerary so she could come meet my students. Wow! Meeting a legend like Miep is more than we could have ever hoped for.

To help prepare the students for Miep's visit, I asked Gerda to share her experience during WWII with the students. Like Anne, who spent her adolescence hiding in the secret annex, Gerda sat perched on a wooden box in a windowless cellar. Not only will the students be able to empathize with Gerda's feelings of persecution and loss, but I hope they'll be able to understand how Anne Frank must have felt.

Diary 41

Dear Diary,

When we began our lesson about the importance of racial tolerance, I had no idea that that lesson would be a life-altering experience. After reading *Night* and *Anne Frank: The Diary of a Young Girl*, I guess you could say I knew about the Holocaust, but I was not prepared for what I was going to be faced with today.

Ms. Gruwell had been talking for a long time about bringing in a Holocaust survivor named Gerda Seifer. Well today, we actually met her. Like Anne, she is Jewish and was born in Poland and she didn't meet Hitler's standards of purity either. During World War II, Gerda's parents made her go into hiding with a Catholic family. She was forced to live in a basement where she could barely stand up. She could hear the SS soldiers marching outside, waiting for their next victim. She is the only survivor in her family. Luckily, she was spared from a camp.

Just as Anne was trapped, Gerda was trapped. Neither Gerda nor Anne could lead normal teenage lives. They lost their innocence due to uncontrollable circumstances. Whenever they ventured outdoors they faced the possibility of being captured by the Gestapo. Jewish people had to wear a yellow Star of David, which distinguished them from others. They were forced to attend special schools isolated from other children. They were ridiculed and tormented throughout the war.

Unfortunately, I know exactly what it feels like to not be

able to go outside, not because of the Gestapo, but because of gangs. When I walk outside, I constantly glance from side to side watching those standing around me. Since I feel out of place, I often put on a façade so that I fit in. Maybe if I look and act like I belong they will not confront me. It is disrespectful to look a gang member in the eye. Imagine what would happen if a prisoner in a concentration camp insulted a Gestapo—they would get killed instantly. After the stories I'd heard from Gerda, I can guarantee that I won't repeat the mistakes of others.

It amazed me how I could empathize not only with Anne Frank, but also with a Holocaust survivor. I'm glad I had the opportunity to hear about the past through Gerda. She is living proof of history. This experience will help me pass on the message of tolerance that Anne died for and that Gerda survived for.

Diary 42

Dear Diary,

To a fifteen-year-old, the only heroes I ever read about ran around in tight, colorful underwear and threw buildings at each other for fun. But today, that all changed. A true hero leapt off the pages of a book to pay my class a special visit. Her name is Miep Gies and she is the lady Anne Frank wrote about in her diary. I can't believe that the woman responsible for keeping Anne Frank alive in the attic came to speak to us in person!

As I entered the Bruin Den teen center, I could feel the excitement. Many of us stayed after school yesterday to make welcome signs to decorate the walls and several students got to school really early to help set up a big buffet. We wanted everything to be perfect.

After the proper introductions were made by Ms. Gruwell, she made her entrance. Everybody stood up and cheered as Miep made her way into the hall. I was thrilled to see her in person after seeing her portrayed in movies and reading about her in the book. No colorful underwear needed—she was a true hero.

After she settled in, Miep began to talk about how she was delighted to meet us. She described to us firsthand how she hid the Frank family from the Nazi soldiers and how she found Anne's diary. When she described how the Gestapo captured Anne and would not allow Miep to say good-bye, it made all of us emotional. She told us about how she tried to bribe the officers into letting her friends go, but they threatened to kill her.

My friend who was sitting next to me was crying. Since we've been studying the Holocaust, it has made him think about all the people he knows who have been killed. His best friend accidentally shot himself, and to this day, he still has nightmares about his death. Miep told everyone that not a day goes by where she doesn't think about Anne.

When she said this, my friend stood up and told her she was his hero. Then he asked her if she believed that she was a hero. We expected her to say yes, but I think she surprised us all. She said, "No. You, my friends, are the true heroes." Heroes? Us? Having her say that made me realize more than ever how special my classmates are. Like she said, we are the heroes and it is up to us to let the younger generation know what's going on. It sure feels good to know that for once in my life my friends and I are doing the right thing.

After she finished and we all had the opportunity to give her a hug or have her sign our books, I realized how lucky we were. Most people will probably never have the opportunity to hear her story in person like we did. A legacy left by one girl, carried by one woman, was passed on to a new generation of teens who have the chance to make a difference like Anne's diary did.

Now after meeting Miep, I can honestly say that my heroes are not just made-up characters—my hero is real.

Diary 43

Dear Diary,

"If you could live an eternity and not change a thing or exist for the blink of an eye and alter everything, what would you choose?" This was one of Ms. G's questions after we read this poem.

Moment

Let him wish his life
For the sorrows of a stone
Never knowing the first thread
Of these
Never knowing the pain of ice
As its crystals slowly grow
Needles pressing in on the heart

To live forever
And never feel a thing
To wait a million lifetimes
Only to erode and become sand
Wish not for the stone
But for the fire
Last only moments
But change everything

Oh to be lightning
To exist for less than a moment
Yet in that moment
To expose the world to every open eye
Oh to be thunder

To clap and ring
To rumble into memories
Minds and spines

To chill the soul and shake the very ground
Pounding even the sand
Into smaller pieces
Or the mountain
Brooding, extinct
Yet gathering for one fatal moment
The power to blow the top clean off the world
Oh to last the blink of an eye and leave nothing
But nothing unmoved behind you

Vincent Guilliano
January 9, 1991

Ms. G gave us this poem, written by someone who had gone to college with her. Ironically, he died shortly after he wrote the poem by drowning in the San Francisco Bay. After we read the poem, Ms. G broke it down to its simplest form, she wanted no part to be misunderstood. She wanted this poem to become our motto in class, and our principle in life.

She told us to be the kind of people that have enough passion to change the world. If we let ourselves be fire, thunder, or lightning, we could alter everything.

We all thought that Ms. Gruwell's lesson was really powerful and all, but us? Lightning and thunder? Not likely. The below-average sure-to-drop-out kids? Please, ever since I can remember, we've been put down and stepped on, and now all of a sudden we have the potential to change the world? Leave it up to Ms. Gruwell to come up with some crazy shit like that.

She tried to convince us that we were capable of anything.

But it wasn't until Miep's visit that it finally made sense. I remember talking about how much we admired her for risking everything to care for Anne and her family. She said that she had only done it because it was the "right thing to do."

Someone stood up and said that Miep was their hero.

"No, you're the real heroes," she answered. There she was, one of the most heroic women of all time, telling *us* that *we* were heroes.

"Do not let Anne's death be in vain," Miep said, using her words to bring it all together. Miep wanted us to keep Anne's message alive, it was up to us to remember it. Miep and Ms. Gruwell had had the same purpose all along. They wanted us to seize the moment. Ms. Gruwell wanted us to realize that we could change the way things were, and Miep wanted to take Anne's message and share it with the world.

That's when it all became crystal clear. Anne's message of tolerance was to become our message.

At that moment, I became like the fire, and like the lightning and like thunder.

Diary 44

Dear Diary,

I can't believe that Zlata Filipovic is coming! Our letters actually paid off. After reading her book, I couldn't do anything but relate her life with mine. It was so interesting to realize that another person my same age, went through such a horrible experience seeking refuge from a war. Even though I didn't physically experience a war, my family managed to escape one just in time from Nicaragua. Blasts of gunfire thundered throughout my country, too.

I can candidly say that in the back of my mind I didn't think Zlata would actually respond to our invitation. I felt like we were writing to a celebrity, and all we would end up hearing in return was a letter from her agent saying thank you and here's a signed photograph. Zlata's response, on the other hand, was much more gratifying. Not only did she personally write back to us, but she also mentioned that she would be more than happy to meet us. I feel like I'm about to meet a person whom I could relate to.

Diary 45

Dear Diary,

March 24, 1996, was the most unforgettable day ever. I had the pleasure of going with my family to the Newport Beach Marriott Hotel to meet Zlata Filipovic and her parents, Malik and Alicia, and her best friend, Mirna. My parents got dressed up in their nicest clothes for the occasion. I wore a suit.

We drove to the hotel not knowing what to expect from the evening. As soon as we walked inside the Marriott Hotel, we felt important and excited to be there. A photographer took our pictures and waiters in tuxedos and white gloves served us appetizers off silver trays. They even served us punch in champagne glasses. Since Ms. Gruwell works there, she made sure that everyone went out of their way to treat us like royalty.

When Zlata came down to meet us, all of us surrounded her as if she was a celebrity. We all wanted to take pictures with her and ask her questions about herself. It was so interesting to see how we had a girl our own age that is such a role model to us. The fact that she was actually here was so unbelievable.

I found out we had a lot in common. We both like listening to music and being with our friends. Zlata left such a good first impression that I'll never forget her. As we continued to celebrate, we had a formal dinner in her honor. The food was delicious. There must have been at least five courses. There were so many knives and forks at our table. I'm glad Ms. Gruwell went over which ones we're supposed to use first.

Before the night was over, Ms. Gruwell told us that this was just the beginning and there's more to come. I left the Marriott with a good feeling and high expectations about our future.

Diary 46

Dear Diary,

My friendship with Mary reminds me of Zlata and Mirna's friendship. They have been through a war together because of race and religion, and they are still best friends. The only difference is that neither of their families want to prevent their friendship. There's not even a war in this country, yet I can't even go to a movie with my friend because she's white. Why does that matter any more? I thought we were in a new era and were getting over the race issue. Yeah, right! I'm living in a big fantasy world. The time hasn't come for people to overcome hatred of others because of something as insignificant as race.

She's the best friend a person could ever have. She's fun, smart, she doesn't just hear me she listens to me, and we have so much in common, but . . . she's white. There's nothing wrong with that, it's not a problem to me, anyway. To everyone else it is a problem, especially my family. More specifically, my father.

My father gets angry when I spend time with her. He says, "Why don't you have any black friends?" or "So you're going over to those honky's house again?" Come on, who uses those words anymore? He warned me to watch my back because those white people always stab you in the back. He has no idea what kind of person she is. I can't believe how incredibly ignorant he is. I think it's because he grew up in an era of pure racism. Worse, he grew up in the South, and racism was all he saw. Does that make it OK to take his anger out on me and my friends? I don't think so!

My father thinks she is turning me into a white girl, because she's my best friend and I hang out with her all the time. She has never done anything negative toward me, and even if she did I wouldn't look at her as if the whole race did something negative toward me.

Color is the last thing that comes to mind when we hang out together. We have more important things to be concerned about.

Diary 47

Dear Diary,

Knowledge comes in strange ways. I never thought that a person who lived over 10,000 miles away could impact me, but tonight, that changed. Zlata has been with us for four days now and we've really gotten to know her well and she's just like us. When I met her, we were wearing the same shoes! I couldn't believe she was wearing Doc Martens. When we started to get to know each other, we talked about the same things. About Pearl Jam and how cute Eddie Vedder was. If I hadn't known that she was Zlata Filipovic, "the famous teen author from war-torn Bosnia," I would have just assumed that she was a normal fifteen-year-old girl who liked to shop and hang out with her friends. The best part is, that she *was* a normal fifteen-year-old girl.

When she came, we were invited to the Croatian Hall where she would be speaking. We didn't want to go empty-handed, so we gathered medicinal supplies, clothes, and even old toys. All these were going to be sent back to Bosnia. This would be our first encounter with people who had been persecuted in Bosnia. We expected nothing less than for them to be accepting and tolerant. I thought they would care less what color, creed, or race any of us were. Unfortunately, some proved me wrong.

As Zlata was speaking in front of the people from Croatia, they were all nodding their heads. "Yes, yes," they would say. She spoke about all of the injustices that one must go through for a simple label or belief. She mentioned her experience as a fourteen-year-old growing up in war-torn Bosnia. How hard it was for her to lose friends because of the way they looked, or what they believed in. At this point, we were the ones nodding our heads.

There is one thing that really stands out in my mind from that night, however. As she was answering questions, a couple of adults asked her what ethnicity she was, Croatian? Muslim? Serbian? I was upset that instead of getting the message that she was trying to convey, they were too preoccupied with what nationality she was. Were these the same adults that preached how wrong racism and discrimination are? Were these the same people that a minute ago agreed that we shouldn't care about labels? Zlata looked around, stared at us, and simply said, "I'm a human being."

That's exactly what we all are. We spend so much time trying to figure out what race a person is when we could just get to know them as individuals. I felt like answering their question with a question. Does it matter? Will it make a difference if she is Croatian, Muslim, Serbian?

She taught me the most valuable lesson that anybody could ever have and to think that she is only fifteen! Ever since that day I've tried not to accept society's labels, but to fight against them.

I have always been taught to be proud of being Latina, proud of being Mexican, and I was. I was probably more proud of being a "label" than of being a human being, that's the way most of us were taught. Since the day we enter th⸢ label, a number, a statistic, that's just the wa ask me what race I am, like Zlata, I'll simply being."

Diary 48

Dear Diary,

Today I went to the Croatian Hall with Zlata and met a little boy named Tony who lived a nightmare because he is Croatian. One night while he was asleep, Serbian soldiers came into his home and shot him in his face; at point-blank range. A Bosnian woman living in L.A. sponsored Tony's trip to the United States to have his jaw reconstructed. When we met him, he had only a medal plate holding his jaw together.

When I saw Tony, I was grateful my family made it out of Peru before we were harmed—or worse, killed. I thought of my three-year-old brother, and pictured him standing in Tony's place, telling this ghastly story. Like the life of my family, Tony's life has been permanently altered by the terror of war. He was a survivor of ethnic cleansing; we survived a revolution that turned into terrorism. Even though the Bosnian war was one of ethnicity and religion, it was just as senseless as the terrorism that ransacked my country. It forced many to leave behind their homes, and their lives.

Although the terrorist struggle in Peru started as a good cause, it turned many people's lives into a nightmare. Just walking by a parked car, you couldn't help wondering if there was a bomb hidden in its trunk. As you passed, you wondered if it was going to explode in your face.

I remember my dad saying, "Everything will turn out OK. In the United States. there are more opportunities, better jobs, and no terrorism." When my Dad said that I didn't really understand what it meant. I was only ten. I only thought about homework, food, TV, and going outside to play with my friends.

I'd been to the U.S. before to visit family, but never thought uld end up living there. Four weeks after my dad told us we were moving, my grandmother called for us. My dad went to the American Embassy to take care of the paperwork for our green cards. We would get our social security numbers and green cards three months after our arrival in the States.

Three weeks before flying to the U.S., terrorists blew up the house next to mine. The explosion woke everyone in the neighborhood. My eyes snapped open as a wave of warm air hit my face. I got out of bed realizing there was only smoke and bright light where my bedroom window once was. I saw my mom running toward me screaming, but couldn't hear her. All I heard was the ringing in my head. She grabbed me, shaking the ringing from my ear. I heard the turmoil in my neighborhood. She carried me outside, my feet were bleeding from stepping on broken glass blown from my window. The firemen told my father that out of twenty sticks of dynamite, ten exploded. If all had ignited, my house would have exploded also. I realized the magnitude of what was happening, and was glad to be moving to the U.S.

My first day of school in the United States was very hard. I didn't understand any English words. Everything was so different. I had had some English classes in Peru, but nothing like this. Everybody spoke so fast, their words were hard to follow. Everything sounded like Rs and Ss. I couldn't talk, read, or write English. The third day of school, some Mexican guys spoke to me. We talked, played, and they taught me English.

Like my first years in the U.S., Tony didn't understand English. My only way to communicate was to play with him. It lifted my spirit to see his joy despite his tragic story. Though it hurt him to smile, he laughed anyway. Though he couldn't understand a word we were saying, he understood that we felt his pain. We too knew what it felt like to live amid war.

When Zlata wrote about Bosnian children becoming the "soldiers" and the soldiers becoming "children," at first I didn't get her meaning. After hearing Tony's story, I understood. In war the innocence of a child is lost, and though the soldiers feel theirs is a worthy cause, they behave like children when trying to achieve their goals. Knowing that a grown man entered a child's bedroom stealing his innocence, makes me sad. They stole his smile. Tony wears the permanent scars of war on his face, just as I wear the scars on my soul.

Diary 49

Dear Diary,

I am so exhausted from yesterday! We got to spend a whole day with Zlata and Mirna. Our marathon day started at 7 A.M. and I didn't get home until 10 P.M. last night. Or was it 11 P.M.? Even though I'm exhausted, I can't wait to spend another day with them!

Our day began with a breakfast by the "Dream Team Moms." These are the dedicated moms who have adopted our class as their kids. After we had breakfast we left in buses to Los Angeles. It was my first time in a charter bus. The buses were air-conditioned, had televisions, a VCR, and lights that we could turn on and off at our seats! Plus a bathroom!! A big difference from school buses!

Soon we got to the Museum of Tolerance, our first stop. For many, it was their first time there, but this was my second time. During our freshman year we went straight to the museum's theater to watch *Higher Learning*. This time we had a private tour of the museum.

The museum focuses on stereotypes, prejudice, genocide, the history of intolerance. There were comic strips to show us some examples of how people are misjudged and how our negative thoughts can lead to violence. Plus there was a section of worn out shoes each representing a victim of the Holocaust.

During the tour, I received a passport with a child's face and name. Throughout the museum you get to find out what happens to them. Each room I went into, I would slip my passport into a computer and it would tell me the fate of the child. Some of my friends had passports where the child died. Many of us cried during the tour.

After we came out of the museum, the ground was wet from the rain. It seems like the rain was a symbol of tears from those who had died. As though they were crying out their tears of sorrows and stories to us.

After the tour, we went to Lawry's "The House of Prime Ribs" for lunch. It is located in Beverly Hills. I was afraid to touch anything because I might break something. The dining tables had a candle with fresh flowers and the napkins folded in the fanciest way. The seats were made of real leather, they weren't sticky or smelly like some restaurants I have been to. Lawry's treated us like royalty! The chef came around with food in a heated cart to serve us prime rib. Even the restroom was decorated with fresh flowers. One thing's for sure, it was a *lot* nicer than our school's restrooms, which constantly smell like cigarettes and have makeup stains on the mirrors and sink. Sometimes you will find the sinks clogged up with paper towels or see wadded toilet paper hanging from the ceiling.

Once we were as stuffed as pigs, we went back to the museum to watch a private screening of *Schindler's List*. Oskar Schindler started out as a man who wore his gold Nazi pin with pride. He couldn't care less about the Jews and others being rounded up and taken away in crowded cattle cars. During one of the Jewish round-ups, he saw a little girl in a red petticoat. She stood out from everyone because the movie is in black and white. She was running away from the chaos and hiding. A few days later he found her dead with a pile of other bodies ready to be thrown into the fire. That's when he started to try to save every Jew he could with the money he had. By the end, he had saved over a thousand Jews.

The movie made *Night, The Wave,* and *The Diary of a Young Girl* come alive. One of my friends actually said he had a flashback about the death of one of his friends. He said that the little girl's red coat reminded him of his friend's blood. It made me realize that senseless violence doesn't only happen in history books or movies.

After the movie, we headed to the Century City Marriott Hotel to have a reception for Holocaust survivors and ourselves. The Holocaust survivor at our table showed us his tattoo and it made me wonder if he ever tried to hide it from others. I wanted to know: What he was thinking everyday in the camp? What was his greatest fears? Did he ever think of suicide? I wanted to ask, but I was too nervous and I thought my questions were stupid.

Near the end of dinner, students introduced the Holocaust survivors sitting with them and told us the most interesting information about their experiences. Some of my questions were actually answered, but there will always be more.

I feel that reading the books gave me a foundation for this piece of history, but today's marathon with the museum, the movie, and especially meeting all the survivors gave me a better understanding of the Holocaust. I'm glad they survived to tell us their stories and pass the baton. My fingertips are still tingling!

Diary 50

Dear Diary,

  Sorry, diary, I was going to try not to do it tonight, but the little baggy of white powder is calling my name. As I chop up the white rock on my special makeup mirror into very fine powder I start thinking about the past week with Zlata and our infamous toast for change.

Zlata left today and I can't help but feel guilty for what I have been doing lately. We're all about changing for the better and I am changing for the worse. This whole week, people have been looking at us as model teenagers who have changed their lives. The local newspapers have actually done stories about us bringing Zlata here and how we've made monumental changes in our lives. That part is true, but then there's me. It does bother me that I am being dishonest, especially to Zlata, but is it lying when I don't say anything?

Ms. Gruwell would be so disappointed if she found out. I definitely can't say anything now because it would really make things worse. I don't know what she would do, especially since Zlata was here. I might as well keep it a secret at this point. I wish she wouldn't trust me so much. I mean how can she trust me if I can't even trust myself? She shouldn't trust anyone who steals money from their family, begs friends for change, and digs through her couch just to support her drug habit. In some sick way I wish I could get caught so all this lying could be behind me. But then reality kicks in when I see that line in front of me. When it comes down to it I'm not ready to change. I know I should stop, but it would be wrong to stop for someone else. When I hear cheesy clichés like "Hugs not drugs," or "Be smart, don't start," it makes me want to do it more. Yack, yack, yack. Come on, get real, how boring! Quite honestly, I'm just not ready to quit yet.

I'm what you call a closet tweeker. To clear things up, a tweeker is someone who smokes or snorts speed. Nobody knows my secret, especially Zlata, and I'd like to keep it that way. It's not something to brag about. I'm getting to a point where I can hide it in plain sight. When Zlata was here, she and Ms. Gruwell had no idea that I was high. I even got high before we went to

Universal Studios with her, but I played it off as much as I could. Even though we were talking about our favorite bands between rides, I don't think she knew.

When I first started getting high, I would be strung out and I couldn't sit still. But now I've learned to control it and I can play it off. I guess that's what happens when you do it all the time. People never see what is right under their noses and believe me I use it to my advantage.

The worst thing about it is that I'm already in out-patient rehab two days a week, but I just have to make things worse by doing drugs more and more, harder and harder. It's so ironic how all this got started. I was put in rehab after our toast for change for possession of marijuana, but now that I'm in rehab, I'm addicted to speed. Where's the change in that? When everyone is changing their old habits I'm making new ones.

My worst fear is that I'm becoming an addict. I mean, can someone like me have an addiction? When I think of an addict I think of someone walking the streets, begging people for change, sucking dick for a score, leaving their babies in the trash still alive. But when I think about it, I'm no better. I'm what you call a model child. A good daughter, one of Ms. Gruwell's favorite students, and now I have an amazing new friend—but I'm lying to my mom, Ms. G, and Zlata. Not exactly model child material.

Now I guess you can call me an addict. No more A's on tests or bringing teachers apples, (like I did that anyway). I'll beg, steal, and cheat just to get a quick line. Sure it has its pitfalls, but you know what they say: "Curiosity killed the cat." Well, not this cat.

For me, a quick line has turned into a fast hit from the glass pipe. The higher the intensity, the better the high. That's my preferred party favor, the glass pipe. It kind of freaks me out because I never thought I would be at this point. Is there time to turn back or am I going to get closer to a dark tunnel with no light and no way out?

I'm actually relieved that this week with Zlata and all the attention is over. Not that it was boring, it was really fun, but I didn't deserve it. With all that behind me, I whip out my straw, sit down on the toilet, making sure the bathroom is locked; bring it to my nose and snort. The burn is a sure sign that I'm on my way to my next high. Oh yeah, it's going to be good. No more headaches, body aches, or stomachaches until of course, the high is over, but only until I reach for my best friend called crystal meth.

Diary 51

Dear Diary,

Basketball for Bosnia was an event to remember. Ms. Gruwell and her students held a tournament at the university to help donate all sorts of food and medical supplies for kids in Bosnia. There were over 500 people in attendance and besides basketball, there was a cheer camp for the little brothers and sisters and a talent show at halftime. I got to play on a team even though I'm not in her class. My team was Anne's Angels (in honor of Anne Frank), and I even got to keep the jersey. No one really cared who won or lost; we were just having fun to help people in need.

I want to get into her class so badly after today. They're so much more than a "class," they act like a family. Ms. Gruwell does things that are so smart, yet so simple. I feel as though I were already part of their team because no one cared what color I was or how I looked. All they cared about was coming together for the same cause. Being accepted for who you are without having anyone snicker at you was great—but it's not something I'm used to.

It brought back a lot of memories from my past. In my honors class, I've never really been that comfortable. I've always been the oddball and have never felt accepted. I feel like I'm always trying to prove that I belong. I remember feeling like that back in the day.

I grew up surrounded by fat people. My mom—overweight; my brother—overweight; my sister—overweight; my aunt, yeah, you guessed it—overweight! As a child, I always thought, Why me? Why did I have to be overweight? Why did I have to be the child that didn't play sports because I was overweight? I couldn't climb the gym ropes, I couldn't swing on the swings, and I couldn't do a pull-up. I thought nothing could be done about my weight. I thought that was the way I was supposed to be, FAT!

Jumping rope and having the other kids yell, "EARTH-QUAKE! Run for cover!" really hurt. People often told me, "Why do you let people talk to you that way? Speak up for yourself," but I didn't have the courage to do so. I was afraid to say anything for fear they might say, "Shut your fat ass up!" So I thought I would save myself the embarrassment.

My sixth grade year was hell! I hardly had any friends and I couldn't look anyone in the face. All I could think about was food. By the time I completed sixth grade, I weighed over 200 pounds. That's a lot of damn weight for a sixth grader. I wore a size 26 to 28 and I had no confidence in myself. I thought I was *ugly!* I had no boyfriend, I didn't go to parties, and I had no social life. I pretty much kept to myself. When some ignorant kids would see me at lunch, they would say, "Your fat ass don't need to be eating shit!" I would just ignore them, but after awhile, the comments were really hard for me to ignore. It was difficult for me to believe that someone would take away my self-esteem, just to gain their own. The only reason why I didn't resort to kicking their skinny butts was because I didn't want to be known as fat *and* a bully, because then *no one* would talk to me.

I felt alone, ashamed, and left out of everything. I would go home after school and think of things I wanted to say to them, but never had the courage to say. I hated them and myself. I felt as if I was in a shell and there was no way for me to get out.

Rather than feeling sorry for myself, I turned to books and

school to feel good. Suddenly, I was getting straight As. School allowed me to creep out of my shell slowly, but surely.

Basketball for Bosnia practically was a rebirth. All my insecurities flew out the window. When the tournament was over, we formed a Soul Train line and danced on the basketball court. I can't believe that I had the courage to go through the center of the line and dance in front of 500 people. Everybody went crazy, they cheered me on and waved their hands in the air. I felt wanted, like I was a part of a family. I wasn't just another face in the class, I had a chance to express myself and be a star!

Zlata's Letter

Dublin, June 4, 1996
My dear friends,

It has been a while since I was spending that crazy little, but at the same time very big and very special week with you. And I still recall the moments, rewind the movie in my head, and remember all of you, read your letters. Listen to the tapes you gave me, look at the presents, look at the stain on my jacket from the flying drink (just kidding!) . . . All the memories you gave me will be with me forever, as they are something one should not forget. And I just want to thank you for all that, for your friendship, your understanding—that is something mankind needs desperately. And you certainly have it together with your strong ambition to make the world a better place by starting with yourselves and your surrounding. You are real heroes.

But I also want to thank you for doing what you are doing today for my country, for children and young people who truly need people like yourselves, who will unselfishly and in a 100% humane way do something for them. Thank you for not forgetting them, for shadowing the feeling of being abandoned the rest of the world gives them. You must know that they will appreciate it greatly, they will appreciate anything you give them, because it is not only the question of the amount, but the gesture brings a lot as well. Offering a helping hand is more than great.

So, not to make this extremely long, as I could, I will just wish you the best of luck for today and the best of fun as well. Enjoy yourselves. Your friends will hopefully know a bit more about Bosnia thanks to you. Go Bosnia Beauties (ha-ha) and all the others.

Don't forget—the strength is in you. You have the power. And you also have the choice where to direct that power to. Just don't forget that.

Once more, thank you for everything—in my name and in the name of all those from a little country of Bosnia who need your help. And special thanks to your wonderful, amazing teacher (let me hear some ovations!) . . .
I love you and miss you all very much.
       All my friendship . . .
              C-YA soon
                With love,
                  Zlata
P.S. Warmest and sincere regard to everyone in sunny L.A. "We must learn to live together as brothers or perish together as fools."—Dr. Martin Luther King, Jr.

Diary 52

Dear Diary,

My life is going downhill, and so quickly I'm not sure if I can hold it up anymore. Let's start from the beginning. The other day my sister and I were looking through some pictures we found in our parents' room. We found this picture of an old man and my mom together at a hotel. They were sitting in their bathing suits together, arms around each other. The crazy part is my parents are still married. It didn't make sense to either of us. I think it hit me a little harder than it did my sister. Though I couldn't decide if I wanted to cry or just start yelling. This was my family my mom was screwing with. We took the pictures to my mom and asked her about the man. She got really defensive and told us to stay out of her room, that we had no right going through her stuff and that he was just a friend. Yeah, right, I didn't believe if for a minute. She wouldn't have been so upset if this guy were just a friend. When my mom went out of town last week with her "friend from work," she was really with this man! That means . . . she is cheating on my dad! Neither of us can say anything to our dad, so we've decided to keep our mouths closed. He is going to find out soon enough. My family is starting to crumble a bit, it isn't falling apart yet, but I know it will soon.

I wanted to rely on Ms. G's class to be my surrogate family, but I'm slowly finding out that it might not be a good idea because we may not be a family next year. Although Ms. G wants to teach us next year, as juniors, the other English teachers don't want to let her. They argue that a teacher who has only been teaching here for a couple of years doesn't have the right to pick her students and teach them for four years. There was a handful of teachers complaining and now we are in jeopardy of not being a class next year.

This can't be happening to me. Now both of my families are falling apart. I'm not going to have anyone left because we are being split into different classes. I can't handle it; I can't lose both my families! This is all I have left. To think it's only because the other teachers are jealous. We are getting all the attention now, newspapers are writing articles about us. Some teachers haven't done anything new in years, and now that we are trying something new, they're becoming jealous. They are trying to hold us down, split us up, and keep us from making a difference. It's not going to work!

Ms. G did what she does best; she talked to anyone who would listen to her about our accomplishments until we had made some headway. They were talking about letting us have our own class. Everyone is worried. I've caught a couple kids crying about it, actually someone probably caught me more then once. All I can think about is us not being together. What would we do? Who would we turn to? As if high school isn't hard enough, this would make it ten times harder. Right now, I have my comfort zone, I have a place where everyone accepts me and I accept everyone, and I can't be without this for the next two years.

It's been a hard time for everyone. We have to keep working in class, although we don't know if we are going to be together next year or not. These teachers can't break our chain, we are linked, not by our hands, but by our hearts and we will always be together. I'm scared, very scared. I hope everything works out.

Diary 53

Dear Diary,

School's almost over, and I just found out that we get to have Ms. Gruwell next year! It's great news for all of us. She fought hard to keep us together! I've been lucky to have her for two years. My mom says, "I've hit the lottery in education." She's the best teacher I've ever had. She truly cares about us and never judges us based on appearances. Now I get to be in her class my junior year!

I have a lot of friends who are in honors English and they've become quite interested in what my class has been doing lately! There have been questions about our field trips and the dinners we attended. After all the years my friends who had made me feel stupid, all are now interested in my class. After all, they used to call Ms. Gruwell's class the "Ghetto Class" because of all the minorities. They have always made me feel like a dumb white boy because I'm not in their honors classes. Well, it looks like they're the losers because they don't know how great this class really is and how many friends I have made because of it. We have had many guest speakers and travel to museums and social functions. I view things much differently than my friends do because of my new experiences, but hey, they're still my friends.

I told my friends that there was going to be room for a couple of more students in Ms. Gruwell's class. I found out they had all signed a waiting list to get into her class the very next day! If my friends are accepted, I hope they will treat Ms. Gruwell and the other students with respect. If not, I'll have to regulate because as far as I'm concerned, they're the ones on probation in my "Ghetto Class"!

ANNE FRANK HOUSE
ANNE FRANK STICHTING

To Faculty and Students of Wilson High School

amsterdam 6 April 1996

Dear Students,
    I thank you with all my heart for the wonderful time I could spent at your institution. The interest and insight shown, both by teachers and students, impressed me immensely. Without any hesitation I state that this visit has been one of my most unique experiences. Several of your faces have been engraved in my heart.
        With warm regards

Miep Gies

Junior Year
Fall 1996

Entry 5 · Ms. Gruwell

Dear Diary,

I can't believe that school starts tomorrow and I'm taxiing down a runway in France. Even though I'm bound to have jet lag in the morning, it's worth it. Since I couldn't take my students with me on my two-week trek, I wanted to bring parts of Europe back with me. So I collected books, museum brochures, and postcards from all the places we studied in class, like the Tower of London and Anne's attic. I can't wait to show them my wooden shoes from Holland, my Blarney Stone from Ireland and all the pictures.

With a twelve-hour flight ahead of me, I have plenty of time to reminisce about the summer. I'll "rewind the movie in my mind," as Zlata would say, and replay the summer from the beginning, pausing on some of the highlights.

The first day of summer seems so long ago. I didn't really have a summer break in the conventional sense because I started teaching at a university. A professor at National University, whose son is in my class, invited me to me to teach a seminar on how to inspire teens to read. It was an emotional two hours. Halfway through the seminar, people started crying. And at the end, the dean of National University offered me a job.

So I taught two education classes during the week and

worked at the Marriott Hotel on weekends, which allowed me to save enough money to go to Europe to visit Zlata and Miep.

My first stop was the Netherlands. One of the perks of being a concierge at the Marriott is that I get to stay at other hotels with an employee discount, so I stayed at the Amsterdam Marriott in the middle of the city. It was my second time to Amsterdam, but since I've met Miep and seen the documentary *Anne Frank Remembered*, it meant so much more to me.

I made the arrangements to meet Miep and her friend Cor at my hotel. I gave her a care package from my students that had a "Miep Mania" jersey from our Basketball for Bosnia tournament, beautifully framed pictures from her visit and the issue of *People* magazine that had a picture of her with my students. Apparently, they made quite an impression on her, and she even said, "Several of your students' faces have been engraved in my heart."

We also talked about Anne. Even though it's been over fifty years since Anne passed away, she said that not a day goes by that she doesn't think about her. As she described their special relationship and all the sacrifices she made during their two years in hiding, I sat there in awe. She told me stories about riding her bike miles in the snow just to dig up turnips and about the time that Anne convinced her to spend a night in the attic. Not only was she generous, but she was also very courageous. She described how she stormed into Nazi headquarters and tried to bribe Gestapo agents to let her friends go after they were captured. Hiding Jews was a crime punishable by death, so she was lucky that she wasn't killed. Although she couldn't save her friends, she did save Anne's precious diary. Now when millions of people think of the Holocaust, they think of Anne.

What impressed me most was her humility. Despite all the accolades she received, she doesn't think her actions were heroic or even out of the ordinary. She told me that what she hopes people will learn from her life "is that every individual, even a very ordinary housewife or secretary, can make a difference." I can't wait to share her simple philosophy with my students that they too can make a difference—like Anne or Zlata.

Miep was so excited when I told her I was flying to Dublin to spend time with Zlata and her parents. She met Zlata a couple years ago on her book tour and said she had "Anne's eyes."

After I spent a few days in Amsterdam trying to see things through Anne's perspective, I flew to Ireland to visit Zlata and her parents. They had just returned from their summer vacation on the Croatian coast. It was the first time they had returned to the Balkans since they fled the war in the winter of '93. Mirna's parents missed her, so she plans to stay in Sarajevo this year to go to school. Zlata and Mirna were inseparable since they left Bosnia, so they're both going to have a hard time adjusting.

Zlata said that so much has changed in Sarajevo since the war began. We spent a lot of time looking at family photos before the war broke out. The soccer field that once held the 1984 Olympics is now filled with tombstones. Even though the buildings are in the process of being rebuilt, Zlata's parents feel like it will take a long time to rebuild relations. There is still a lot of animosity and racial tension.

Although Zlata's book sheds light on the problems occurring in Bosnia, it wasn't until she left that she realized the magnitude of this war. So we spent hours talking about politics, looking at photos, and making predictions about what will happen when all the American soldiers leave.

Even though Zlata's the same age as my students, she seems so much wiser. Sometimes she's very philosophical and at others she's a typical teenager. After we'd spent hours talking about politics over a traditional Bosnian meal, she wanted to take me shopping in Dublin and show off her adopted city. She took me to see a punk rock band, helped me pick out Doc Martens and she and her friend, Daragh, made a video for my students.

We got so close on this visit that we all cried when I left.

After leaving Dublin, I took a quick tour of London, but I couldn't wait to get to Paris to meet Zlata's cousin, Melika. Before moving to Ireland, Zlata and Mirna went to school with Melika in Paris. We met at the Eiffel Tower and I instantly felt like I was meeting a part of my family. As with my time with Miep and Zlata, sightseeing was secondary to sharing stories and photographs and building a relationship.

Since this trip will really help bring "World Literature" to life, I've got to think of a clever way to bring "American Literature" to life. I wonder if we'll befriend any literary icons this year or travel to any historic locations. Last year is going to be hard to top.

Diary 54

Dear Diary,

When I was born, the doctor must have stamped "National Spokesperson for the Plight of Black People" on my forehead; a stamp visible only to my teachers. The majority of my teachers treat me as if I, and I alone, hold the answers to the mysterious creatures that African Americans are, like I'm the Rosetta Stone of black people. It was like that until I transferred to Ms. Gruwell's class. Up until that point it had always been: "So Joyce, how do black people feel about Affirmative Action?" Poignant looks follow. "Joyce, can you give us the black perspective on *The Color Purple?*"

Maybe I am just looking at this all wrong, maybe I should feel complimented. I mean, I am being trusted to carry the weight of millions of people's voices, right? Wrong! I don't feel complimented. How the hell should I know what the black perspective is on Affirmative Action or *The Color Purple?* What is it, magic? Black people read, and *poof*, we miraculously come to the same conclusion? The only opinion I can give with some degree of certainty is my own.

I know some people would say "Now, Joyce, it's not every day one finds an African American in advanced placement and honors courses." People think that I should know that better than anyone else, considering I'm in these classes. As if I don't notice, or better yet, could forget I'm the only black person around. Hum, must have slipped my mind.

I remember the teacher I had before Ms. Gruwell. Let's just say for a teacher she isn't very tactful. I dealt with all sorts of rude and stereotypical statements, but one day she took it too far. I was in class looking over our reading list for the year, along with our essay assignments, when I noticed a saddening lack of diversity. I asked her why, and her response was "We don't read black literature in this class because it all has sex, fornication, drugs, and cussing." Whoa there, slow down lady, a simple "it's inappropriate" would have sufficed. But no, she had to take it to the extreme. I almost overlooked the blatant ignorance of her statement, but did she have to say it in front of the entire class? I mean, ouch!

I held my tongue, until lunch, when I told my friend. Her response was that I should tell my mom, tell the principal, tell the superintendent, but tell someone. I told my mom when I got home. I tried to tell her in a nonchalant, offhand sort of way. Can't you just see it, me at the dinner table in between swallows of chicken and broccoli casually mentioning the day's events.

"How was your day, Joyce?"

"I don't know, the same, I guess."

"Tell me about it."

"Well, I had lunch with Alisa, and took a chemistry quiz. Oh, by the way, my English teacher's a bigot."

There's a brief pause, followed by fork clinking and jaw dropping. She just looked at me. Then she asked me what I did. And I told her, "Not a damn thing!" Well, actually I can't curse in my mom's presence, so I said, "Nothing." The next day I was called to the principal's office and there was my mom with a list of books written by and about black people. I was told that my teacher has been contacted already and the principal personally apologized for her words. My mom gave me the list of books and sent me off to class with a kiss and a hug.

OK, what was I supposed to do? Walk into class with a smile and my new book list and present it to the teacher like a shiny red apple? "Mrs. Bigot, I just wanted to present you with this list of wonderful books. I hope they are all free of drugs, fornication, sex, and cussing. Furthermore, I want you to know that I hold no grudge against you, and I am really looking forward to your enlightening lectures for the next two years!" Yeah, right. I couldn't imagine another term with this woman, and as long as I stayed on the honors English track I would be stuck being the spokesperson for the rest of my high school career.

I told Alisa about my dilemma and she told me all about her English class. She told me that her teacher actually earned the title of educator. She puts everything into her classes, cares and listens, and above all else, refuses to label people. I wasn't really interested in all the other things, I just knew I wouldn't have to keep sending Gallup polls out to Negroes all around the country.

And that is how I found myself starting my junior year in Ms. Gruwell's class. It's my personal tale of mystery and misgivings, hatred and heroism, scandal and sacrifice. Well, actually it's a tale of how one woman, with an blind eye to stereotypes, had the eraser that took "National Spokesperson for the Plight of Black People" off my forehead. She replaced it with "Spokesperson for Joyce Roberts."

Diary 55

Dear Diary,

For the past month, we have been studying different American writers like Ralph Waldo Emerson and Henry David Thoreau. Emerson wrote about being self-reliant. He once wrote, "Who so should be a man, must be a nonconformist." Our class is really intrigued by Emerson because Ms. Gruwell is encouraging us to be independent thinkers and to question authority. I am amazed at how much his philosophy applies to me. For the past four years I have blamed myself for something I couldn't control. It was just one of those unexpected tragedies, that just smacked me over the head as soon as I turned around. I have constantly blamed myself for the death of my grandmother.

I was only twelve years old when my grandmother died from severe burns that were allegedly inflicted upon her by my father. She was burnt from head to toe. Allegedly my father had poured kerosene on her and lit the kitchen stove. She caught on fire immediately. When I saw her, she had blisters all over her body and all her hair was burned off. Her skin was black and it was peeling off. She had tears running down her cheeks. I could smell her raw, burnt flesh.

I felt like my heart was about to burst and my stomach was going to erupt at any moment, because I had a feeling she was going to die. The thought of losing the two people I loved most in the entire world made me feel dead inside.

The helicopter came and took her to another hospital. My aunt and I stood there until the helicopter disappeared. I felt so weak that I could hardly stand. I looked at my aunt. She was shaking. I didn't want to go home, I knew that eventually I would have to face my dad. As I approached my dad's house. I saw a scene that looked like an angry mob was ready to strike at anytime. I could see my dad standing in the window with a machete in his hand. I hated him. He made me tremble with fear because I knew he had tried to kill my grandmother. The crowd was yelling at him, and he was yelling back.

Finally, the police came and knocked on the door. I stood there, trying to move so my dad wouldn't see me, but my feet had control, and they wouldn't let me move. Tears were running down my cheeks. I watched as they handcuffed my father, read him his rights, and put him in the back of the police car. I watched as the car drove out of sight. I knew then that my life would change forever.

I looked around at everyone, trying to hide the embarrassment that was already written on my face. "Why did he do it? What made him so crazy?" I asked myself. I had so many questions, but no one could answer them. I don't even think my dad could answer them. He had threatened to kill me, but he had killed my grandmother instead.

After the death of my grandmother, I couldn't look anywhere except down. Whenever I walked, the ground was all I saw. Family members constantly reminded me about my grandmother's death. I looked for ways to stop the hurting and constantly asked myself questions like, "How could my dad do something like that? How could he leave me with the guilt? I wonder what he's thinking? Is he thinking about me?"

My dad spent only three months in jail. Sometimes I get so confused that I'm not even sure if he actually did kill my grandma. Maybe it is just too hard for me to accept the fact because he's my father.

When Emerson ended his essay with "to be great is to be misunderstood," it made me think about how many people have always misunderstood me. No one really understood what I was feeling. They were so caught up in what they thought about me that they didn't really care. It really bothered me that they didn't even try to understand me. Deep down inside I was just a scared little girl who was simply misunderstood. Maybe it's not so bad to be misunderstood. Now it's time for me to learn to hold my ground and be self-reliant.

Diary 56

Dear Diary,

A carton of milk was thrown, someone shouted "Fuck Niggers," a big crowd formed, and the fighting began. There were people punching other people and there were people throwing things at each other. It must have lasted for about three minutes, although it seemed like three hours. Somehow I managed to find my way out of the crowd without hitting anyone or throwing a thing. It wasn't necessary for me to join in the fight because their reason for fighting was stupid. When I stood away from the crowd I saw staff members and policemen breaking it up. The tardy bell rang a minute later, indicating that lunch was officially over. The crowd was reluctant to go to class because they wanted to see what happened to the people who started the fight.

Two people went to the principal's office, one was African American and the other was Hispanic. The principal suspended them both, hoping to get rid of the problem as fast as he could, but his decision made the problem worse. Friends of both races now held grudges against each other.

After school, I walked to the bus stop by myself. I noticed there were some Hispanics at the next bus stop where some African American people were waiting. When the bus arrived everyone got on the bus, and another fight broke out. This was round two. Some guy started swinging a stick that came from one of the art classes at school. There were at least twenty people from each side fighting on the bus. I got off and stood behind a bench. There were so many people on the bus that it started to rock back and forth. The bus driver told them she would call the police, so the African Americans got off the bus.

As they were waiting for the next bus, a Hispanic boy crossed the street to the bus stop. He didn't see that a fight had just ended, but he did see the angry tension in the crowd as he walked past the bus top. As he walked by the crowd someone stepped in front of him and asked him "What did you say?" The boy had said nothing at all. The boy didn't respond, but tried to walk past. The boy who confronted him suddenly punched him in the face. He fell unconscious into the bushes then everyone rushed him at once. There were twenty angry boys against one. Someone grabbed him by the neck and dragged him out on the street. They started kicking, and punching him in his ribs, face, and anywhere else they could reach. Someone picked up a metal trash can and slammed it into his face. Traffic was being held up, a bus arrived at the stop across the street, it stopped, and the bus driver got off to help the boy. He screamed, "Stop it, you punks." Someone turned around and punched the bus driver in the face, the bus driver ran to a store nearby and called the police. A lady got out of her car and also tried to help the boy, but got hit in the face for her efforts. As soon as the lady got back into her car the police came, and put an end to the fighting.

The boy lay unconscious, his arms, legs, and back were all broken. I watched as he was taken to the hospital and watched as the culprits were arrested.

"Why didn't I do anything to help him?" I asked myself. Maybe it was because I was scared of the consequences. Most likely, I would have been mauled by the crowd. Even though I could have been hurt, I wish I had done something. If Ms. G finds out that I just stood by and did nothing, she'll really be pissed at me. After all, I wasn't being very "self-reliant." I just hope she doesn't find out.

Diary 57

Dear Diary,

Today I finally grasped the true meaning of self-reliance. In class Ms. Gruwell handed out a self-evaluation sheet. We were asked to write the letter grade we felt we deserved, then write a brief comment on why we thought we deserved that grade. Immediately and without hesitation, I wrote "F."

I have been having some trouble at home and have had to miss a lot of school lately. I just learned that my mom has a disease called lupus. All I know is that it affects her kidneys and makes her too weak to watch my younger brothers, or do anything for that matter. So instead of being at school, I'm usually home helping Momma because she needs me. No matter what my reasons are, I thought Ms. Gruwell should fail me. I was sad, embarrassed, but a little proud that I had been honest.

I sat in my chair, disappointed by how my situation had ended. Little did I know it was in fact just the beginning. Ms. Gruwell approached me and asked to speak with me in the hallway. At first I thought she would drop me, but since I was already in what the others teachers called "dummy" English, where else could I go? I figured she would simply give me the same speech other teachers had given me: "You're failing and I know you're bright, so get it in gear. OK?" Sometimes I just wanna say, "No shit, really? I'm failing, so how do I change that?" But in light of the many times I've been blown or brushed off, I keep it to myself. I walked into the hallway and immediately she turned to me and said, "What's this?" She flashed my evaluation in my face. "Do you know what this means?" I didn't answer. I didn't know what to say. Just when I thought she was at her boiling point, she turned it up a notch by adding, "FUCK YOU! That's what this is! It's a fuck you, and a fuck me, and a fuck everyone who's ever cared about you!" Immediately our conversation became a road-trip to hell with me riding shotgun. I was thrown off, confused, flabbergasted, and to put it simply—shocked.

No one in my life has ever given me the facts so boldly. I had never had a "pep talk" like this. After my jaw seemed to wind itself back into its proper place, what she said began to sink in. She went on to tell me that "until I had the balls to look her straight in the face and tell her to fuck off, she was not going to let me fail, even if that meant coming to my house every day until I finished the work." I couldn't tell her off, so I just stood there with tears in my eyes.

What she showed me today is that a truly self-reliant person takes action, leaving nothing to chance and everything to themselves. She showed me that excuses will not bring about success and that adversity is not something you walk with, but something you leap over. The only obstacles are the ones you allow. A chain is only as strong as its weakest link. A truly self-reliant person finds his weak link and strengthens it. I want to be a self-reliant person, now and forever.

Diary 58

Dear Diary,

Our class is reading the part in *The Catcher in the Rye* where Hodlen Caulfield talks about his friend's suicide. Holden, who usually doesn't give a damn about anything or anyone, seemed to be really upset about the death of his friend. I never thought about the consequences or the effect that suicide would have on anyone else before. All I thought about was my own losing battle.

I have a problem. For the past two years I've been tormented by an illness that runs in my family. When I was four, my mother was diagnosed as "clinically depressed" because of a chemical imbalance. Luckily, she sought help before it was too late. She received medical attention and was cured with the help of a drug treatment called Amitriptylin.

Now this illness, our family's enemy, has returned to claim yet another victim. Against my will, I have been taken prisoner, and feel like I'm being punished for a crime I did not commit. My worst nightmare is now becoming my reality. Suicide is something that's always on my mind, "24/7." There isn't a day that goes by without the enemy shooting suicidal thoughts through my mind. I am left injured and confused. Without notice, the enemy takes control of my mind and body and I become its puppet. My thoughts, as well as my feelings, are re-created into my worst fears. I start crying and screaming for no reason, raging with unexplainable anger stored deep inside of me. Then I am left feeling worthless, without any hope of living.

I even tried to take my life once, because I thought there was no other alternative. It was the day my mother and I got into a huge argument. Now that I think back, it seemed so fake. Like one of those corny after-school television specials. After the argument, not knowing what to do, I ended up in the kitchen. I felt a cold breeze as I entered. There I was, standing in the dark, holding a kitchen knife to my wrist. My heart began to beat faster and faster as I held out my arm. I pulled back my sleeve, exposing my wrist. My mind blacked out. I looked down to see that the knife had barely cut into my skin. The knife was too dull.

Diary 59

Dear Diary,

I'm going to tell you about the crazy mess I got myself into a couple days ago. It all started about a month ago when I was assigned to read the *The Catcher in the Rye*. I took one good look at the plain white cover and set it on my desk where it managed to collect dust. I thought to myself, "What can this book teach me?"

I really wasn't up to reading this book, but somehow I managed to pick it up. Like usual, I read the ending first. After taking a look at the type of vocabulary J. D. Salinger uses, I was hooked. I thought, "Hey, this is my type of book!" I instantly developed respect for the author because of his unique style of writing, not to mention the fact that he didn't throw in some stupid preachy message. (You know, an attempt to save today's youth.) Those sugar-and-spice-and-everything-nice type of endings make me want to barf.

Well, I read the whole goddamn book. I was surprised how much I was able to relate to the main character, Holden. When Ms. Gruwell was trying to hype the book, she mentioned that our class was full of Holdens. Now I know what she meant. Like Holden, I think that everyone around me seems phony. I go to school with a bunch of conformists. Everywhere I look I see duplicates of the so-called perfect pattern. The teachers are the operators running the mind-control factory.

As for my parents, boy, do they think my every move is a deliberate plan to irritate them. My parents speak to me like I'm a child too wet behind the ears to know anything about life. I felt the need to escape. I was fed up with all the rules forced upon me. I didn't want to play their crummy old game. So this is where my journey of breaking loose from the "system" began. Well, my attempt anyhow.

One night, a couple of girlfriends and I were sitting around watching TV and talking. You know, girl stuff. Then the phone rang. It was my mother. She just called to see what time I'd be home. I swear she's a damn detective, always tracking me down. I told her I would be home in an hour. That was that. Well, an hour passed and I surely didn't feel like going home. So, instead of heading home, my friends and I decided to take a drive to the beach. I don't know how, but somehow between my friend's house and the beach, we ended up in Las Vegas. I guess we must have taken a wrong turn somewhere? No, I'm just kidding, that was the explanation I gave my mother. Unfortunately, she didn't buy it. The truth is my best friend had never been to Las Vegas and it seemed like a good idea at the time. We arrived in Las Vegas to witness the sunrise from behind the casinos. Once in Las Vegas we cruised around taking pictures and more pictures and even more pictures and that's pretty much it. It's not like I could gamble, I'm only sixteen. Soon after that I decided to call home. I was bored, and besides, I had been gone all night. I figured my mom would be a bit angry. OK, so she was furious and even threatened to call the Las Vegas police and report my friend's license plate number. Well, that totally ruined our road trip. After that heart-to-heart talk with dear old Mom, we decided to try something we hadn't the night before. Following an exquisite breakfast at one of Las Vegas five star restaurants, Burger King, we headed home.

Unlike Holden, I was spared from the "institution." Even though I provoked her by pleading, "Send me anywhere, somewhere, a rehab of some sort. Anywhere that isn't here." "But there is nothing wrong with you," she insisted. And then I said, "I just need to get away, I'm fed up with everything, everyone!"

The farthest she sent me was to my goddamn room.

Diary 60

Dear Diary,

Tonight the wildest thing happened: I got offered a job from John Tu! I can't believe I'll be working for a millionaire. How I got the job was crazy.

We were having a big party at the Bruin Den with all our parents. Ms. G's really into family and we're always having parties where all our families get together and have a big love fest. Her dad, her stepmom, and her brother are practically part of our family now. This party was another opportunity for our families to meet John Tu and thank him for all his help.

After the party was over, I asked him if he wanted a ride to where his car was parked. It was only about five blocks away, but I didn't want him to have to walk late at night with his wife and his two kids in our neighborhood. With him being a millionaire and all, I was afraid he was going to get jacked.

When I offered him a ride, I didn't think he'd actually say yes. When he did, I was like "damn!" I froze because I have a '78 Oldsmobile—which can't touch his top-of-the-line Mercedes. When he entered my car, I felt really embarrassed because my car only has one seat in the front. The passenger seat was stolen. There is just a big old gap in the front. I don't even have a radio, or a rearview mirror. My front window has a big-ass crack on it, too. Since it gets me from point A to point B, that's all that matters. When John got into my car, he said, "Damn, this is comfortable! It feels like a limousine!" He stretched out on my upholstery. My backseat is a far cry from leather, but he crossed his legs as if he owned my bucket. Then he said he wished that when he was my age he could have driven a car like this one, but instead he drove a bicycle. Wow, he hadn't always been a millionaire like I thought! He actually earned his money through hard work. That really got to me. It was as if he was telling me not to just stay at my level and drive a $200 "bucket," when I could shoot for driving a Mercedes.

When we reached his car, not only did he say thank you, but he also asked if I was interested in a job at his computer company. A job? I'd never had a job before. He said I would learn something new . . . and now I can't wait to begin my new career, and turn my life in a different direction!

Diary 61

Dear Diary,

In class today we discussed how double standards exist for men and women. We talked about how men can get away with whatever they want, but when a female does the same thing, then she gets degraded and even dissed. Ms. G introduced the word called "misogyny" and everyone in the class was like "What?" A guy in the corner even said, "Misogyny? Did you say massage my pee-pee?" and started laughing.

Ms. Gruwell structured a debate called "Misogyny or Mayhem?" She started by having us analyze the cover of Snoop Doggy Dogg's album with cartoon characters representing a male and female dog. The male dog is on top of "da dogg house," and the female dog is on the bottom with her ass hanging out. Throughout the cartoon, the female dog is called a hoochie and a ho, and they even kick her out of the dog house in the last illustration. All the girls felt like this cartoon showed how men think they're on top of everything. I think it's about time men start respecting women, instead of degrading women to the point where it's unbearable. I don't know why women allow men to brainwash them and use their bodies as objects instead of cherishing them as if they were treasures. But it's never going to change until women start respecting themselves more.

If you were looking for someone to give you an example of misogyny, my family would be the prime illustration. My male cousins were advised, "Make sure you put a hat on that Jimmy!" or "Get as many girls as possible!" Because I'm the only girl in my family, the only advice I was given was to keep my legs closed. Therefore, when I lost my virginity, it was the end of the world.

My boyfriend and I had been together for two years before

we decided to have sex. Then when it came time for what was supposed to be my special moment, I thought there would be caressing and passionate kisses. Instead, it was a five-minute bang, bang, bang. I looked at him after we were finished and asked him, "Is that it?" I thought losing my virginity was something that would be worth while. Instead, it's something I now regret.

Now I'm not a virgin and everyone looks at me as though I am a tramp or a ho. Of course, if I were male, I would be congratulated. I wish that things were different, but they aren't.

Diary 62

Dear Diary,

Today marks a turning point in my life. As soon as I walked into Ms. G's second period class, I picked up *The Color Purple*, a novel written by Alice Walker. I began to read, kept reading, read some more, and found myself unable to put it down. It was so intense and complex. I read slowly, wondering who she was, where she had gone. I'd never seen her before, had never been where she'd been. Yet in the midst of it all, Celie seemed strangely familiar. Life wasn't easy for Celie, but she knew how to survive. She needed little to get by. Come to think of it, I do know who Celie is . . .

My Uncle Joe was unlike any other uncle. He was nice, caring, a good listener, understanding, very handsome, and best of all, he always knew just what to say whenever I was miserable. He was always there for me when I needed a warm, sincere, loving hug. Basically, he was my hero. I loved Uncle Joe with all my heart.

We lived in a very small apartment complex, so Uncle Joe, my younger brothers, and I all slept in the living room. Moonlight filled our tiny room and the scent of a freshly cut Christmas tree filled my nostrils. Life couldn't have been better, or so I thought . . .

"Hmm? What is that? Who's touching me?" Whatever it was, I didn't like it . . . it was Uncle Joe. What was he doing to me? Whatever it was, I wanted him to stop. I opened my mouth to tell him to stop, but the words wouldn't come. It was as if a ton of bricks had fallen on me, knocking the air from my lungs, making me unable to speak.

I felt his body right next to mine and his breathing got stronger and stronger. He was touching me in places I didn't know could make me feel so dirty. I didn't move a muscle. I made my body as hard as a rock, as he slowly slid his hand up my shirt caressing my back and the side of my breasts. He kept on trying to make me lie on my back, but he was unsuccessful.

He got closer and closer. I could actually feel his skin touching mine. The feel of his sweat and his lips on my skin made me want to cry. A gigantic lump formed in my throat and to this day, nothing makes it go away. Uncle Joe wasn't being rough with me, which made it hard for me to decide whether or not what he was doing to me was wrong. It tore me up inside to think he would actually do me any harm. I was only a little girl, but I knew what he was doing was wrong. But why? Uncle Joe is the most righteous person I've ever met . . . After Uncle Joe invaded me, he got up for a drink of water. As soon as I heard the water running in the kitchen, my hatred for him grew. It was as if he was thirsty and exhausted from fulfilling himself and making me feel like the dirtiest being alive.

I had to think fast. "What to do, what to do?" I got up to go sleep on the couch before he came back. I didn't want him to do any more than he already had. Uncle Joe came back and took his tanktop off. He saw me on the couch and asked what was wrong. I looked at him for a few seconds. "Nothing . . . I just can't get to sleep." I wanted to cry out. I wanted the entire universe to know

I was scared. That I needed to be held; that I wanted to die . . . but who could I run to? The only person I could talk to was hurting me.

I sat there for a long time while Uncle Joe fell asleep. I didn't dare blink. The next morning, I heard my parents get up and get ready to leave for work. I'll never forget that feeling of hopelessness when my mother kissed me good-bye. Uncle Joe baby-sat my brother and me every day. But today was different and he was acting as if nothing had happened. He was being his usual "charming" self.

I was so angry, I couldn't think straight. I refused to do anything he wanted me to do. He acted like he wanted to hit me. My face hot with rage, I ran into the living room crying, yelling how much I hated him. It wasn't so much that he had changed the way I felt about myself. He had destroyed the only thing I believed in. He destroyed my belief in him.

All he had to do was apologize, and once again I was charmed. His eyes seemed so sincere. He really believed he had done nothing wrong. The hours felt endless. My only relief was when my mom came home. Only then did I dare to take a shower, trying hard to scrub away the permanent filth. As soon as I got out of the shower, I pulled my mother into her bedroom and told her everything. My relationship with Uncle Joe has never been the same since.

Celie was violated, tormented, humiliated, degraded; yet through it all, she remained innocent! Out of all this horror, Celie was given courage. Courage to ask for more, to laugh, to love, and finally—to live.

Now I'm certain who Celie is. Celie is and always has been me . . . and with this in mind, I will survive.

Diary 63

Dear Diary,

If you look into my eyes, you will see a loving girl.
If you look at my smile, you will sense that nothing is wrong.
If you look in my heart, you will see some pain.
If you pull up my shirtsleeves and look at my arms, you will see black and blue marks.

We just started reading the book *The Color Purple* and as Ms. Gruwell read aloud I just wanted to cry.

Celie's situation reminds me about an abusive relationship I had with my boyfriend that changed my life. I, too, became wood and every time my mom asked me, "Did you have a good time, honey?" as I'd walk through the door, I'd simply answer "Yeah." Then I'd go to my room and look at my body to see all the marks showing just how good of a time I had.

When I crawled into bed sometimes I would lie there and try to remember what had happened. I would try to think of what I did to cause it? Why did I make him so mad? What should I have done? When would it stop? Where would I draw the line? The first shove, the first time he slapped me, when he started calling me names, or the time he squeezed my arm so hard I had a bright red handprint around it?

At first when the abuse started, it was a slight shove or a twist of my arm. Gradually it became more intense. Each time he pushed harder or dug his nails into my arm deeper as he twisted it. I thought he was just playing around and being a little aggressive, but then he started yelling at me and calling me names. His voice was frightening and his words ripped through my body. His voice could make me shiver and become too scared to move.

One false move and he was a time bomb waiting to explode. In each situation his wires got triggered and he'd go off. When he exploded, he would hit me, shake me, push me, squeeze my arms, and yell things like "You stupid bitch, you can't do anything right."

When we'd get into an argument, he'd yell "I want to hit you so bad!" That's how it always went: I would do something to make him angry, he would get this horrifying tone in his voice, and this crazy look in his eyes, then he would hit me. Sometimes he would stop just as he was about to throw another punch, and look at his fist, then look at me and say, "Oh my God, babe, I'm so sorry." Just like that and he would hold me saying how sorry he was, and I would stay there too shaken to move.

When hitting wasn't effective anymore, he moved on to control. He began locking me in his garage or bathroom so I couldn't leave. Sometimes he'd push me out the front door and tell me to leave, but as I started walking down the street, he would come running after me. When I went back, he'd act as if nothing had happened. I always went back, too—back to his house, the abuse, and him.

We would be kissing pretty heavily and he would get a little too excited. He would want to have sex and I always told him I wasn't ready. He would start pulling my clothes off, saying, "We are going to do this!" Then he would just stop and push me aside and order me to get dressed.

He made me so nervous, that I would get sick, literally sick. When he called and I heard his voice over the phone I would get this nauseous feeling all over my body. Then when I was on my way to his house it would get worse. My stomach would turn and I would have to ask whoever was driving to pull over so I could get some fresh air. I threw up a few times before I even left my house, and twice at his house. He thought that I had a nervous stomach. He never knew it was because of him.

I still don't know why this happened or how things got so

bad. It got to the point that I didn't know what to do. I couldn't tell anyone. Every time we were together, it seemed to get worse. The worst point of the relationship was when he ran after me with a butcher knife, yelling "I'm gonna kill you!"

The whole time this was happening it felt like a bad dream. A dream I could never wake up from. Unfortunately, we gave each other what we were both missing. He had anger all built up inside that he needed to release on someone and I was a ball of emotions just looking for someone to love me. He was the security I needed.

We were like a fire triangle, he was the oxygen, I was the flame, and together we made the fuel. All mixed together we were a fire. Somehow we needed each other to keep going. It ended like someone pouring water on our fire. It went out all of a sudden and without warning.

As fast as it started, it was out.

Diary 64

Dear Diary,

Reading *The Color Purple* really makes me uncomfortable because Celie is always getting beaten up by Mister. Every time I read about Celie being beaten up, I flashback to when my mother was recently beat by my alcoholic stepdad.

I always knew I had to be careful and protect my mom because my stepdad is a professional alcoholic. He is a little guy, but when he's drunk, his size doesn't matter. He doesn't care about anything and tries to destroy anything that gets in his way. When he's drunk, he really scares me, so I try to keep him in control. Unfortunately, that doesn't always work.

Things were starting to get pretty hostile between them, so I made it a point to come home from school as soon as possible.

One day when I got home my mom told me that things were already out of control and that he'd been yelling at her. We went to my aunt's house for dinner to let him cool off.

Later that night, as I was lying in bed thinking about what we'd read in Ms. G's class earlier, I began to think about my mom in the other room. My mother, like Celie, could not defend herself against a drunken alcoholic. I felt that I should stay up and listen for any arguments that may arise.

Suddenly the book came to life when I heard her calling for me. Seconds later, I heard *thump! slap!* and "Get off me!" She called for me. When I opened the door, he was holding her arms down slapping and hitting her. Without even thinking I rushed to him and threw him off her. I took a quick glimpse as she ran out the door and I could see her eyes were full of tears and fear. My body raged with anxiety and anger.

I could feel my stomach twisting and turning, and my hands and arms were shaking like they'd never shaken before. My mind and body felt like they were ready to explode on this human piece of crap, who was trying to hurt the person I love the most. I asked myself, "What should I do? Should I turn around and beat the shit out of him? But what if he tries to attack me? Or should I get my mom and my little sister the hell out of here?" I only had a few seconds to decide. I decided to get my sister ready and put her in the car first, then I went back inside for my mom.

Celie, who coincidentally, was in the exact same role as my mother, didn't have somebody to stop Mr.——— from abusing her. Seeing how scared my mom was made me think about all the women like Celie who have no one to rescue them. After seeing the fear in her eyes, I vowed I would never let anyone physically or mentally abuse her again.

On the way to my aunt's house, I could see that same color again, like it was haunting me. The color purple was coming from my mother's eye where my stepdad had punched her. That's when I began to understand that the color purple isn't just a color or the name of a book.

Diary 65

Dear Diary,

I can't believe what I did today! I told them everything! Well, not everything, but almost everything. It's unbelievable how much I revealed. I had a feeling Ms. Gruwell was going to pick on me. I knew she was going to make me get up and talk to everyone. I just knew it!

Ms. Gruwell took some of her students from Wilson to her college diversity seminar at National University. We were supposed to teach graduate students about diversity in the classroom because they were going to be the future teachers of America. We didn't know we were in store for an emotional healing. A healing that no amount of money spent in a psychologist's office could buy.

I'm still in shock. I was always taught not to tell anyone about anything that happens our household, but tonight I guess you could say that I spilled the beans. I knew Ms. G was going to pick on me because of the topic we were discussing. I knew there were at least two or three more people who were in more or less the same situation that I was in. But she picked me. I still can't get over it. I tried to scoot down in my chair and hide behind the person that was in front of me, hoping Ms. G had forgotten I was there. No such luck. She pointed her finger around the class and asked, "Where is she? Oh, there you are. Why don't you stand up and tell my college students a little more about your experience with homelessness?"

My legs were shaking as I stood up. I didn't know what I was going to say to a roomful of strangers. Why did she have to pick me to speak to these people? I didn't think they'd listen to my story, and if they did, I thought they'd forget it once they went home. My intent was to say a couple of words and sit down. I wasn't going to elaborate and go into detail about my life. I wanted to say something like "It's not fun being homeless and I wouldn't try it if I were you." Of course, Ms. Gruwell wouldn't let me get away with saying something like that.

So I decided to tell the class about my father. I also told them that I didn't think he deserved the skin God blessed him with. I told them how he makes my mother go out because he doesn't want to get up off his butt and get a job to provide for us. I explained that "going out" means that my mother stands on the corner with a "Homeless! Will Work for Food" sign. She stands outside for hours with that sign, hoping people will give her some money to feed her children. She goes out in the hottest and coldest weather just to make sure we had something to eat. When my mother comes home, he has the audacity to take the money and go buy beer and drugs, more specifically cocaine. My mother has to lie and say she only made half the money she really made so she can get us something to eat for the day. I don't know why she puts up with his shit. She has the education to get a good career. If it weren't for my father she wouldn't have done drugs and believed that she couldn't do any better than standing on a street corner asking for money.

I went on to ask the class, "Do you know what he does? He gets all of his beer bottles and recycles them so that he can go and buy more beer." Well, you can't say he isn't trying to help the environment. He sells our food so that he could get more drugs, leaving us hungry. After I laid my life out like an open book, I couldn't help but break down and cry. Talking about my father made me realize how depressing my life really is. It never bothered me before tonight, because I guess I'm used to it and I've never expected it be any other way.

At that point, I was crying hysterically. I couldn't help it, but then neither could anyone else. I noticed there were some males in the corner who had actually stepped out of the room because I guess they had a little "something in their eyes," but I still kept talking.

"He is a selfish bastard," I said, heaving and gasping for breath. He doesn't care about anyone but himself. He claims that he cares for his precious son, but he doesn't try to get a job and make sure his son has food in his stomach or clean clothes on his back. He doesn't care that his precious son has to go to school with the same clothes he's been wearing for the past week. He doesn't care that we have to wash our clothes in the sink with the soap we use to bathe with. He doesn't care that we had to sleep on the streets because he couldn't pay rent for the hotels we were living out of. He doesn't care about his son or any of his family— all he cares about is his drugs.

By that point, I was seething mad and not caring what I told people about my father. I was getting everything off my chest and it felt damn good. I continued to tell the class that my father had molested my sister and how angry I was that my mother didn't do anything when she found out about it. In fact, she doubts that my sister is telling the truth. That's shows how much power and influence my father has over my mother.

After years of keeping everything in, my heart felt like a grenade. It exploded, full force, and left me emotionally drained. I was relieved, but felt horrible just the same, because I told these strangers basically every detail of my life.

When I finished my story, I clumsily sat in my chair because I could barely stand straight. My friend sitting next to me took me into her arms and gave me a much needed hug. Ms. Gruwell's college students were so comforting that they didn't feel like strangers anymore.

I can't believe what I did today. I told them everything! Well, not everything, but almost everything. It's unbelievable

how much I revealed. I knew she was going to pick on me I just
knew it . . . but I'm happy that she did.

Diary 66

Dear Diary,

Tonight, while I was sitting in Ms. G's class at National University listening to other students' stories about their families, I
couldn't help but remember my own. Rather than listen, I began
to look out the window, staring at the cars driving by when I
thought about my brother Kevin's death a year ago . . .

Kevin was placed in a Children's Hospital to undergo a brain
biopsy for a misdiagnosed tumor. The surgery lasted all night. I
spent that night looking at the big Hollywood sign in the dark
from the seventh floor of the hospital. I saw people driving around
in their cars, going about their business, not aware that they just
passed by a hospital that was filled with children who were ill or
near death. All I could do is sit in the waiting room, waiting.

Kevin got out of surgery early the next morning. He was
placed in the ICU and only two people were allowed to see him at
a time. I didn't know what to expect when my mother and I
walked in. When I saw him, he was hooked up to various machines. Parts of his hair was shaved off and his head was ban-
daged. The sight was gruesome. He hadn't woken up from the
procedure yet. He looked like a mess and I didn't know what to
do. I just stood there and looked at him. I was afraid to touch him.

After Kevin recovered in the ICU, they discovered that he
was paralyzed on the left side of his body. He was moved to the
Physical Therapy ward. The ward was on the sixth floor of the
hospital, which was lit up and colorful. It seemed happy, unlike
the people in it. The ward was filled with children who were sick
and unable to walk or perform basic activities, like playing with
toys. Now Kevin would be one of them. He stayed at the Physical

Therapy ward for three months. He was hoping that he was going to be able to walk again, but he never did. I was in so much pain watching him attempt to do a simple task, which was impossible for him.

Every day my mother drove to the hospital and stayed there. When I went with her, I spent the day looking at Kevin in his bed or in Physical Therapy. When I had a chance to run off, I would. I ran up to the roof, looked at the city, and thought about Kevin. I also thought about my dad. I wanted him to take me away from this place. Unfortunately, my father didn't have any idea that Kevin was even in the hospital, because my parents were divorced. They haven't spoken to each other for two years. My mother thought it would be best if we didn't tell him about Kevin's illness. I wanted to tell him so I could feel like everything was going to be all right. But things weren't going to be all right— and this secret was my ball and chain.

From the hospital, I could see the blue ocean in the distance, the same ocean that my brother and I used to play in. I hadn't seen the ocean for about a year. I miss it.

When Kevin was released from the hospital, he lived with my mother and me in a one-bedroom apartment. The neighborhood was bad. He was placed in a local hospice program. In a way, being in the program made things easier to deal with, but Kevin wasn't getting any better. There were still nights spent in the hospitals.

Kevin was bed-ridden, having seizures and hallucinations. No matter how bad the situation got, and how many times the doctors told me he was going to die, it just didn't sink in.

I knew Kevin was suffering, maybe not physically, but mentally. How can a person cope with the fact that they came to the hospital walking and left four months later in a wheelchair? As I sat there watching him, I wondered what he was thinking. The doctors and medical staff had no idea of his mental status. Was he sane or was he delusional? If he was sane, in his physical state, it must have taken a toll on him, but what if he wasn't? What if he was just a vegetable? Did he know who I was? Did he actually see me? I had so many questions, but no answers. I was afraid to sleep because I wasn't sure when Kevin would have his next seizure. My worst fear was that I would wake up and find him dead. That thought alone was enough to keep me awake at night.

Months passed by, and Kevin saw his last Christmas and New Year, which was the worst time for all of us. We spent it in the hospital watching him choke on his food and water. A couple of days after the holidays, Kevin began to lose his reflexes and couldn't swallow his own saliva. There was nothing we could do. We couldn't help. We didn't know what would happen next.

The last time I saw Kevin alive he was in the emergency room. He was asleep and he looked like an angel. There were no seizures and no more choking. For once, he seemed fine. I thought the nightmare was coming to an end. There would be no more hospitals, doctors, pills, or pain. Now there were only two roads he could take, or that God would allow him to take. One was recovery, by some type of miracle, and the other was death.

As we walked into Kevin's hospital room the next day, the foul smell of death was choking me. I was shocked to see that Kevin's body was placed in the ICU with five other critically ill patients, even though he was dead! The nurse pulled open the curtains around his bed to show Kevin's lifeless body to my mother and me. The nurses had already "cleaned his body" and placed him in a white body bag. Only his head was poking out. My mother broke down in tears and I stood there in disbelief . . . He's dead. He's dead.

Junior Year
Spring 1997

Entry 6 · Ms. Gruwell

Dear Diary,

I just got off the phone with Zlata and I told her that she's the inspiration for our latest writing project. Using her as our muse, the students will begin compiling the diaries they've been keeping into a collaborative book. She still keeps a journal and feels honored to be passing the baton.

Zlata said writing was her salvation during the war and it kept her sane. She suggested that writing might be one of the best vehicles for some of my students to escape their horrific environments and personal demons. Even though they're not held captive in an attic or dodging bombs in a basement, the violence permeating the streets is just as frightening—and just as real.

For some of my students, my classroom is one of the only places where they feel safe. Room 203 is a place where they can seek refuge from all the mayhem. Outside my classroom walls, anything can happen.

Many of my students say they live in fear and are constantly looking over their shoulders. It's not uncommon for them to stay until seven or eight o'clock at night doing their homework. If it gets too late, I feel obligated to drop them off on my way home. There have been times that I've been really scared. I've seen prostitutes propositioning men right in front of my students; I even had a crack dealer approach my car once and try to sell me rock. I've seen gangsters hanging out drinking 40s or playing dominoes. My students always seem to point out the makeshift altars of where the latest casualty went down. There are usually flowers and candles adorning the bloodstained concrete.

I always feel guilty when I drop them off and then head to Newport Beach. Although they're only about forty minutes apart, the cities are worlds apart. Some of my students have security doors and bars on every window. I don't even lock my front door. I've never had to worry about drug dealers loitering on street corners or helicopters patrolling from above. The parks aren't strewn with hypodermic needles or broken glass.

Since their fears are legitimate, I need to let them keep their anonymity. Some of their diary entries deal with subjects like murder and molestation. By using numbers rather than names when we compile our diary, I think they'll feel more comfortable and it will probably be safer for all of us. To ensure that no one embellishes or sensationalizes their stories, I'm going to ask them to sign an honor code.

This project makes me feel a certain sense of personal responsibility—resembling the commitment Miep Gies felt to the Franks. Now I understand what Miep meant when she said, "I simply did what I had to do, because it was the right thing to do." This writing project feels like the right thing to do, and it will be worth making some personal sacrifices. Although I haven't dug up any turnips in the snow like Miep did, I have dug up corporate support. I've asked several powerful adults to get onboard and help see this project through.

John Tu was the first to pledge his support. He thought it was a good idea to protect the students' anonymity, too, but he was concerned that people might recognize one another's handwriting. After several hours of discussing alternative solutions, he offered to supply the class with a set of computers. Thirty-five to

The Freedom Writers have a dream! On the steps of the Lincoln Memorial in Washington, D.C., following a candlelight vigil honoring family and friends lost to violence.

Our fearless leader, Ms. G.

U.S. Secretary of Education Riley, speaking to us when we presented our manuscript in Washington, D.C.

Miep Gies, the courageous woman who sheltered Anne Frank and her family, signs copies of her book, *Anne Frank Remembered*, and Anne's book, *The Diary of a Young Girl*.

With Miep.

Zlata, her best friend Mirna,
and the Freedom Writers.

Zlata and Ms. G
at the Croatian Club.

Holocaust survivor Gerda Seifer with our big supporter John Tu, who sponsored our Basketball for Bosnia fundraiser.

Freedom Writers and Senator Barbara Boxer.

In our Basketball for Bosnia T-shirts (left to right): three Freedom Writers, a Freedom Writer dad, Ms. G's brother Chris, and more Freedom Writers.

A group of mothers
we call "The
Dream Team"
surround Ms. G.

Another late night in
Room 203 working on
one of the computers
donated by John Tu.

Dr. Carl Cohn,
Superintendent of the Long
Beach school district.

War correspondent and author Peter Maass when he came and talked to us about his book on Bosnia, *Love Thy Neighbor.*

The Spirit of Anne Frank Award was presented to the Freedom Writers on January 15, 1998.

Linda Lavin (who played Mrs. Van Daan in the Broadway production of *The Diary of Anne Frank*) presents the Spirit of Anne Frank Award to the Freedom Writers.

The Anne Frank Center USA

Spirit of Anne Frank Awards

Outstanding Youth Award

Freedom Writers

Presented January 15, 1998

Leo S. Ullman, *Chairman*

Grayson Covil, *Executive Director*

The Anne Frank Center USA presents

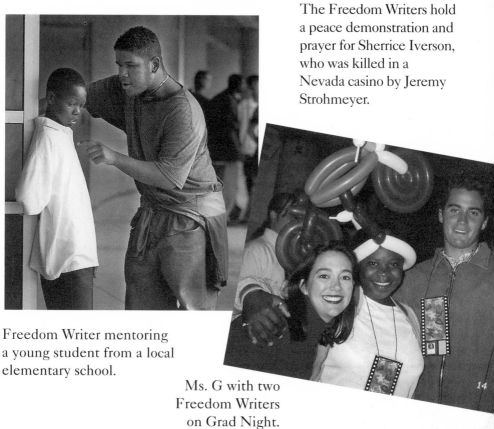

The Freedom Writers hold a peace demonstration and prayer for Sherrice Iverson, who was killed in a Nevada casino by Jeremy Strohmeyer.

Freedom Writer mentoring a young student from a local elementary school.

Ms. G with two Freedom Writers on Grad Night.

14

Connie Chung and the Freedom
Writers prepare for the "Prime Time
Live" taping.

Graduation!

be exact. Our computer lab in the library only has twenty out-
dated computers for the entire student body. After I managed to
pick my jaw up off the floor, we came up with an idea. Since the
"Toast for Change" wiped the slate clean for many of them, their
grades have gone from Ds and Fs to As and Bs. John and I came
up with a contract stipulating that once the computers arrived the
35 students with the highest grade point average would win a
computer when they graduated. With computers in my class, the
sky's the limit.

To help me design an honor code, John recommended that I
get advice from a lawyer. Realizing that I barely had enough
money to pay for school supplies, let alone legal expenses, John
suggested soliciting a big law firm because sometimes they do
work pro bono. Pro bono is a nifty term for "free." But he was
right. With some help, I found a senior partner in one of the biggest firms in the country, who offered to help us. I told him that
we could have a fundraiser to help pay for his advice, but he
laughed and said, "Erin, I'm a lawyer. Who's going to donate
money for a lawyer? People think we're sharks." But our lawyer
dispels the stereotype. The kids love him because he spends
more time in a baseball cap than a suit. And when he told one of
my students he had tickets to the "Rage Against the Machine"
concert, she turned to me and whispered, "Doesn't he realize
that he *is* the machine?"

So with computers on the way and honor codes being drawn
up, I'm going to kick off our diary with a special visit from two
people who have been immortalized in Anne Frank's diary. I've
helped arrange for the kids to meet Anne Frank's best friends,
Jopie and Hanneli (a.k.a. "Lies") who she wrote about before she
went into hiding. Hopefully, meeting Jopie and Lies will get
them excited about starting our new writing project—and reaf-
firm the power of the written word.

Diary 67

Dear Diary,

My mom always says, "Silence will get you nowhere in life." Today she was right. I had the opportunity to sing to Anne Frank's best friends, Jopie and Lies, but I didn't. Two people were needed to sing the song "Hero," but I never told anyone that I could sing. I really wanted to sing to them because Anne Frank is my hero and the song would have tied in perfectly, but the thought of telling anyone scared me. So I let that chance slip right out of the palm of my hand.

When the girls sang, I was sad because I had the chance to do it and I didn't take it. Everyone cheered, but I felt so disappointed that I wasn't on the stage. One of the girls who volunteered was in the conceit choir, but she was not in Ms. G's class. She hadn't even read the book, so she didn't know the symbolism of the song. I did—and I was ashamed that I didn't stand up.

After the song, Jopie and Lies told us about how they knew Anne. They both went to school with Anne before she went into hiding. They were inseparable, kind of like the Three Musketeers, until the war tore them apart. Luckily, Jopie didn't have to go to a concentration camp, but Lies did. Ironically, while she was at Bergen-Belsen, she had the opportunity to talk to Anne, who was dying of hunger, disease, and sadness. A fence separated them and Anne was sick with typhus. Anne kept saying, "I have no one left." Lies threw a bag of food to Anne across the barbed-wire fence. Even though she would not have food for herself and she risked getting killed by the Nazis, she didn't care, because she saw that Anne needed help and she could not deny a friend. Somebody grabbed the bag and ran away with it, leaving Anne in that horrible situation. She died a few days later. When Lies was liberated from the camp, she found out that Anne's father, Otto, was the only one who survived from the Frank family. Otto treated Lies, who had lost her family as well, as an adopted daughter. Both Jopie and Lies were shocked to read Anne's diary. They never knew that they meant so much to her.

After I heard their moving stories, I felt really guilty. After all, Jopie and Lies risked themselves for their friend and I didn't even have the guts to say that I wanted to sing to them. Maybe I didn't deserve to be there because I wasn't as brave as they were. Lies helped her friend in the camp, knowing that if an officer saw her she would be killed. No one was going to kill me just for saying that I wanted to sing, but I made it seem that way with my cowardliness.

Bad things have happened because people hold back information. Women get beat up by their husbands and no one can help them because they never say who did it. Children get abused and we sometimes think that everything is normal because they act as if there is nothing wrong. The Germans knew what was going on in the camps, but the world found out too late because they held back that information. There are many tragedies that could be stopped if only we spoke up more often. From this point on, I will not be silent.

Diary 68

Dear Diary,

This is my first year to have Ms. Gruwell as my English teacher. I am one of the transfers, or the "lucky ones," on "Gruwell's List." However, now that I'm in, I am terrified because I feel that my writing capacity is not at the same level as the other students. They have had so much more experience writing than I've had; writing essays and crafting letters to people like Zlata and Miep. They know what to expect from Ms. G and all her crazy writing schemes. I don't.

Today Ms. Gruwell assigned a new writing project. We each are going to choose one of our favorite journal entries and combine them into a classroom book like the letters they'd previously sent to Zlata. Ms. Gruwell wants us to pick an entry about an event that changed our lives. In my case, there is only one that really sticks out, but I want to forget it. Not because it is embarrassing, but because it is the most painful one . . .

I guess it was foolish to think that my brother would be here for the rest of my life, but I did. I had a brother, but I took him for granted. I thought that I would go to high school with him, see him get his first job, and grow old with him. It didn't happen that way. It has only been nine months since he died, and now my teacher wants me to open the floodgates and lose control of my emotions by writing a book? I just can't do that. I don't want to remember!

Silence is my way of staying strong, for my brother and for me. I want to forget everything, lock the door and hide the key where no one could find it . . . Writing about it will only make it worse!

Diary 69

Dear Diary,

Ms. G came up with a new writing assignment that she thinks will bring the class closer together; we have to create a book of events that have changed our lives. It has everyone in class so excited about the thought of emulating Anne and Zlata.

Someone even suggested that we could bind our stories into a book or diary. Unlike everyone else, I am not excited about the new assignment. For the first time I am feeling alienated from the rest of the class.

I have great respect for Anne Frank for writing about her life in the attic, but to me, my neighborhood is somewhat like her attic. I would rather write about something fictional, because I do not want to be reminded of where I come from. Writing about where I come from will bring up a lot of things that I want to suppress.

As I look up at the sky, there seems to be a black cloud lingering over my neighborhood, even on the sunniest day. I picture myself coming home to a wonderful house with white picket fences, but slowly my picture starts to fade. With the smell of marijuana in the air, the mumbling of drug dealers trying to make their sales, the horrific sounds of gunshots, and the sight of graffiti, which is more popular than Vincent Van Gogh. The reason why my neighborhood is filled with violence is because I live in the projects.

The projects are the farthest thing from the fictional *Brady Bunch* neighborhood. On *The Brady Bunch*, kids play together peacefully in their backyards, all the lawns have green grass, and neighbors even go camping together. Parents get together to compare their kids' report cards, and gang violence is something they read about in a newspaper.

In the projects, little kids are bad! Rather than play, they destroy. They set trashcans on fire, they knock on people's doors and run, and they turn their neighbors' water hoses on in their backyard so it will flood. Most of the kids in my neighborhood do not know their ABCs, but could sing you a rap song word for word. As for green grass, the grass is dead. The only grass that's alive is the grass they smoke. But grass isn't the only thing that they smoke. I see crackheads getting high in the "cut" smoking their pipes. In fact, I don't even borrow sugar from my neighbors. Becoming friendly with your neighbors will end up getting your house robbed. As for parents comparing their kids' report cards? Being smart and getting good grades makes you an outcast in the projects. If I tell anyone that I got a good grade on a test, then I'll be eating my teeth. Instead of reading about gang violence in newspapers, I'm the kid you see on the news telling a reporter what I've witnessed.

At sixteen, I've probably witnessed more dead bodies than a mortician. Murder plays a big role in my project. Every time I step out of my front door, I'm faced with the risk of being shot. Just recently, while I was sound asleep, I awoke to the sound of gunshots. It was 2:30 in the morning. After the gunshots stopped, a woman screamed, "Help me, please . . . why, why, why?" I looked out of my bedroom window to see a man with a bullet wound in his head the size of a quarter and blood oozing out of his head like ketchup coming from a Heinz bottle.

Besides gang violence, domestic violence, or spousal abuse, is common. So common, in fact, that people ignore it, turn the other cheek, or go back to bed. I have watched men pistol-whip their girlfriends or smash their heads through car windows. Damn! I have seen a lot of crazy stuff. Stuff that makes me thankful it's not me.

It's easier for me to pretend I don't live where I live or see what I see. That's why I go to school so far away from home so I can escape my reality. Like Anne Frank, I live through the pain of being stuck in my house because I don't want to become a casualty of war, gang warfare that is going on outside of my bedroom walls. I sit in my room wishing I could fly away from all of the madness. Writing about my pain will only make it worse.

Diary 70

Dear Diary,

John Tu donated thirty-five computers to our class, and what a difference they make! Ms. G said we're not limited to just using them on English assignments. She's going to let us use them for projects for our other classes before and after school. The most amazing part is that Ms. G and Mr. Tu created a contract stating that whoever has the highest grade point average from now until graduation will win a computer for college. That means that I have a chance to get a computer if I keep my grades up. For some reason, I feel like I'll do better than I have the past two years.

It feels good to start off with a clean slate. Not many people get a chance like this since most people seem to make judgments based on the past. Unfortunately, the education system tends to dismiss kids based on their past and not on their potential. Throughout my years of education, only Ms. Gruwell took action to help me with my learning disability. As a matter of fact, when I told one teacher in jr. high that I thought I had dyslexia, he told me that I was just lazy. Yeah, right! Me, lazy? I would end up with the same routine before every vocabulary test or important assignment. I would spend a week trying to memorize words that, no matter what I did, I couldn't spell right. On test days, I would turn in the test, and get an F. All I could do was hope that I'd do better on the next one.

It only got worse in high school, where there were more spelling and essays tests, with more complicated words that seemed too impossible to memorize. Finally, I just started to think, "Why should I even try? I am just going to end up with an 'F' anyway." It seems that an "F" was going to symbolize what I would end up in the future. I felt especially hopeless and depressed when I had to take an essay test where spelling counted toward my grade. I wanted to do well, but no matter how many great answers I had in my head, if I couldn't spell words right, I was going to fail. It wasn't like I could ask someone sitting next to me how to spell a word, and I couldn't just bust out the dictionary, because that would be considered cheating. That's why I always hated turning my essays in, because the teacher would look at me as if he knew that I was going to fail. On one essay test, my sociology teacher even told me that he "didn't expect me to do well anyway." When he told me this, I felt hopeless because I couldn't prove him wrong, at least not yet.

When I heard that we were going to write stories, I can't tell you that I was too happy. I started to picture me with a dictionary, looking up words all night long. Since Ms. Gruwell was my new English teacher, I didn't want her to think that I was stupid like the other teachers did. This was my chance to prove the other teachers wrong. Then I heard the bad news: She expected us to crank out a story in a couple of days. My friend said that it would be easier for me now because we had the computers. I was still scared because I didn't want anyone to know that I couldn't write. As I turned on the computer, I still was uncertain if Bill Gates's creation was going to help me in any way . . .

At the end of the day, I was surprised to see that I didn't have to substitute a word in my story just because I couldn't spell it. Thanks to spell check, now I feel like there are no limits or boundaries enclosing my ideas and feelings. Sitting in front of the monitor with my fingers on the keyboard makes me feel powerful in a way I never have before.

Diary 71

Dear Diary,

To inspire us in our new writing project, Ms. G gave us a letter she received from Miep after her trip to Amsterdam. It really

ANNE FRANK STICHTING

To the students in the class of Erin Gruwell at Wilson High School
Long Beach, California
c/o 1703 Clay Street
Newport Beach, CA 92663
. U.S.A.

Dear Erin and students,
        What a heartwarming surprise Erin brought to
Amsterdam. I enjoy the beautifully framed pictures very much and now
look forward to the album, that will be sent to me. Erin also gave
me beautiful flowers and best of all she told me with great enthusiasm
about the courageous way in which you secure your personal future.
I am deeply impressed by the fact that although many of you endured
a lot of hardships, you nevertheless don't give up, but struggle
towards a brighter future. You are wonderful individuals and will
contribute a lot to your society and also to a better world for all.
        Many of you I still remember, your eyes, your
smiles, your words, your warmth. Thank you for that wonderful experience. I deeply regret that those who are in trouble are often blamed
for their ill-fate. My message is that if you have difficulties, you can
be absolutely innocent. Think of Anne Frank. She really was in great misery.
Did she deserve that ? No, she was innocent, Therefore Anne Frank
stands symbol for the innocence of those who are in trouble !
        With warm regards

        Miep Gies

inspired the whole class to keep up with our work and gave us the
impression that the sky is the limit.

The class was very thankful that Miep Gies took the time
to write to us. I admire her for the nice things she did for Anne
Frank. I think we are very similar to each other because we both
had innocent friends die. Even though fifty years have gone by,
Miep still thinks about Anne and all she went through in the

secret annex. Not a day goes by that she doesn't think about Anne.

I had a friend who was shot in the eye and killed in cold blood. It's been a year since he died and like Miep, not a day goes by that I don't think about him. I think to myself, "Was his death in vain?" No! I have to do something about it because he was an only child. Now I want to write his story so others will know his death was not in vain!

Diary 72

Dear Diary,

"As his penis twirled in my mouth, thoughts of the popcorn he promised me ran through my mind . . ." As I read these words, I began to wonder who the author of this story was. My mind began to think, "Damn, I've been through the same thing." Bad things always happen to the wrong people. I read the sentence repeatedly, then scanned the room to see any body language that would reveal who wrote it. I looked, yet no one gave me any evidence who the author was.

I can't believe that I got a story to read and edit that I could have told. I stared down at the words and began to think back on the terrible act of violence I suffered at the hands of a family member. I felt a sense of relief that someone else had been molested, someone else had a story to tell also. I was supposed to edit the story, but after reading it over and over, I felt the words needed to remain the way they are. Untouched. The words held power.

Then it hit me like a ton of bricks. Did someone know I had been molested? Maybe Ms. G knew. Or maybe the others. Oh shit, what if they all knew? Why does it seem that everyone is looking at me? Damn! After all this time, has my little secret been discovered?

Then Ms. G decided to read the story aloud, so everyone would know the degree of individuality put into our stories. She told us this was our chance to speak up on the tragic things that have happened to us in our lives. Some girls left the room, too overwhelmed with emotions to stay and hear the rest. Some stayed in the room and cried. But not me, however. I remained cool, cool as a cucumber. A muscle didn't even move. I hardly even breathed or blinked. I just sat still and asked myself, "Why in the hell did we have to do this damn editing anyway?"

The more I stared at the words, the more I began to realize I have been blessed through someone else's misfortune. Maybe someone will feel the same way after learning about my experience. I wanted to reach out to her to let her know she wasn't alone. I wanted to tell her I know how she feels, to show sympathy, to be a true friend to her. I never found her. But now I know that I am not alone—and that has made a difference.

Diary 73

Dear Diary,

Today we were given another damn story to edit. When I was handed this story, I just thought, "Oh wow, another story to edit. Gee, this is great! I wish I could do this every day." When I started to read the story, all of a sudden everything hit me: "I sat on the operating table, shivering . . . my stomach flipped as I lay back and placed my feet in the stirrups." How was I so lucky to get a story about abortion? It was my secret come to haunt me once again. It was as if my subconscious was speaking to me about everything that I kept penned up inside of me.

This story was so graphic and depressing, describing details I never thought about before. I wonder if my girlfriend went through all the things that the girl went through in the story. She wrote about how a counselor walked in and took her hand. "If you need to, just squeeze my hand," she said and held her tightly. I wonder if my girlfriend had anyone there to support her. It makes me sad that I wasn't there to hold her hand. Was it lonely and bleak in the office? She said, "I wanted to erase this place from my mind." Did she have all those terrible thoughts going through her head? How could they make these places so dark and dreary? It has to kill the girls inside to even step into the office, because she wrote, "With the death of my unborn child, part of me died."

I wish my girlfriend had told me all these things. It would have been so much easier to know that she was pregnant in the first place. I suspected she was, but before I knew the facts, she had an abortion. Even though the decision was up to her and she knew that I would support her no matter what she chose to do, I just wish that I knew beforehand so I could have at least gone with her.

Now that I'm sitting in class thinking about what she went through, all I can say is that I'm glad we're still together. And as always, what didn't push us apart brought us closer. With something like this, I will always look back and wonder what would have happened if we kept it? Where would I be now? All there is in life is questions and temporary solutions, and even though this was a major solution—it will always stir up questions.

When I finished reading the story, I didn't feel so alone. Somebody in my class shares my secret. I actually wrote her an anonymous note and simply said, "I feel your pain—you're not alone!"

Diary 74

Dear Diary,

My mom always told me that "one person can make a difference that can change the whole world." It sounds unbelievable to me that one person can be a catalyst for such a change. She also told me that when she was young, during the sixties, there were many men and women that made significant changes that affected her life, as well as the world around her. Rosa Parks was one of those incredible people that changed the world.

Rosa Parks is an African American woman who was living in the segregated South. One day she was coming home from a hard day's work and had to ride the bus. At that time African Americans were not allowed to sit in the front of the bus, and when the front section filled up, they had to give up their seats in the back to white passengers. Most people don't know that Rosa Parks actually sat in the black section in the back of the bus that day. When the white section filled up and the bus driver ordered her to stand, she refused. No one had ever challenged that racist practice before, but she was tired, her feet hurt, and she just didn't feel like getting up. Even though she was a law-abiding citizen, she felt so strongly that she should be able to sit that she refused to move from her seat and was then arrested.

Her bold action astonished many people. They believed that if this small, lone African American woman could take such a courageous stand, then they could, too. Many people believed she had done nothing wrong, so they started to boycott the buses. No one rode the buses for weeks. Rosa Parks opened the door for one of the most famous boycotts of our time and introduced the struggle for civil rights. I can see from this one person's act that my mother was right.

After listening to my mom's account of Rosa Parks's protest, I thought about the power she had. The power to challenge segregation and to stand up for what she believed was right. Rosa Parks was a true catalyst for change and she was only one person.

Hearing about Rosa Parks and her protest showed me that there is hope for me and all the students in Ms. G's classes to truly be catalysts for change. Imagine if there were 150 Rosa Parks standing up for tolerance, what a difference we would make.

Diary 75

Dear Diary,

I feel like I finally have a purpose in this class and in life.

That purpose is to make a difference and stand up for a cause.

Ms. G showed us a video during Black History Month, about a group of Civil Rights activists, in the 1960s, who were inspired by Rosa Parks. They decided to challenge segregation in the South. Rather than boycott buses, they took their challenge a step farther. They integrated their bus and traveled from Washington, D.C., through the deep South.

There were seven whites and six blacks on the bus, most of them college students. They were called the Freedom Riders, and their goal was to change segregated interstate travel, along with everyone's life forever. The Freedom Riders had faith that what they were doing was right, and they wanted the world to know that change was necessary and that being tolerant of each other is good.

I can picture myself on the road with that bus. I can visualize pulling into the bus station in Montgomery, Alabama, to discover the unsettling quietness. Even though they didn't expect a warm welcome, no one was to be seen at the station, not even the attendants. All of a sudden, Ku Klux Klan members were everywhere. Hundreds of them surrounded the bus, some carried bats or metal poles, and others held vicious German shepherds, growling and ready to attack these unarmed people. The mob was just waiting to get their hands on the riders. The Freedom Riders were barricaded on the bus. The mob, armed and hungry to attack, was just waiting for their first victim to step off that bus.

By choice, the seating arrangement on the bus was integrated: Blacks sat by whites, and vice versa. They were breaking a law that had been established in the South. This was unheard of! Jim Zwerg, a white man, stood up from the back of the bus. He wanted to be the first person to step off, even though he knew at the other side of the door was a mob of bigots drooling for a victim. What was he thinking? He felt this was his chance to fight back, nonviolently, and show his feelings to others. These strong feelings put his life at risk. Jim took that first step off of the bus, and the mob pulled him into their grasp. It was as if he had been swallowed up and disappeared, like bees on honey. Jim was almost beaten to death. He suffered a cracked skull from being hit with an iron pipe, a broken leg, and many cuts and bruises. During the moments the mob was beating on him, the other Freedom Riders got a chance to run for shelter.

I was impressed that Jim made a choice to be on that bus when he didn't have to. After all, he was white and could sit wherever he wanted and risked everything when he didn't have to. He wanted to fight for others who didn't have the same privileges or rights as he did, which made me realize that's been my role for the last two years. Since I'm white and my parents make a lot of money, I probably could have gotten out of Ms. G's class if my parents had made a big enough fuss. I'm sure that because of Jim's choice of riding the bus with black people, a lot of his peers must have thought he was crazy; after all, he didn't have to, so why get himself into trouble? I guess in my way I've been like Jim, and I didn't even know it. By making the choice to stay in Ms. G's Class since my freshman year, I've forced myself to fit the cause. People gave those riders a chance to get off the bus, and they didn't, and I'm going to face intolerance head-on as well.

The way I feel about segregation in school is the way Jim must have felt about segregation in the sixties. I want people to interact with different cultures and races. I don't want segregation like you see in class or in the school quad. The way Jim must have felt when he stepped off the bus is probably the same way I felt those first couple of days in the class. I remember feeling scared, like a wimp. I was the only white student in the class. I felt helpless. But after I stayed in the class and toughed it out, a lot more white students transferred in, just like more people joined the Freedom Rider movement after Jim's first step.

At the end of the video, a fellow classmate asked the question, "They fought racism by riding the bus?" That was it! The bells were ringing, the sirens were sounding. It hit me! The Freedom Riders fought intolerance by riding a bus and pushing racial limits in the deep South. Then somebody suggested that we name ourselves the Freedom Writers, in honor of the Freedom Riders. Why not? It's perfect! But those are huge shoes to fill, so if we're going to take their name, we better take their courage and conviction. It's one thing to ride a bus, but they eventually had to get off and face the music. So, it's one thing for us to write diaries like Anne and Zlata, but if we want to be like the Freedom Riders, we need to take that extra step. Just like Anne's story made it out of the attic and Zlata's out of the basement, I hope our stories make it out of Room 203. Now when I write, I'll remember Jim's work and what he risked his life for. Like him, I am willing to step forward, unafraid of who or what lies ahead. After all, history tells me that I am not alone.

Diary 76

Dear Diary,

"Me, cleaning my mother's blood off the wall, represented the 'tornado' breaking and destroying her face (I liked to call my mother's boyfriend the 'tornado'.) After he would hit, everything would look like it had been caught in a whirlwind—our apartment, our sanity, and my mother's face. I was cleaning up after the tornado hit my house and diminished everything. Washing my mom's blood, which was shed from time to time; a sacrifice to make him happy. He lived for blood—her blood, en-

joying every fist that hit her flesh, and every scream that took place. While he broke televisions, stereos, VCRs and the dining room table, it didn't compare to the breaking of her mind. My mom was never the same, and neither was I . . ."

Damn! That was really deep. I think now that we're "Freedom Writers," we're taking the "freedom writing" part to heart. We've decided to bind all our diary entries, and call it *An American Diary . . . Victims of an Undeclared War*. Someone said he refused to be called a "victim," and we all agreed, so we came up with *Voices* instead.

Since we titled it *An American Diary . . . Voices from an Undeclared War*, we felt that someone should hear our voices, but who would be the right person to listen? We wanted to shoot big! The mayor? No. The governor? Hell no! (Some of us are still upset about Proposition 187!) The President? Nah. We wanted somebody who had a direct effect on education. Ms. G mentioned some guy named Richard Riley. Supposedly, he's the top dog in his field. I think he's the United States Secretary of Education.

He claims he wants to get to know America's youth, and as part of America's youth, we would give it to him straight. He's adamant about changing education, and we're adamant about revolutionizing it. He's perfect, but there's a catch—he's in Washington. Just when we were about to leave that idea alone, someone said, "That would make it even better because that's where the Freedom Riders started their mission." It made perfect sense, but one question: How the hell are we gonna get there?

Since we became the Freedom Writers, people have been acting even crazier than ever. They stay after school, and even come in at lunch. Last night we didn't leave here until 10 P.M. and the custodian had to kick us out. We tried to bribe him with pizza, but it didn't work. That's nothing compared to the other night, though, when we almost got arrested. We were editing stories, and before we knew it, it was 11, at night! Fred made all of us, even Ms. G, climb out the window so the alarms wouldn't go off. Somebody must have seen us, 'cause within thirty seconds Ms. G's car was surrounded by five cop cars. They thought that we were jacking our own computers. They found it hard to believe that we were studying, and it was even harder to believe that some of us hoodlums were still at school. What was worse is that they didn't believe Ms. G was our teacher. Maybe it was because she looked somewhat like us. She was wearing my big-ass sweats because we had made her change out of her suit to be more comfortable. Her hair was up in a ponytail, so she looked like a teenager. They must have thought that her car was our "G ride." They were about to arrest us all, until we found Ms. G's "Teacher of the Year" plaque in the back of her four-runner.

It's weird, but this incident brought us all closer together; how many people could say that they almost got arrested with their teacher? The fact that Ms. G was willing to get arrested to help us complete a writing assignment was a sign of loyalty, and we respect her more for it. It's ironic how Ms. G is helping us write about an undeclared war, and that night she was helping us fight it.

She proved to us that she was down for us, so now we had to be down for her. We have to trust her, even if it does mean doing the impossible to make our trip to Washington, D.C., possible.

Diary 77

Dear Diary,

We decided to have a concert in order to raise money for our Washington, D.C., trip. There is no better satisfaction than watching our small ideas become a big show; I am so excited. The people who bought tickets to our Echoes of the Soul fundraising concert did not simply support one hundred and fifty high school kids, they supported a cause. Tonight is our night to shine. We'll have Latin dances, singing of all types, Cambodian dances, a fashion show, and even skits. The diversity of ideas, traditions, and spirit is the true purpose of the Freedom Writers.

It used to be that no one believed in us, but now our whole community is behind us and cheering us on.

Diary 78

Dear Diary,

I read this poem at the Freedom Writers concert:

An Innocent Freedom Writer

A young black boy filled with innocence and care,
looking for someone, but no one is there.
His first day of school, the father's not around,
to comfort his son when he's sad and down.
Looks up to his brother who knows money and power,
watching his back every single hour.
An innocent boy is now twelve years of age,
and finds himself locked up in a human-sized cage.
An innocent young man is now a criminal mind,
having nightmares of murders every single time.
But this time you'll think this fool should see the light,
but he's jumped in a gang and they nickname him "Snipe."
Kicked out of the house and left in the cold.
Have you been through this at eleven years old?
He says to himself "no one cares for me,"
then makes his bed in an old park tree.
The next time a park bench, how long can it last?
Will he forget this dreadful, dreadful past!

He goes to Wilson High with a messed-up trail,
and meets a guardian angel named Erin Gruwell.
He learns about the Holocaust, Anne Frank and the Jews.
Now the time comes that he should choose.
He meets Anna, Terri, Tommy, and others.
These are the innocent boy's new sisters and brothers.
A 0.5 now a 2.8—
Change is good, for those that wait.
He's back to innocence, but still has fear,
that death is upon him and drawing near.
But people say it's hard to see,
this life of emotions is all about me.
All this is true, because I'm not a liar
just a brokenhearted male with a label—Freedom Writer!

Diary 79

Dear Diary,

I think I'm pretty lucky. I have a good life, a loving family, and a beautiful home. My friends, however, are not as fortunate as I am. Some have been in trouble with the law, have family disputes, or are just alone and have no one to turn to. I did not find out how much other teenagers go through until we started writing and editing our stories. The more I read, the more I found out about my peers' personal problems. Even though I don't have my own sad story, I am willing to help, listen, and encourage other Freedom Writers to tell their stories. People should hear what they go through and understand that no one comes from a perfect home. I believe that the passion behind our stories will speak as loud as the words in it.

We have the same passion and hope as the Freedom Riders had when they traveled from city to city across the South. Freedom Riders stood out among the crowd, trying to bring an end to segregation between whites and blacks by traveling from Washington, D.C., to New Orleans. Without the collaboration of both the Caucasians and the African Americans they would not have won the battle. They worked together as one to win the war against ignorance. Our camaraderie has more than just two sides, and I feel really fortunate to be a part of this new movement that's not just black and white. We are following in their footsteps by traveling from California to Washington D.C., announcing to everyone that we are strong and we will be heard. Our trip to Washington is to prove the passion behind our cause. Just like the Freedom Riders, we are going to fight for what we believe in.

Being able to look into another person's life is one thing, but doing something about it is another. I feel that we have the potential to help those who fear to speak for themselves. But speaking out is not always easy. We may face a lot of close-minded people along the way. So, just like the Freedom Riders, who didn't give up when their bus got bombed or when they were beat up by the Klan, I hope we'll stand strong like the Dylan Thomas poem and "Not Go Gently Into That Good Night."

We want people who are adults to take the time to listen to teenagers and respect what we have to say. So we came up with the idea that the best way to tell our side of the story is to give our diaries to Secretary of Education Richard Riley. If we could hand-deliver our stories to Secretary Riley, then one more person will know the problems teenagers face day by day. Unfortunately, a lot of adults are too blind or cold-hearted to see our pain. But blinding yourself to the realities that our teenagers go through is like seeing a murder and turning the other way. I am not going to let that happen. I will fight along with the other Freedom Writers to stand up, speak out, and "rage against the dying of the light." Hopefully when we're in Washington, Secretary Riley won't turn us away or stay blind to our cause.

Diary 80

Dear Diary,

I can't believe I'm here in our nation's capital! I'm so excited. I have never felt so free. But at the same time, I'm scared about my dad coming back and finding out that I'm gone! He's in Mexico and I don't know when he's going to come back. If he was home, I wouldn't have been able to come. He's very strict and old-fashioned. I'm not allowed to do anything after school. I've had to miss every trip that involved the Freedom Writers. I didn't get to go to the Marriott to meet Zlata, I didn't get to go to the Museum of Tolerance and see *Schindler's List*, I didn't even get to go to Medieval Times. Every time my friends came home from a field trip, I felt so left out. Everyone had something to share, and I didn't. I would listen, look at their pictures, and hide my tears. Every time Ms. G tried to get me to go, I always said "No!" I already knew what my dad's answer would be: "No!" During my sophomore year I used to beg to go, but my dad would always say, "You already know the answer, so don't ask!" From that point on, I just stopped asking. It hurt too much to hear him say "No!"

When the Washington trip first came up, I just assumed I wasn't going. The thought of getting away ran through my mind many, many times. I never realized that my wish would actually come true. Every time Ms. G asked for a final headcount to reserve our plane tickets, I never responded. Deep down inside, it was killing me. I'd never been on a plane before, never stayed in a hotel or left my house for that matter. I'm like a prisoner in my own home! I'm not even allowed to talk on the phone. If I do, my dad disconnects it. If anybody calls me, he tells him or her "She doesn't live here" and hangs up. Then I get screamed at.

Three days before the trip, a miracle happened. My dad left for Mexico because my grandma got sick. I got up the nerve to ask my mom if I could go. I was afraid she'd say no, too. Even though she was scared of my dad and said that we were both taking a huge risk, she wanted me to go. If he came home, he would beat her and me up for sure. He'd never let me leave the house again. He would probably hold a grudge and blame everything that went wrong on me! But for some reason, even though she was scared, she said I had to go. She said that I deserved it, and I might not ever get this chance again. Wow! I couldn't believe my mom was willing to sacrifice so much for me.

It was the first time in my life that I felt hope. I wanted to go so bad. I prayed that it wasn't too late. So, the first thing I did the next morning was run to Ms. G's class. Luckily, the baseball team made it to the playoffs, so our star athlete wouldn't be able to go on the trip. Ms. G said I could have his ticket!

From that point on, everything was a blur. I had never felt so free. I was so nervous, running from place to place trying to pack. Since I'd never been on a vacation, I had no idea how to pack. What should I take? What was I going to wear? I never even had sleepovers when I was a little girl, so this was all new to me.

All this was new for my mom, too. She was so scared because I'd never been away from her a day in my life. What if something happened to me? This trip was really for the both of us. I want to share everything with her, every detail: what we ate, what we saw, who we met. Everything!

This morning when I left, all my relatives were there to say good-bye. Tears rolled down my cheeks as I kissed my mom good-bye. At that moment, I had doubts about my departure. So I asked my mom, "Are you sure you want me to go?" I thought she'd change her mind, but I was wrong. She hugged me and said, "Make good use of this opportunity and don't let me down. I'm so proud of you." Her words gave me so much motivation and in- spiration, that I can't explain. Now I was ready to say good-bye and leave Long Beach. I headed off on my adventure, an adventure that I'm sure I'll cherish for a lifetime. Her excitement gave me the courage to hop on a plane for the first time. Yeah! I was afraid, but it seemed like nothing else mattered. I can't wait to share everything with her when I get home.

Diary 81

Dear Diary,

I'm writing to you from Washington, D.C. We went to Arlington Cemetery today where J.F.K. and many soldiers were buried. As the bus pulled up, I could feel a flood of tears forming in my eyes. I saw the cemetery filled with rows of graves. Like these soldiers, I, too, have witnessed many die. Many of my friends have been shot in the head, and stabbed a number of times, yet their deaths will never be recognized like these men and women. To me, my friends are soldiers, not soldiers of war, but soldiers of the street. With them, it wasn't a fight for territory, it was a fight for their lives.

I didn't want to enter the cemetery to see the rest of the graves and memorials for the lost soldiers. I was not being disrespectful, but it made me think back to when I was twelve years old and my father died of AIDS. He never had a headstone to commemorate his life. To this day, he still has nothing but a section of grass that you have to use a map to find. He was just another number, another statistic, someone that no one knew.

It makes me sad to see the media only concentrate on the deaths of famous people. I've always asked myself, "Why do only famous people make the headlines?" The media makes a big deal out of a movie star breaking a leg or fracturing a toe, but if a man with as much wisdom as my father passes away, no one cares.

Diary 82

Dear Diary,

I would say this has been the best night of my life! As we pulled up in our bus at the Lincoln Memorial, I felt as if I was a part of history. It was raining, but we still wanted to see the statute of Abraham Lincoln. It has always been my dream to see the world-famous statue of Abraham Lincoln.

At first I didn't understand why Ms. G wanted us to go to Washington so badly. But now that we're in our nation's capital, it hit me! I will never be the same! I finally realized what being a Freedom Writer really means. Everyone was standing around the monument reading the passages on the wall. We all wanted to know what each passage meant, when it was written, and who wrote it.

After that I heard a small voice excitingly yell, "It's time to go back outside in the rain." I knew Ms. G was up to something, because she's always trying to do something spontaneous that has some kind of symbolism in it. This time, it would be the most symbolic of all. We went outside and stood on the stairs of the monument and held hands facing the city, facing the world.

To think that Dr. Martin Luther King recited his famous "I Have a Dream" speech here where he dreamt that someday "little black children and little white children . . . will come together." Ironically, when I looked at the Freedom Writers holding hands in the rain, I realized that we are his dream come true. Then all of a sudden, one, two, three, we screamed "Freedom Writers have a dream!" The rain stopped and the sound of our voices echoed across the city!

Diary 83

Dear Diary,

As I walked with my group down Pennsylvania Avenue, my eyes filled up with excitement, my lips followed what I saw with a smile, and my heart was full of enjoyment to be in a city that is so different than Long Beach. At that moment I felt as if I had entered a place were violence and hate did not exist. But in a few seconds that safe feeling would be all taken away . . .

"Damn! Check out this swastika, can you believe it? Just blocks away from the White House and the Holocaust Museum." "Look, there goes another one on that wall," I overheard as we walked down Pennsylvania Avenue. Those feelings I had within me were now found at the tips of my toes. I knew those symbols meant hatred and represented Nazi organizations. My judgment about Washington being perfect was wrong. I guess I kind of judged it for its cover.

Anyone can cover up the swastika with paint; but then again another idiot would probably come back and spray it again. I know from experience. It's sad to say that I once was much like this idiot that sprays on walls, but had different causes. We both destroyed property, but what was being sprayed was way different. The swastika he sprayed is a symbol of hatred. I used to hit up streets with a spray can to get name recognition, not spread hatred.

Early the next morning at my breakfast table my homie and I knew something had to be done. Then we both made up a Freedom Writers logo. So the next time we saw a swastika spray painted on a wall or newspaper stand we could represent ourselves, the Freedom Writers, without destroying property. I then took the logo we came up with to the hotel concierge and asked if he would be nice enough to make several copies of it. I also asked if he would be willing to give us masking tape to tape our logos and not destroy outside property. Then we left the hotel armed with logos and tape in our hands. We attacked the first swastika we saw on the streets. Everyone joined in and surrounded the symbol. Once we had covered it up with our logo, everyone filled up with joy and started to clap. Once again my eyes filled with excitement, my lips followed what I saw with a smile, and my heart filled up once again with enjoyment because we had made a difference and I felt safe again.

Diary 84

Dear Diary,

We took a trip to the Holocaust Museum today. Inside the museum, many memories from my past resurfaced. We sat in a room to watch a movie on how Jewish people were treated during the Holocaust. They were beaten, starved, and forced to watch their loved ones killed before their own eyes by Hitler's troops. As I watched the movie I began to zone out . . .

"Please get off me!" I screamed at the boys who were at least two feet taller than me and had extremely deep voices.

"Shut up you fucking nigger, your kind don't belong here," they screamed as they kicked me harder and harder.

I couldn't believe what was happening to me. I was being beaten to the ground for being in the wrong place at the wrong time, and not to mention for being the wrong color. Each blow was more powerful and furious than the one before. I tried to open my eyes, but I couldn't. I wanted to see their faces. Who could do this to me? Then in that brief moment, my body went numb. I blacked out. I don't know how much longer they beat me, but when I came to, I was in the middle of the street. I got up to go home and as I walked, no one tried to help.

When I got home, my cousins were asking me what happened. I chose not to say anything. It hurt too much to do anything, so I just went to my room, and cried myself to sleep. I slept for about four to five hours. I would have slept longer, but I was awakened by an unfamiliar smell.

"Johnny, what the hell are you burning in there?" I asked.

"I don't know where that's coming from, it's not me or anything in here," he said.

I got up to see what was going on. What was burning? Was the neighbor's house on fire? I could hear the crackling sound of the wood being burned. As I walked into the living room it was lit up as if a small lamp was on.

"Johnny, call the police, I think the neighbor's house is on fire," I said.

I moved toward the door and the light from outside began to hurt my eyes, and the closer I got to the door, the warmer it got. I opened the door and I saw five people dressed in white robes. One of them was little and petite. In each of their evil eyes, I saw the reflection of the fire from the cross that was burning on my aunt's lawn.

I stood, staring at them, as if it were an illusion that I was seeing. I closed my eyes, thinking that the vision would go away, but when I opened my eyes, the cross was still there. I came to realize that these were the same people who had beaten me earlier that day, and they continued to beat me, not physically, but emotionally. I stepped back, but careful not to take my eyes off of them, and I closed the door, and waited for help to arrive. My heart was beating so fast as I sat on the couch, nervous, and scared for my life.

"Hey, come on," a classmate said.

When I looked up, the movie was over. My palms were sweaty and I felt as though I had just gone through the same experience again.

It seems as though everything tied together; the Jews and a

little girl, both victims of a hate crime, and now the graffiti we saw in the nation's capital. I guess some things never change . . .

Diary 85

Dear Diary,

Yesterday I was up all night having fun with my roommates. I was planning to go to bed earlier, because we were supposed to be ready to leave for the museum at 8:00 A.M. but my roommates wouldn't shut up. I put a pillow over my head and tried to tune them out. I tried to go to sleep, but I couldn't. I couldn't stop thinking about the Holocaust Museum. I wondered what it's going to be like? I was so curious, but at the same time I was scared. Scared of what I might see. My roommates didn't fall asleep until 4:00 A.M. so when the alarm went off at 6:30, I thought I was going to die.

God! I can't believe what I saw at the Holocaust Museum. I tried to hold back the tears as I walked through the museum, but I couldn't help it. As I walked through the entrance, I thought about Renee Firestone and Gerda Seifer, two Holocaust survivors who were visiting the museum with us. I couldn't stop thinking of the pain and suffering they went through.

As I walked from room to room, I saw videos about thousands of people being buried in a single grave. How could this have happened? Why didn't someone stand up for these people? How did people just allow them to die? I asked myself these questions as I headed to the next room. I looked at the wall and something caught my attention. It was a quote from a German preacher that summarized the outcome of what happens when no one takes a stand. "They came for the trade unions, but I was not a trade unionist, so I didn't respond. Then they came for the Socialists, but I was not a Socialist, so I didn't respond. Then they came for the Jews and since I was not a Jew, I didn't respond.

Then they came for me and there was no one left to speak out for me." Next to this quote there was a picture of the concentration camp. I looked at that picture for a while repeating the words in my head. The more I thought about it, the more I cried.

Gerda caught up with me and started telling me about the cattle cars that the people were squeezed into. We walked into the next room and she just stopped. She started crying and when I asked her what was wrong, she raised her arm pointing at the cattle car right in front of us. We had to cross through a real cattle car in order to exit the room. She was afraid. She must have imagined her friends and family being shoved into one just like it. I asked her if she was OK. She took a step forward and then started describing how crowded the cars were. She told me that many of the people died before they even got to the concentration camps. When we finally got across it, both of us were crying. Gerda grabbed my hand and thanked me. But I should be the one thanking her.

On our way back to the hotel, I saw the swastikas that we had covered. Before, if I saw something bad happen, I probably wouldn't have done anything. I used to think, "If it doesn't affect me, why bother?" With the covering of the swastikas, and everything that happened today, I now know that there is not a day that will go by, when if I believe something is wrong, I won't do anything about it. It is better to take a chance and make a change, than it is to pass and pity.

Diary 86

Dear Diary,

As we walked through the double doors and entered the cold and scary room at the Holocaust Museum, silence fell upon me as I looked at the death of millions. I never saw so many people dead in one place at the same time. What made it even worse was that it was for no reason at all. I was shocked when I saw all those dead people, but I was particularly devastated when I looked at all the twin carcasses. Quicker than a bolt of lightning, it was as if I was going through the same pain and suffering as those innocent twins who were so exploited and mutilated. The more pictures of identical twins I looked at, the more it seemed as if I, I mean, we were there.

They say one twin can't last without the other. I couldn't believe that all those twins were forced to test that theory. Dr. Mengele, a doctor at Auschwitz, was obsessed with doing experiments with twins. Rather than using lab mice, twins became his human guinea pigs. He became the Angel of Death and tortured every twin on the European continent that he could get his hands on. It made me wonder how it would be if I were to lose my twin. Would I have tried my hardest to run away if Mengele singled me out? Would I have tried to fight him? I really don't know because I wasn't there, I wasn't in their shoes. Or would I have even tried to do anything to save any of the other twins? These are some of the questions that ran through my mind as I saw those kids lie there helplessly.

The more evil I saw that this man had in him, the more angry I became. All of these horrific pictures of children with their arms and legs cut off of their bodies and put together on another adult or child's body was like looking at a collage of bad dreams that was put together like a picture puzzle. How could one man crush so many dreams? He must have been a man with no heart, and no mercy. He got pleasure from someone else's sorrow.

Being at the museum made me think about how much I really need and love my twin sister. Even though growing up as a twin has had its good points and bad points, at least I always have someone to talk to, share clothes with, and experiment with. My twin gets on my nerves sometimes, but I would never dream of trading her in for anything in the world.

Kids these days have the chance to dream about what they want to be and want to change. It's the changes that affect people's lives for either good or bad. Unfortunately, Dr. Mengele took so many people's chances from them when he took "change" into his own hands. Taking dreams away is the problem, making them happen is the solution. Unfortunately, those twins never had a chance to dream the same dream we are making come true . . . change.

Diary 87

Dear Diary,

The big day is here. I can't believe this is my fourth day here in Washington, D.C., and I am actually meeting Secretary of Education Richard Riley. It has been a long day and there is still more to come. We've just got back from visiting a couple of museums and getting a tour of the Capitol. This has been the longest and most exciting day of my life.

What am I going to wear? I have to look nice for tonight's dinner. This is the most important night of all. The people from the Marriott even had a rehearsal for us. I never realized how important this man really is. Now I know that he represents a lot in education. I wonder what he looks like. Is he young or old? Either way, I know I should never judge a book by its cover, like Ms. G taught me. "He has to be a really important and educated man to be the Secretary of Education," I said to myself. I can't wait to meet him. He will probably be surprised when he sees all of us, a diverse group of teenagers in front of him. I hope he gets excited when he finds out that we came all this way to hand-deliver a copy of our book to him. I also hope he can help us pursue our future education.

"This is going to be a boring night, you know, long speeches on things I don't even know or understand. This is for grownups, what am I doing here?" I said to myself at the beginning of the dinner. Richard Riley said, "You are the future leaders, don't give up," His words really got my attention. I couldn't believe he was the Secretary of Education. I imagined him differently. I thought he would be stuck up like all those other important people, but I was wrong. He's cool. I didn't think he would tell us about his life, but he did. He talked about his life and how he relates to some of us. He told us about all the struggles that he had to overcome to become who he is today. I can't believe I'm here, only five feet away from the most important man in education. Hopefully he will take a good look at us and realizes that it will only take a few of his words to change our future. He seems like he's moved by what we have accomplished.

He made me realize that with education you can become whoever you want. He made me see things from a very different perspective. "I hope one day I can become someone important like Richard Riley," I said to myself while he was walking away. Tonight has been a really good experience. I even got a rose from my date, which was very exciting. Hopefully many nights like this will come, but for tonight the memories will stay in my heart forever.

Diary 88

Dear Diary,

This is the poem I wrote that Ms. G asked me to read to Richard Riley at the dinner. I couldn't believe that I was sitting at the head table with all the big shots. I sat next to Ms. G's parents. Her stepmom, Karen, held my hand because I was so nervous. When I finished reading the poem, I got a standing ovation.

Stand

Stay Black—
    Stay Proud
Stay White—
    Stay Proud
Stay Brown—
    Stay Proud
Stay Yellow
    Stay Proud . . .

Don't be afraid to be what you are,
'cause all you can be, is you!
You'll never be anything else but you,
so be the best you, you can be.
Keep it *real*—
            by all means,
                        at all times.

Whether a lawyer, a doctor, a football player,
a toilet cleaner, a garbage handler, a panhandler—
keep it *real*
            and still—
                        be the *best* you can be.

Have pride, have dignity, *stand!*
Stand proud, talk proud, act proud, be proud!

Don't lay down,
back down,
bow down,
run away,

sell out yourself,
sell into criticism.

Be *real* and *realize* that the ones who criticize,
best recognize that you are you—
take it or leave it.

"MMM HMM!"
I knew you'd get it.
Get what?
The stuff—
the stuff called pride, that attitude, that aura,
your identity, your self, your pride, peace of mind,
worry free.

See, *I can't be you*, but I'm a damn good *ME!*
Righteous.

Diary 89

Dear Diary,

We gave our book to the United States Secretary of Education, Richard Riley, tonight. As I watched him come into the Marriott ballroom, I couldn't help but notice how different we were. He is a rich white Southern man from South Carolina with a Southern drawl, and I'm a young black male trying to make it in life, living check by check. But I realized we were both there for the same reasons—we care about the future of kids in America. As I sat there listening to his speech, I realized he actually cared about us. More important, I realized that this man would actually read my diary entry.

By reading my diary, he will know all the things that I went through and maybe be in a position to do something about it. As I was listening to him tell us about how he fought against discrimination in the South, I couldn't help but remember the night that my brother got shot, purely based on our race.

We were just driving on the freeway when a car full of Mexicans drove up next to us. All of a sudden I saw sparks flying, glass shattering, and blood splattering. A bullet actually ricocheted all through the car. Another bullet went through the backseat of the car and grazed my friend in the back. My brother, who was driving, was shot four times. Twice in his chest, inches from his heart, once in his thigh, and once in his calf. He turned to me, with his shirt soaked in blood, and said, "I can't breathe no more. I can't drive!" He pulled off the road while my two friends were yelling in the backseat, "I'm shot! I'm shot!"

Trying not to panic, I pulled my brother into my seat. Then I jumped into the driver's seat, which was full of blood, and started looking for a hospital. I finally pulled into a gas station to call the police to tell them my brother got shot. While I was by the phone, I couldn't help but notice that there must have been about twelve bullet holes in the side of the car. The car was totaled. It looked like it had been through a war. In two minutes an ambulance came and they took my brother and my friend to the hospital. Then the police took me to the hospital.

The hospital was only a block away. When I got there, the doctor took me into the room to see my brother. He had tubes all in him. I didn't know what to think. Then my brother made this joke from a movie. He said, "The doctor told me I'm never gonna walk again." I knew that was a line from a movie, but I didn't know whether to laugh or to cry. Then my brother went into surgery for six hours so they could remove the bullets. Apparently his lungs collapsed. I thought he was going to die. If he died it would have been for the simple fact that we were black and in the wrong place at the wrong time.

Luckily, he came out of the surgery OK and was only in the

hospital for one week. His doctor told me that if I didn't react like I did by getting my brother to the hospital so soon, he would have died. The doctor said, "That makes you a hero!" I guess it does. It made me realize that a real hero should try to prevent this from ever happening again.

I guess that's why I want Richard Riley to read my story. I want him to know that the guys with guns were absolute strangers. All they saw was our color because they were ignorant. If they were educated, like I am, they'd learn to see past shades and beyond exteriors and see people. I guess that's why the Freedom Writers had to write about our lives and share them with him, because he's in a position to educate kids like that.

Unfortunately Secretary Riley can't change what happened to my brother and me, but maybe he can help us spread our message so it doesn't happen to another innocent teen.

Diary 90

Dear Diary,

Last night we had a candlelight vigil for our family and friends we've lost to senseless violence. Right after we dedicated our bound copy of the book to the Secretary of Education, Richard Riley, we all held hands to form an unbreakable chain and marched out of the hotel toward the Washington Monument. The chain we made was so long that we held up traffic while crossing the busy intersection on Pennsylvania Avenue. When we were crossing the street, some guy asked what we were doing. Someone said, "Changing the world," but the weird thing about that is the fact that this candlelight vigil was one of the stepping stones used by us to get in a position where we can truly make a change for the better and influence others to change, too. So we really were changing the world.

When we reached the Washington Monument, we formed a

huge circle around it and we all began to sing "Stand by Me."
During that moment tears of mourning began to fall from everyone except me. I didn't want to think about the painful memories
of close friends whose lives were blown away like dust in the
wind. We held hands again and walked back to the hotel after we
pinned the buttons that had names of people who were killed because of violence on a tree in front of the Washington Monument.

The pain that everyone was feeling didn't hit me until we arrived back at the hotel. I just couldn't hold it in anymore. I began
to think about all the times that I was almost killed and the fact
that my name could have been on one of those buttons. Right at
that moment I felt like I was going to have a nervous breakdown.
My heart was beating fast as the tears ran down my face because
all of those painful memories that came back. I had constant flashbacks of all the guns put to my head, all of the bullets that barely
missed me, and all the times I thought to myself, "Just give up,
they're gonna kill you anyway." But I couldn't give up, I didn't
give up, and I will never give up!

Diary 91

Dear Diary,

I'm thousands of feet in the air in a "Freedom Writer Only"
plane, on my way home from Washington, D.C. As I look at the
clouds, ice crystals build up on my window, and my eyes become
heavy with fatigue. (It was hard checking in our baggage and then
running to the plane. The girls' bags were ten times heavier than
when we left.) I'm sitting here thinking, "OK, so this is what it's
like to fly first class." This is my second time on a plane, the first
was when we went to Washington. Me, on a plane? If I'd never
met Ms. G, this would have never happened!

"Yeah right," my sister said when I told her I was flying to
D.C. Even my stepdad was skeptical. I saved my plane tickets,

just so I would have proof that I'd actually gone, to show him when I get home. Actually, I saved just about everything—my movie ticket, a handkerchief from the hotel, even the soap and shower cap!

You're probably wondering how one little female high school teacher brought such drastic changes into my life. Well, I have about four hours before we land in LAX, so I'm going to sit here and tell you a story of how my life was changed by this "little" high school teacher . . . Just thirteen years ago, I felt helpless, like I'd never be free. Thirteen years ago may seem like a long time ago, but to me, it seems like yesterday . . .

"Give me some money!" A deep, booming voice yelled at my mom.

"I don't have any," my mom cried.

"Yes you do! I know you do! You just got your welfare check. You better give me some money or I'm gonna fuck yo' son up!" Afraid this man would hurt her child, my mom foolishly gave him all the money she had in her purse. It couldn't have been more than twenty dollars. "Yeah, I thought you didn't have any money, you lying bitch! When I get back, that little nigga better be gone," he said. I sat trembling on the couch, his prized possession. "And get the hell off of my couch!" He grabbed me by my shirt and threw me across the room. Then he picked me up by the neck. All I could think of was why is he was doing this to me. I didn't do any thing to defend myself, it's kind of scary having a six-foot-four giant, with arms built to play football, grab you by the neck and throw you into the trunk of a car. While in the trunk I could hear my mom screaming. I could hear the sound of his fist smashing against her face.

I stayed in that grease-infested trunk for at least a day. It was morning when my mom finally let me out. The daylight burned my eyes. My pants were soaking wet with a combination of dirt, car oil, and urine. We didn't have any soap or hot water, so my mom bathed me with dishwashing liquid, in a tub of ice-cold water. All of my mother's welfare money supported her maniac boyfriend's cocaine habit. There was never any money left for food, just enough for Top Ramen noodles; it was our breakfast, lunch, and dinner. Most of the time we had to eat that raw.

My mom was eight and a half months pregnant. With all the stress in her life, she had to be rushed to the hospital in premature labor. And I was stuck in the house with a child abuser, woman beater, murderer, drug user, and ex-convict. I was constantly being hit. Constantly being told I would never be anything, I ain't shit, I'll never be shit. I knew there would be trouble as soon as my mom left for the emergency room. The second this thought entered my mind, this madman started yelling at me. "It's your fault that she's gone! Don't start that crying shit. I ought to beat your ass."

I was home by myself most of time my mom was in the hospital. My mom's boyfriend exchanged all her jewelry with his dealer so he could buy his drugs. When my mom came home, the rent and all the bills were overdue, so we were evicted. We were given a week to move, but we didn't have anywhere to go. We couldn't move in with my grandmother because her boyfriend caused too much trouble. Our only option was his mother's house.

We left everything behind—which wasn't much—and moved into a dingy garage. For two years we lived in a garage with the gardening tools, old furniture, a tiny black and white TV, and a lone mattress in the center. There was no heat, no air-conditioning, no fan, and no restroom. It was just mom, her new daughter, her boyfriend, and me.

When we finally got our own house, her boyfriend took the bedroom, and my mom, my sister, and I slept in the living room. So in essence we'd come full circle. The only difference this time is that I'm older, I understand more, and I have more fear in my heart due to previous beatings. At least once a week there was an argument between the two either over money or me living in the house. Sometimes they just argued over why there's money in the house and no cocaine. For years he sold drugs out of the house where my mom paid rent. Where my mom paid the bills and bought food.

After living in such chaos for so long, I began to believe my mom's boyfriend. Maybe I wouldn't amount to anything, but Ms. Gruwell helped me prove him wrong by making me realize the things he said were not true, and that nothing that happened between him and my mother was my fault.

Diary 92

Dear Diary,

I have finally taken a real vacation. I have always had to go to summer school and I've never had time off. Well, thanks to the Freedom Writers, I got to go to the nation's capital. I had the best time I ever had in my life. My only regret is that I didn't have a camera during the whole trip to capture this once in a lifetime opportunity.

Everything in Washington, D.C., was great! It was my first time in a really nice hotel. I got to stay up late and didn't have to worry about my parents telling me to go to sleep. The first two nights, I never slept because I kept thinking my parents were going to call. They never did.

On my way home from Washington, D.C., I finally fell asleep on the plane. I dreamed about the events that happened and how things were going to be when I got home. When we got off the bus, it wasn't what I expected. My parents were there! At first, I just thought that maybe they were out getting gasoline for the car or eating out, but not to see me. Boy, was I surprised when they came up to me, gave me a hug, and asked me about my trip. I felt so welcome. This is something I'm not used to. Before I left, my parents always used to make me feel bad. They always thought I was bad, and I was constantly in trouble. I always argued with them and sometimes I even hated them! But tonight I forgot about all the bad times and I felt close to them.

When we got home, I walked in the house wondering why there was a lot more cars parked on the street. Everybody was at my house—from my closest relatives to people that I've only talked to once or twice. This was the first time since my sister got married that everybody was here. Were they here to see me? When I walked in, everybody started congratulating me! I felt really happy, as though nothing in the world would ever put me down. I wish I had taken pictures for them to see, but they were so excited just listening to me. And all their eyes were looking at me!

I sat in the middle of the living room telling them about my trip. I told them about how amazing the Capitol building was. I mean, I have never seen such beautiful paintings and magnificent sculptures. I described how the Lincoln Memorial was the biggest statue that I'd ever seen. I also told them about the cruise we took up the Potomac River. There was so much food that I ate until I could no longer get up. While I was outside on the deck, waving hello to everyone, it started to rain. But that didn't stop anybody from having fun! Everybody went inside the boat and started dancing and singing. I also told them how I was hoping that we would get a tour of the White House. But at least I got to see the White House in person, even though it was from behind the front gate.

As I was describing Washington, they had the look of envy in their eyes. Tonight, for the first time in my life, I was the main attraction in my house. Everybody was congratulating me and congratulating my parents for having such a "good," "smart," and "fascinating" son. They said I am a role model for the family and hopefully for the world.

Diary 93

Dear Diary,

As I entered the school this morning, still tired from our trip, I noticed that everyone was acting weird, like something crazy happened. There were media vans in front of the school and the first thing I thought to myself was they were there to welcome the Freedom Writers back and to write an article about us. But they weren't. So, I asked one of my friends, "What the hell happened?" He replied, "You know Jeremy Strohmeyer?" I said, "Yeah, Jeremy 'Strombocker,' " which is the name we used to call him when we joked around with him. Then my friend said, "Well, Jeremy was arrested."

Apparently Jeremy had brutally raped and murdered a seven-year-old girl in a Nevada casino. He had taken a Memorial Day weekend trip with a friend, another student at our school, and the friend's father to Las Vegas. On the way, the father stopped at a casino in Prim, Nevada. While the father gambled, Jeremy and his friend hung out in the arcade. Jeremy began playing tag with the little girl, followed her into the women's restroom, where he raped and murdered her in a bathroom stall. The friend with Jeremy was also in the restroom at the time, but he left and did nothing to stop this crime.

At first I was shocked. I couldn't believe it. I considered Jeremy an acquaintance because we had been on the same soccer team and we'd see each other around school. How could he possibly do such a thing? The more I heard, the more confused I felt.

Jeremy had a dark side to his personality. He had child pornography on his computer, and he was abusing drugs. This is a lethal combination. Although not an excuse, such things can make a person with such a dark and disturbed side commit acts they may never have if not under their influence.

I saw the media bombarding our campus with questions. We realized pretty quickly that they were not after our story. The Freedom Writers might as well have been on Mars for all the attention we got. It's ironic that while the Freedom Writers were taking a symbolic stand against violence in our candlelight vigil at the Washington Monument, a murder was being carried out. No wonder young people are so easily stereotyped. The media seems to focus more on the negative rather than on the positive things that young people accomplish. It makes me sad that this horrible murder moved the Freedom Writers' story to the back cover, while Jeremy's got the front page.

Diary 94

Dear Diary,

Today I heard the news; along with the news, I heard the rumors. Jeremy and David killed a girl in Las Vegas. No, wait: It was just Jeremy, while David stood by and watched. Or was it that Jeremy murdered her without his best friend knowing about it?

Once school ended I decided to sort this whole thing out. I watched the news, and finally learned the supposed truth. David watched Jeremy drag the girl into the bathroom stall and he left before Jeremy killed her.

What a case of tragic irony. One hundred and fifty students travel to Washington, D.C., to actively acknowledge the violence in Long Beach; two travel to Las Vegas, where one eventually murders a young girl, and the other leaves while she is struggling.

How could David walk away without helping her?

This is a question that I can't answer. Although I've never been in that type of situation, I do know that what he did isn't right. It should never be solved with the "just look the other way," normal approach to solving trials.

In any and every situation, nonaction is never a sane and rational approach. To illustrate this point, picture living in a small town filled with normal people, just like you. Every day loaded trains come in, make their deliveries, and leave. Factories constantly bellow smoke. Then one day you notice the trains aren't making simple deliveries anymore. And the factories aren't bellowing mere smoke. Would you rock the boat and speak out, or would you remain silent, as the people of Auschwitz did?

The saying is true, "If you're not for it than you're against it." David Cash wasn't for saving the life of that young girl, in the same way many Poles weren't for saving the Jews. They watched the trains and smelled the ashes, ignoring tragedy. David had a chance to be a hero, to both Jeremy and that little girl.

Diary 95

Dear Diary,

I was late to school this morning because we had just come home from Washington, D.C., very late at night and I wanted to tell my mom everything we had done. When I got to school I had to go through the front door instead of my usual route. Guess what I saw? Swarms of news cameras! I was so excited! I thought they were all here because the Freedom Writers had just come back from our trip! I guess I was wrong! I found out they were really here because of a kid at our school named Jeremy Strohmeyer, who had gone to Las Vegas and raped and murdered a seven-year-old girl while we were in Washington.

I walked into school and there were mixed reactions throughout the campus. Some people were even crying. By this time, I was in shock. With news cameras surrounding the campus and students crying, I didn't know what to think. Not a person on campus could concentrate on their schoolwork with all the chaos and confusion. There was gossip circulating the halls about what "really" happened. People were saying it was because of drugs, specifically speed, that led Jeremy to murder a seven-year-old girl. Bullshit! I used to be a "tweeker," but not even at my lowest point would I ever murder anyone. The only person I was murdering was myself. How can they even factor that in? He may have been strung out, but don't blame the drug, blame him.

When I finally got to Ms. G's class, everyone was furious. The Freedom Writers decided to have a peace march similar to the one we had in D.C. where we circled the Washington Monument and prayed for all the victims that had died on account of violence. We thought we should do it again, this time in front of the school, and in front of the cameras. We wanted to show that we can all unite and stand together for a positive cause and think about the person who really deserves some attention, the seven-year-old child who lost her life. Why wasn't anyone talking about her? She's the innocent victim in all of this.

As I went to each class, I told people and those people told others. By 1:00 the whole school knew of the peace march, including the administrators. We were told that if we participated in the march we would be in trouble and that it was not allowed. The principal didn't want to call any more attention to the situation at hand. When we heard that we couldn't believe it. Why wouldn't they want us to show a positive side to our school? We felt that our school should not be judged by the actions of one; so we did it anyway.

There have been more positive people that have come out of our school than negative ones. I figured that was a perfect reason to hold hands and walk together as one. Students who were stoners, football players, and even girls from my cheerleading team were planning to join the march.

The plan was for all of us to meet right after school as soon as the bell rang. As the group started to form I felt a feeling of unity.

We were all together for one cause. Some faces were familiar and some were not, but none of that mattered. All that mattered was the label the media had put on our school, the little girl who had lost her life and that all of us were there together. As I stood there singing I thought about how in Washington, D.C., we did the exact same thing for almost the same purpose. I lifted my head high as I looked around to see all of us holding hands.

The media didn't want to notice us in front holding hands. All the news cameras cared about was bribing students to talk about Jeremy. "Was Jeremy violent?" "Do you think drugs drove him to commit murder?"

So we sang and prayed until the news cameras left. I didn't see us on TV tonight. Instead I saw the negative publicity, the questions they asked students, the humiliation we would have to deal with when all of this chaos is over. But at least for a brief amount of time, we stood strong for what we believed in.

Diary 96

Dear Diary,

The end of my junior year is coming up right around the corner. Next year I want to be very active, and end my senior year with a bang. How can I manage to do that?

Then Ms. Gruwell says, "Next year you guys, I want you to be very active and I want the Freedom Writers to be widely represented throughout Wilson High School. Student Council, athletics, and any other extra curricular activities."

Wasn't I just thinking about that?! Well, since I'm not very interested in sports, I think I'll give student council a try. But what will I run for? I don't want to be Governor of Publicity—that sounds too easy. I want an office position where I can have some sort of authority, because I know I like to be in control. How about Senior Class President? . . . Yeah, Senior Class President.

So, the next day I went to the meeting, entered my name on the ballot, and started my campaigning. The Freedom Writers supported me 100 percent, so at that moment, I knew I had at least 150 votes in my favor. Now it's the rest of the school that I have to worry about. So I campaigned and campaigned up until the day of the election.

"Vote for me if you want to have a bomb-ass senior year! I have nothing but good things to offer you." Those were the words that I shouted at school the day of the election, so that people who forgot today was election day would vote for me.

And then there was the period that I had to wait for the results. I had to wait around for at least a week or so until the spirit rally to know if I was the winner or not. At the spirit rally, I was a nervous wreck, but since I'm a smooth kind of gal, I didn't let it show. Then it was time for the announcements.

"And your next year's Senior Class President will be . . ." It was loud and I couldn't hear the name that was called. Then I felt all kinds of pats on the back and people were hugging me.

"Get up there, girl, you won. You won."

And the whole crowd was cheering my name and going crazy for me. As I walked up to the stage, I said, "You love me, you really love me."

This is such a great accomplishment, I feel that I can do anything if I put my mind to it. Maybe next week, I'll try out for the cheerleading squad.

Diary 97

Dear Diary,

I feel as though chaos is stalking me, sliding its slimy tentacles into every crevice of my life. It has already conquered my home life, now it's trying to destroy the Freedom Writers, too. Every time I begin to get comfortable, someone goes and changes the rules on me. The whole reason I came to Wilson in the first place was to escape the uncontrolled environment I was raised in.

If "raising" is what you call it. My mother's parenting capabilities consisted of "I'll give you twenty bucks and the keys to my car if you leave me alone this weekend." It wasn't that she was a bad mother, she "was just tired of playing the role of mother," as she so bluntly told me one morning. How could she teach me to be responsible if she wasn't responsible herself?

Maybe it was her drinking, maybe it was her drugs . . . Maybe it was me. All I know is that absolute and complete freedom gets old very fast. My mother was simply tired of raising me, so I raised myself. There would be times I wouldn't see my mom for days, even weeks. Sure I always knew where she was, but that is never the same thing as having a real parent there. I missed the little things; curfews and rules were nonexistent. Whenever I asked her when I had to be home, she would reply "By Monday," even if it was Friday. Imagine being fifteen years old and feeling as though your own mother could care less about you. I not only wanted but needed guidance.

After a while I would give myself curfews so that people wouldn't know my mother was oblivious. It is hard raising yourself. If it was easy, then we wouldn't have parents. But we do, or most people do at least.

I began to feel so alone. All my life it had been my mom and me and now it was just me. I became very depressed, escaping reality any way I could.

The Freedom Writers filled this huge hole I had by giving me a safe place where I always knew someone cared. We are in jeopardy of not being able to be a class next year. Losing these people would be like losing a part of my family. I can't go through that again.

Diary 98

Dear Diary,

I just found out that we are going to be an official class our senior year of high school. After all the commotion from some of the teachers at school, we were worried that we would be separated. Why would the teachers want to separate us? Can't they see that we are so much more than a class? We are a family. Fortunately, the school superintendent, Carl Cohn, supported us all the way.

The Freedom Writer family has worked hard to stay together and the word "together" is very symbolic for me! I had a normal family once, with a father, a mother, and a couple of sisters. Our home was filled with love. What happened? My mother felt she needed more freedom, so she disappeared. I still don't know where she is. She left when we all needed her, especially me. In the long run, I hope that she will understand all the pain that she has caused in the family. My sisters and I stayed with my father, of course. He was the only one that showed love and pride for his girls. Then he met Ms. "She Thang" and allowed her to move in with us. For some reason, when I met her I felt the same feeling that I felt the day I lost my mother. I knew something was going to happen, because my father just expected my sisters and me to accept her as our mother. We were still trying to cope with our actual mother leaving us and now Dad had a new woman in his life.

My dad had three kids with his new wife and in the process, he forgot about his eldest daughters. So my sister and I moved out and moved in with my aunt. The youngest stayed with my father. My aunt was like a second mother and she received us with open arms when we walked into her home. I loved that feeling. It was as though I was starting a new life. Until her son introduced her to his friend from jail. She became real close to him over the phone and as time went by, they fell in love. They spent a large amount of time speaking to each other on the phone while her son was out causing trouble.

My aunt's niece and her friends would bring drugs in and out of our home; they would stay up at all times of the day and night, while my sister and I would stay locked up in our room. The two of us had the opportunity to become really close, so at least something positive was coming out of all this negativity.

My aunt continued to be her sweet self with me only until her boyfriend got out of jail. Suddenly, she was constantly out and I felt as though she totally forgot all about me and I couldn't understand why. She started to play favorites with her niece and for some reason it all made sense: They were planning on moving out together, but my sister and I weren't included. So, we did what we had to; my sister moved in with the neighbors and I'm living with a cousin who offered to take me in. She has been one of the best things that has happened to me in my entire life. I'm only hoping that nothing will happen to cause me to lose her, too.

Unlike my biological family, the Freedom Writers understand me and have been there for me for a long time. They have actually had the time and patience to listen to me, to help me, and to support me. Even though my mother left me when I was young, I have had many people try to fill the role of a mother. Many have not accomplished the position very well, but Ms. Gruwell has succeeded. I appreciate her and the Freedom Writers for what they have done and given me. They have helped me become a stronger person.

Senior Year
Fall 1997

Entry 7 · Ms. Gruwell

Dear Diary,

Getting permission to teach senior English has not been an easy feat. I forgot that the reason I had these students as freshmen in the first place was that I was told, "Things are based on seniority around here." Since I have no seniority to speak of, teaching seniors sort of rocked the boat. Luckily, my superintendent, Dr. Cohn, and the president of the Board of Education, Karin Polacheck, realized that this particular boat needed rocking.

Dr. Cohn & Karin Polacheck accompanied us to Washington, D.C., and since "they're down" for the cause they immediately became part of our family. The kids even got Dr. Cohn out on the dance floor while we cruised up the Potomac River on a tour boat. He's been a great role model for my students. Since there seems to be an absence of men in some of the kids' families, many of them look up to him as an adopted father figure. As an African American with roots in Long Beach, he saw the value of supporting our unique family.

My primary focus this fall will be to get the Freedom Writers thinking about their future—where they want to go to school and what kind of career they want to pursue. When Secretary Riley told my students "everybody deserves a college education," I interpreted it as a personal challenge to make sure that all the Freedom Writers would go to college. Our trip to Washington and Riley's speech made the kids feel almost anything was possible, but the idea of going to college is completely foreign for a lot of my students. Since many of them will be the first in their family to graduate from high school, their parents aren't pushing them to go to college.

Since my parents went to college, it was expected of me that I would go too. We talked about college at the dinner table, my parents paid for me to take SAT prep classes, they took me to visit colleges and they even helped me fill out my applications. As I became more familiar with my students and their circumstances, I realized (sadly) that the same thing doesn't hold true for most of the Freedom Writers since some of their parents don't speak English and can't help them fill out applications; and others can't afford to pay the application fee.

What I need to do is let them know that I understand how difficult all of this is and introduce them to different options. I realize how daunting the process is and I don't want them to feel overwhelmed. To help level the playing field, I plan to take them on college tours and bring in specialists who can help them fill out financial aid forms and prepare for those dreaded standardized tests.

Since being a "mom" to 150 college-bound kids will be overwhelming, I've decided to rally the troops and elicit more help. Since my education classes at National University have become so popular, I was able to create a special college forum in the fall. The seminar will have seventy-five graduate students who will each be paired up with two Freedom Writers. The idea is to have the Freedom Writers be a "case study" for the graduate students, and in exchange, my grad students will help mentor them.

Since the biggest obstacle in their way is money, Don Parris
and I created a nonprofit organization called the Tolerance Education Foundation. If anyone decides to donate money to us,
they'll get a tax writeoff and they'll be helping a kid go to college.
Not too shabby!

Diary 99

Dear Diary,

My mother always uses little clichés like, "What doesn't kill you makes you stronger!" If living in the projects is supposed to make me a stronger person, then I would rather be weak. I've spent most of my life living in poverty, being afraid to walk out of my front door because of the risk of being shot. My neighborhood has a way of demolishing any hope I have for a brighter future. "I was born poor and I will probably die poor. No one from my neighborhood has ever made a difference and I probably won't make one either." This was my mind-set. For so long, society has told me that because of my neighborhood and the color of my skin, I would never amount to anything.

The thought of college terrified me. At times we barely had enough money to pay our rent, I knew that we couldn't afford college. In addition to that, no one from my neighborhood had ever successfully completed college. If anyone ever did attempt to go to college, it's because they hoped to get the financial aid money. When they couldn't, they would drop out. Most people in my neighborhood figured they weren't smart enough. No one else in the 'hood has graduated from college, why should they be the first to try? This was my mind-set until I met a courageous woman named Cheryl Best.

"Adversity makes warriors of us all." Cheryl said. "I grew up in the projects and despite what others may have thought of me I never let them bring me down. I've witnessed it all, and I didn't get caught up in the negativity surrounding my neighborhood. If I could make it in the projects I knew that I could make it anywhere." That was the first time in my life that I had heard someone talk about living in the 'hood in a positive manner and with a smile on their face. I started to think about all of the horrific things I've witnessed. Crackheads getting high right in front of me, and drug dealers making more money in one day than a stockbroker makes in one week. I realized that like Cheryl, I too have never wanted to be caught up in the negative lifestyle that surrounded me. For a brief second, Cheryl made me feel as if I was a warrior, destined to make it out of the undeclared war that I call home, the projects.

Not only did Cheryl live in the projects but she also survived an ordeal that is so horrific, it seemed like something invented in a horror movie. Cheryl was kidnapped, raped, driven to a desert, and had acid poured all over her body. She was left to die. Cheryl refused to give up on her life. "As I lay there helpless, my life flashed before me. I realized that I had overcome too many obstacles in my life to just give up and die. I had too much to live for." I heard her describe the horrible ordeal she went through. The fact that she survived made me speechless. Cheryl got up from the ground even though acid was eating away at her skin. She began to walk toward the sound of moving cars that were on the highway, about one hundred feet away from her. The acid had blinded her and she had to rely on her other senses. Once Cheryl reached the highway, a motorist spotted her and took her to the hospital.

I pictured in my mind what Cheryl went through. I thought that if that had happened to me, I would have given up and asked the Lord to take my life. Cheryl didn't; she believed that she had too much to live for. She not only survived that ordeal but she learned how to read in braille, since the acid had left her permanently blind. She didn't stop at learning braille. Cheryl decided that she wanted to go to college. The media had reported what happened to Cheryl, and people were so inspired by her that people donated money to help pay for reconstructive surgery. Cheryl went to college despite all of the odds against her and she graduated with honors. After hearing Cheryl's story in person and watching her talk about what happened to her, as if it were just another obstacle she had to overcome, I knew that I could go to college and that I was somebody. Like Cheryl, I had witnessed, been through, and experienced too much in my life at such a young age to give up on my future.

Diary 100

Dear Diary,

The words "Eviction Notice" stopped me dead in my tracks. I looked at the notice in disgust, and realized what my mother told me was true. It didn't really dawn on me until I saw the notice; it didn't seem real. I felt a big lump in my throat, and looked away. I knew that if I read the fine print I would start crying. It would probably say that we only had one week to pack our stuff and leave. The last time we got only five minutes.

This is my last year in high school. Why did this have to happen to me now? I only have one year left before I graduate and I don't have a place to live. I don't know what I'm going to do or where I'm going to go. I don't even know if I'm going to be able to go to college. I think I will get a full-time job to help my mother. My mother doesn't have a plan in mind and doesn't know what to do. I'm stressed, I have knots in my stomach, and I have to start studying for school. But where am I going to study? I won't have a place to stay in a week. I'm scared.

I can't believe this is happening to me again. It's been such a long time since I last got evicted. The last time this happened we lived in a good apartment in a nice neighborhood, and we finally had somewhere stable to live. One day the manager knocked on the door and simply told us to get all of our things together because we only had five minutes to get out. In shock, I rushed to grab all of my belongings. Then we lived in hotels. When we finally ran out of money we had to resort to the only place we didn't have to pay rent, the streets. This gave me a new meaning of the saying "to sleep under the stars." When we finally got a place to lay our things, we put all of our clothes on the ground to make a pallet for us to sleep on. It was so cold I don't know how I went to sleep. I thought, "What if someone sneaked up on us in the middle of the night? What if something bad happened? Where were we going to use the bathroom?"

Even though I'm scared, I have to do something. Maybe I should drop out of school and get my GED after we get a place. It probably wouldn't be so bad having a full-time job, perhaps two. I'm confused, I don't know what to think. I have to go and find out if there are some family shelters nearby. Hopefully Ms. Gruwell can help me. It seems like hope is the only thing I have to hold on to.

Diary 101

Dear Diary,

I feel like crying and running out of this house and never returning. I have no idea where I am going to get $800! The landlord keeps on calling me and asking me if I have the money for rent. And just today, I received a letter in the mail saying that if I don't send in my car payment within five days my car will get repossessed. Tomorrow it is going to be two months since my cousin was murdered and my parents left the country. Since then, I've been the head of the household, taking care of my younger sister and myself, working my mom's job, baby-sitting to get extra money, cooking, cleaning, doing the laundry, and trying to keep my grades up in school.

Yesterday, my science teacher told me that I'm failing her class and I need to pass the class to graduate. I feel so depressed, all my life I was an A and B student and now I am failing. I've never gotten an F in my twelve years of schooling. My teachers always told me I was an example for the rest of the students. I was always known as one of the most responsible students in my classes and I feel like I'm letting everyone down. I haven't been attending school on a regular basis either. When I do show up, my teachers look at me like they want to lecture me about how irresponsible they think I am. The teachers' disapproving looks really hurt. I feel like they've turned on me. I try to explain to them that I'm going though really bad times, but they don't seem to care. All that matters to them is that I am not doing their work. Most teachers don't want to be bothered with the reasons why. In my yearbook class, I volunteered to do the Freedom Writer page and I did. I did it at home, but when I finished it, it was after midnight. Unfortunately, the day it was due, the collection agency showed up at my door trying to get the money and I didn't make it to school. The following day I showed up at school and my advisor didn't accept my yearbook page. She said it was too late and someone else had to do it for me.

These few months have been the worst of my whole life. My senior year was supposed to be the most fun of all my years, but I guess things happen for a reason. I hate to pour out all my problems to you, diary, but I have nowhere else to turn. After all, I always dreamed of going to college and being someone in life. Now I feel like I only have one alternative—dropping out of high school and getting a full-time job to help my parents with all their payments until they come back home.

After my advisor rejected my yearbook page, it made me want to say "Forget this!" This was just enough to make me want to quit everything I was doing. At the end of the day, out of desperation, I went to talk to Ms. Gruwell and my fellow Freedom Writers. I told them I felt like dying and was going to drop out of high school. I just broke down in tears. They just hugged me and listened. They didn't judge me or put me down like the others. I couldn't believe how understanding they were. They even convinced me to stay in school and offered to help me catch up on my assignments. Despite all this drama, I've decided not to give up. I'll get the money for rent somehow, I'll catch up in my classes and I'm even going to make time to go with everyone on a college tour with Ms. Gruwell. With such a loving "extended" family, I got back the strength to fight for my dreams: to graduate from high school and go to college.

Diary 102

Dear Diary,

Everyone in Ms. G's class is talking about their college application essay that was due today. The essays are supposed to be about a significant event that occurred in our lives. I thought to myself how lucky all the Freedom Writers are to be able to say, "I'm going to college." For me that statement is impossible to say because of one little reason: I am an illegal immigrant.

I wish my essay could have been about the most significant event in my life; how my family immigrated to America. My mother brought her children here to provide them with a better life. My mother kept us away from my drunk and abusive father, she wanted us to have a better future, and the opportunity in life that she never had—to have a successful education. Who would have thought that getting an education would be so tough? The irony is that I was brought here to get an education, yet at the same time, I feel like I am being deprived of an education in the future.

When I read *The Joy Luck Club* by Amy Tan, it made many things clear to me. I could identify the mothers in the book with my mother. Even though I'm not Chinese, I can relate to the feelings the four daughters had toward their mothers. Even though there were cultural differences between them and their mothers, they still appreciated all that they had done for them. Now when I think about this book, it makes me appreciate my mother that much more. If the girls in *The Joy Luck Club* were able to overcome all the obstacles that they were faced with, why can't I overcome mine?

The memory of my journey, or should I say my struggle to America, is buried deep inside of me. I was four years old when I was lifted into the arms of two strange men. They guided me down through the Río Bravo in the dead of night, from Mexico to Texas. The river is called the Río Bravo, meaning the "angry river," because its huge waves are very strong. It has taken the lives of many people who have tried to cross it.

Sometimes, I close my eyes and I can hear the wind blowing against the trees surrounding the river. I remember sitting on a hard tire in the middle of cold, murky water. I was terrified that the river would swallow me alive. All I wanted at that moment was to be in the arms of my mother, who was on another tire behind me with my younger sister. After my brothers, sister, mother, and I made it across the river, we were taken to a man's house. He was a "coyote" and was supposed to help us get through our second obstacle—the border, without getting caught by Immigration. I guess you could say he knew what he was doing because I am here today.

Since I'm an illegal immigrant, the obstacles didn't stop once I got across the border. My freshman year, I thought I was going to kicked out of school because of Proposition 187. Now I can't get a part-time job, or apply to college. On one occasion, I even blamed my mother for all of the troubles that I've had, because I don't have the necessary papers to be in this country. Blaming my mother was the biggest mistake I've ever made. She only wanted what was best for us. If she had known that in this country of "dreams" everybody talked about, things would be harder than they seemed, she wouldn't have brought us here. She would have raised us in our own country to the best of her ability.

To this day I can't decide whether my journey here was taken in vain. I was brought here to have a golden opportunity, but unfortunately, it's not being given to me. I know it won't be easy, but I won't stop until I have gotten what I came here to get: my education. You know, come to think of it, my journey here was for that purpose. I must fulfill my dream of becoming an educator and helping young people like myself.

Diary 103

Growing up, I always assumed I would either drop out of school or get pregnant. So when Ms. G. started talking about college, it was like a foreign language to me. Didn't she realize that girls like me don't go to college? Except for Ms. G., I don't know a single female who's graduated from high school, let alone gone to college. Instead, all the girls my age are already knocked up by some cholo. Like they say, if you're born in the 'hood, you're bound to die in it.

So when Ms. G. kept saying that "I could do anything," "go anywhere," and "be anyone"—even the President, I thought she was crazy. I always thought that the only people who went to college were rich white people. How did she expect me to go to college? After all, I live in the ghetto and my skin is brown.

But Ms. G. kept drilling into my head that it didn't matter where I came from or the color of my skin. She even gave me a book called *Growing Up Chicano* about people who look like me, but made it out of the ghetto.

In class today she made us do a speech about our future goals. I guess some of her madness was rubbing off on me because I found myself thinking about becoming a teacher. I began to think that I could teach young girls like me that they too could "be somebody."

I had planned to tell the class that I wanted to become a teacher, but after hearing what everybody else wanted to be . . . a lawyer, a doctor, an advertiser, I announced that "Someday I'm going to be the first Latina Secretary of Education." Surprisingly, nobody laughed. Instead, they started clapping and cheering. Someone even told me that they could picture me taking over Secretary Riley's job. The more they clapped, the more I began to believe that it was actually possible.

For the first time, I realized that what people say about living in the ghetto and having brown skin doesn't have to apply to me. So when I got home, I wrote this poem.

They Say, I Say

They say I am brown
I say
I am proud.

They say I only know how to cook
I say
I know how to write a book
So
don't judge me by the way I look

They say I am brown
I say
I am proud

They say I'm not the future of this nation
I say
Stop giving me discrimination
Instead
I'm gonna use my education
to help build the human nation.

I can't wait to read it to the class tomorrow.

Diary 104

Dear Diary,

Ms. G made us do an oral report in front of the class about what we wanted to be. Her plan was to get us thinking about our careers in the future. We filled out cards with all kinds of information about our first and second choice of careers. I went through three to four cards, with my first choice changing every time. As much as I'd changed cards, my second choice remained the same.

So the time came when it was finally my turn to stand in front of the class and talk about my future. As soon as I got up there, I started talking about my dream to be a filmmaker and make movies. I went on and on about my dream but then I added, "but realistically I would like to be a . . ." Ms. G automatically butted in when she noticed me disregarding my dream. "What do you mean 'realistically'? Why don't you go for what you love? Follow your dream." Then it sunk in. I can do this. I want to make real films that will impact people in their everyday lives.

I'm in the same position as some as my favorite filmmakers like Richard Rodriguez and Quentin Tarantino, who had people doubt them because of where they came from. Before today, if I told people I wanted to be a filmmaker, they thought I was insane and would suggest a career that was more "realistic" for a poor Latino kid like me. Luckily, Ms. G. and the Freedom Writers don't see being poor and Latino as an obstacle to becoming a film-maker. They believe I can achieve my dream. And with their support, I know I can.

Diary 105

Dear Diary,

Historians say history repeats itself, but in my case I have managed to break the cycle because I'm going to graduate from high school and go to college, an opportunity my parents never had. My father only went up to the second grade because his father, my grandfather, needed help farming and taking care of the cattle. In the two years he spent in elementary school he was not taught to read and write. His teacher instead sent all of the "poor kids" to play outside or to work in the garden. He saw kids like my dad as working hands. This was and still is common in the rural areas of Mexico.

My mother only went up to the sixth grade because it was not the custom for a woman to get an education. Her dreams of becoming an accountant were shattered after my great-grandmother did not let her go to high school. Instead she was sent to sewing classes, so she could become a "true woman" and not suffer when she got married.

Because of their educational experience, my parents were extra hard on me. When I was four years old my parents made me practice writing my name, numbers, and made me memorize the colors. As I grew older they made me read every day, do all my homework, and little by little, this became part of my daily life. While other kids spent their afternoons playing outside, I would be inside my house studying or reading a book.

Now Ms. G. is cracking down on me too. Since the beginning of the year Ms. G has been talking about how to get into college and what different colleges are like. The thought of going to college scared me. But, Ms. G recognized our fears and planned a field trip to visit different colleges. We started our day by going to National University. There we learned about financial aid, college life, and the process of getting into college. After spending half the day at National, we went to visit a small private college and a big university so we could experience how different they were.

After the trip, I decided that I would go to a community college because the campus and the classes are smaller and more manageable than a large university, you get to interact, and have a better relationship with your professors. I am planning to transfer to a big university in two years. For now, I will worry about taking the first step.

I feel like the traveler in Robert Frost's poem "The Road Not Taken": "Two roads diverged in a wood, I took the one less traveled by, and that has made all the difference."

I am the traveler that came upon those two roads. I had a choice: I could take the road that is more traveled by the members of my family and get a job, or I could take the road less traveled and be the first to go to college. I decided to take the road less traveled because I knew it would be better in the long run. I know that my decision to go to college will affect my sisters' decisions and they will not be as afraid as I was of traveling this road.

Diary 106

Dear Diary,

Colin Powell once said, "The best method of overcoming your obstacles is the team method." Ms. Gruwell is an advocate of the team method, which is why she began a mentoring program between her graduate students at National University and the Freedom Writers. Each college student would mentor two Freedom Writers. Ms. Gruwell thought we would all learn from each other. The mentors would share their wisdom that comes with age and experience and we would share our knowledge about diversity to help make them better teachers.

The first night at National University, Freedom Writers were put in pairs and then assigned a mentor. My partner was named Becky and our mentor is Sara. For the rest of the night we talked and got to know each other. Sara was very interested in our goals. Becky wants to be a pathologist and I want to be an aeronautical engineer.

To help me learn more about being an engineer, Sara drove me to the Jet Propulsion Lab in Pasadena. There I met John Matthews. Mr. Matthews is an engineer, and he showed us places that aren't usually seen on the tour. One of those places was a room where model rovers were displayed. These rovers were used to help simulate the rover on Mars. I felt like a kid in a candy store!

After watching all the scientists on television hype about the rover, I actually had a rare opportunity to be so close to all the action. I could almost see myself working with the engineers on the Pathfinder Rover Mission. "This could be me in four years," I thought to myself. I was so awestruck that I couldn't think of anything to ask Mr. Matthews, but Sara was right by my side asking the questions she thought I might want answered. Thank goodness I have a mentor like Sara!

I then had the privilege of being taken to a small room with a few computers that engineers used to map out the location of the rover, using information that the rover sent back! I was allowed to move the rover on the computer, now that it had lost its communication with Earth after over ninety days. Everything was so overwhelming that Mr. Matthews lightened the mood by taking me to an area where enlarged 3-D pictures of Mars were displayed. Mr. Matthews explained how some of the rocks on Mars received their names. For example, a rock named Yogi received its name because the rock resembled a bear.

After seeing the technical and nontechnical sides of the job, I began to picture myself working on a mission like this one. I could now see myself doing this for a living. My dream is slowly becoming a reality, but my next and most important step lies ahead of me . . . in college.

Diary 107

Dear Diary,

Today at Butler Elementary School, the Freedom Writers mentored the kids. I feel so happy right now because we made a difference that will probably change some lives. These children are like lotus plants. A lotus flower doesn't grow in a swimming pool, but grows in a muddy pond. It lives in a dirty environment, but amid the muddy pond lies a beautiful flower emerging from the water. I hope with guidance, these kids can become as beautiful as the lotus flower.

Butler is located by the most dangerous, gang-infested park in Long Beach. In the past there have been shootings, drug dealings, and other illegal activities. On the corner there's a liquor store next to a small plaza. The school building is fenced in. It is a dull, drab, ash gray; it looks very old, even though it was built several years ago. In front of the school are houses with graffiti and barred windows. At night it is unsafe to walk around because of the gang activities near the area. Most of these children live near the school and have witnessed a drive-by shooting by the age of ten.

One of the teachers from Butler read an article about the Freedom Writers in the *Los Angeles Times*. The article was inspiring and many teachers throughout the country responded by inviting us to speak at their schools. They wanted their students to hear our real-life success story.

There we were in an auditorium in front of an audience of

fifty kids. There were kids from every ethnic background; blacks, whites, Hispanics, and Asians. Usually Ms. Gruwell would accompany us, but today we were on our own. Today we were given the torch to carry our message of tolerance and education to these kids. To start off the assembly we presented a video documentary of the Freedom Writers in Washington, D.C. After the video we answered their questions about the trip and gave them the historical background of our name and foundation. Later on we played an icebreaker game. The kids were on one side of the room and we were on the other, and down the center was a white line that divided us. Each one of the Freedom Writers had to go down the line and read a sentence from a piece of paper. Some of the questions asked were, "Who's wearing a green shirt?" or "Does anybody know what they want to do in the future?" If any of the questions applied to them, then they would have to stand on the white line. As we got toward the end there were some personal questions. We asked them, "Has anybody seen someone get shot before?" Almost everyone stepped on the white line. At that moment we decided to share some of our personal experiences with the kids.

One Freedom Writer told about his experience of being in a gang and living on the street. Another person shared his experience of quitting school and realizing that life isn't a fantasy world. When one of the Freedom Writers talked about her friends who had been killed, a little girl in the corner started to cry. I tried to pull her aside to ask her what was wrong, but she started to cry more and more. She stayed in the room to tell her own story of how her friend had gotten killed. After that confession, more of the children started to tell their stories. Some of the stories were similar to what the Freedom Writers had experienced. We talked to the children more and asked them if this was how they wanted to live their lives. There was a simultaneous "No!" By the end of the day, all of the children were declaring that they would become "doctors, lawyers, and teachers!" but they also promised to come back to the community they lived in to fix the problems. We gave them hugs and words of encouragement to hold on to their dreams and goals and to always soar high.

It's amazing. I remember when we got back from Washington, D.C., Ms. G said that kids will think of us as heroes and will want to become Freedom Writers, too. We laughed at Ms. G's analogy, and did not take her seriously. We have come to learn not to doubt Ms. G.

Diary 108

Dear Diary,

I didn't realize writing was so hard. It's very tedious and overwhelming, but satisfying at the same time. The writing assignments I do for Ms. G's class require draft after draft until everything is perfect. I can't begin to imagine how hard Nancy Wride has it when she goes through everything over and over to finish a story. That's what she does, she tries to make her work perfect for the *Los Angeles Times*.

Nancy Wride is a wonderful reporter who just wrote a story about us. It seems as though she really cares about our past and our future. She is a tiny little thing, but she's all heart, and she is very thorough with her work. She makes sure what we say is reported accurately word for word in the newspaper.

When Nancy's story was published, it felt as if the entire world had read it and then decided to call Room 203. We've had to assign a student to act as receptionist in each class period. We've been receiving so much mail from people all across the country, and we have no idea what to do with it all; the donations for our college fund are amazing and quite touching. People have thanked us for the work we have done in educating others and ourselves. Even people in prison wrote to us, telling us that they hope our future is successful, because they were doubtful about their own. Children wrote to us saying they look up to us and adults encouraged us to keep going. I never knew that one article could get such a response. A journalist from the Associated Press called us and wants to do another story. I wonder what the response to that article will be.

Diary 109

Dear Diary,

I've received lots of letters from people in prison before. In fact, all through my childhood I got letters once a week from my dad when he was doing time. I didn't get emotional about them; the letters were just a reminder that my father was still in prison. So it never crossed my mind that a letter from a complete stranger would make me cry.

My mom has always told me that the past always comes back to haunt you. Well, she's right. My past always seems to find me. Only this time it hit me where it hurts the most, my family. I received a letter from a complete stranger, a prisoner from West Virginia who read an article in the newspaper about the Freedom Writers, and who was able to remind me of the values and the rules with which I was raised. He reminded me of the barrier I had to break to be where I am today.

With his letter I was reminded of all the years my father spent in prison. Leonard is only eighteen years old and he is facing life in prison for a crime that he did not commit. The worst part is that he has a little girl that's eight months old. She is going to grow up without a father just like I did. Leonard is innocent, but because of the way he was raised, he is going to stay in prison for the rest of his life. He, like me, was brought up to believe that you don't rat on your homeboys. That's why my father spent so many years in prison—he refused to turn in his friend—and I so many years without a father.

Maybe Leonard's daughter will develop a phobia of birds being locked up in cages. Every time she sees them, she'll be reminded of her father in the cage that is his jail cell. The same image I used to have when I was a little girl. Since he reminds me of my dad, I'm going to write back to him and encourage him to do the right thing. He must tell the Judge he is innocent so he can be a father for his daughter.

In his letter to me, he quoted Anne Frank by saying that he, too, felt "like a bird in a cage and sometimes just wanted to fly away." That is the power of the written word. Leonard didn't know who Anne Frank was but he quoted her, because I had quoted her in the newspaper. The power of the media to reach people in every corner of the world is amazing.

Diary 110

Dear Diary,

I used to think my father was a coward because he left my mom when she was pregnant. Even though my father and mother were never married, I assumed he left my mom because he didn't have a job at the time and he couldn't afford to take care of me. Sometimes I thought he was a bad person who did drugs, drank all the time, and stayed home doing nothing. Most of the people who knew my father put these thoughts in my head.

My father has missed so much of my life, especially the last few years while I've been a Freedom Writer. He missed my trip to Washington, D.C., to meet the Secretary of Education, and I think the biggest thing my father will miss is my graduation in June.

When Ms. G made us read the book *Jesse* by Gary Soto,

about a teenager who had a father but lived with his stepfather, it made me think about my real father and what it would've been like to have him around. After we finished the book, Ms. G made us do an assignment dealing with other cultures where we had to interview fellow Freedom Writers about their family heritage. I was afraid of what I would say when one of the Freedom Writers interviewed me. I didn't want to do the assignment because I grew up not knowing anything about my family's past. My father was never there to teach me about my roots.

I think I am Latino, so I interacted with friends and other classmates who are Latino, so I could learn about some of my past. When I met my friends' fathers I began to wonder about my dad. Do I look like him? Is he tall like me? Do we have similar interests? So I thought about trying to meet my father.

After I learned about my culture, I asked my mom if we could go meet him. For days and days I kept asking her, but she kept saying "No!" Then one day when there was no school, my mom surprised me and asked, "Do you want to go meet your father?" I was shocked! My mom felt it was time that I knew who my father was, since I am getting older. I never thought she would take me to meet him after saying no so many times. I was so happy! I started jumping up and down as if I was a little kid.

On the day that we went to meet him, I was nervous but happy. After all the years of not knowing anything about him, this would be the day I would find out why he left my mom. It took us a while to find where he lives. When we finally found him, my mom approached the door and asked if my dad lived there. The owner of the house, who was my grandmother, told my mom that my dad lived here. I had a big smile on my face because now I knew where my dad lived. My mom and my grandmother started talking and my mom told her why we were there. My grandmother told my mom that my father was very sick and that he did not want to see anyone. I asked her if I could just say "Hi" and then we would leave. She said no. I ran to my mom's car and I cried.

This was supposed to be the time when I finally got to meet him after all these years, and I was hoping we could spend the day together. I got out of the car and went up to her one more time and asked her "Please, I would like to meet my father, I do have the right, you know!" My grandmother still kept saying no. I told my mom I wanted to leave and I went to the car and waited. I was so disappointed that my mom and I drove all the way to his house to see him, but ended up going away not knowing the truth about why he didn't want to see me.

Now I know my father is a coward. A coward because he had someone cover for him. He could not face his own son like a real man. From this experience, I don't want to try to meet him again. Learning from my father's mistakes, I know I am not going to be a coward like him.

Diary 111

Dear Diary,

"Jingle balls, jingle balls, Jingle all the way . . ." That's right! Balls, not bells! Literally speaking. I watched the most popular guys at my school that I once thought were gentlemen, standing in front of these freshmen girls yelling obscenities at them. The random chanting of "Touch my balls, you slut," or "Look at my fucking balls, you stupid bitch!" sprayed the air with the sour stench of beer. After being hazed into the most popular sorority at our school, these innocent girls didn't stay innocent for long.

All of the older girls that are a part of this sorority, including myself, watched the guys as they laughed and yelled at the pledges. I was there watching and wondering how this ritual went and I reminisced back to when I was a freshman pledging for this sorority.

A couple of my senior friends invited me to join this sorority in the fall of my freshman year. I didn't think much of it, so I thought, "Hey, why not?" It would be a good way to meet people and make new friends. My best friend and I happened to be the lucky ones. We got the presidents of the sorority as our "big sisters," which meant that throughout pledging, we escaped a lot of the hazing. Luckily, I never had to do what my fellow pledges did. I didn't even know about some of the pledge nights, and I didn't care.

After every pledge night that I missed, I would hear all the horror stories from the pledges. The pledges, who weren't as fortunate as I was, would always laugh and joke around about what happened to them the night before. "You are so lucky you didn't have to go last night," one of the pledges said. "We had to play a game called Jingle Balls. Well, the most popular senior guys were standing in front of us . . ." Then they went on to tell me how all the guys were screaming at them and telling them what to do. They said the guys had their balls out of their pants and the pledges had to kneel in front of them and sing. They told me how they had to sit on guys' laps, sing to them, and even kiss them. At the time, I thought, "That sucks!" but it didn't affect me because I was at home. But what none of us realized was how demeaning and degrading this actually was. Unfortunately, it was the price we were willing to pay to be popular.

Now that I'm so-called "popular" I stood in shock listening to the young girls sing "Jingle balls, jingle balls, Jingle all the way . . ." I couldn't believe it! I watched the pledges on their knees, inches away from the guys standing in front of them with their balls out of their pants. The freshmen girls were singing this song, in disgust, as the high school participants crowded around to watch. After a couple of minutes, the males were getting frustrated. I didn't know why at first until I heard, "The fucking bitches are closing their eyes. Make them open their eyes!" The senior girls disregarded their comments and continued watching. When they went through this ceremony four years ago, the males were allowed to wipe their balls on the pledges' faces, but this year the girls were spared this. The irony being that the seniors thought they were actually saving the girls from being too exploited. Slowly everyone lost interest and this game ended, but the hazing still continued . . .

As I watched the people participate in hazing, I suddenly realized how unnecessary all of this was. I couldn't understand why these freshmen were putting themselves through this torture just to be "popular." And yet, I was an active member of this sorority and I was allowing all of these awful things to happen to them. Why didn't I say anything? Why didn't I do anything? Being a Freedom Writer, I couldn't understand how I just stood by and let all of this go on. I wish I had spoken up and told them how unnecessary all of this really is. Suddenly, I realized that "popularity" was just a word and has no meaning in real life! At that point, I knew I didn't want to be a part of this group or any group that degraded or humiliated people like that ever again. But I guess popularity always has and always will take its toll on people.

Diary 112

Dear Diary,

It's Christmas time 1997, and I'm really excited about getting together with my dad. Every moment I'm with him, I realize how important he is to me and how lucky I am to have him. I understand that there are people out there who don't even know their fathers, and I cherish every moment spent with him.

This makes me think of the time that I almost lost my dad.

"Sean, what happened? Who is that on the phone?" I couldn't hear what my brother was telling my mom, but right af-

ter he spoke to her and handed her the telephone, she walked to
her room and closed the door behind her.

I was thinking about what could be bothering my mom
when she interrupted my thoughts and slowly began to talk to
me. "Teres, I have to tell you something and when I do, baby
please try to stay calm. The phone call I received was from the
hospital. They called to inform me that your dad has been shot.
He was shot in the head and is now in critical condition. I am so
sorry, baby." I couldn't breathe after she told me this. The pain
that my stomach was feeling when my mom began to tell me had
now traveled up through my chest, into my throat, and took a seat
right in my head. I didn't know what to think, what to do, or what
to say. I thought I was going to die because of the lack of oxygen
my body was receiving. I began to cry so loud that I would have
thought everyone around would have heard me at that moment.
What else was there to do but cry?

While in the elevator, on our way to the sixth floor of the in-
tensive care unit, I thought about how my dad would look. Would
his head be distorted? Where in his head did he get shot? What
would I say to him? Will he know who I am? As I exited the elevator, I walked slowly to the doors where my dad was placed. Walking through seeing so many sick and diseased people made my
stomach hurt. I saw my grandmother and for a split second, I
didn't know whose bed she was at until I saw the person in it. My
dad looked horrible. His head was huge and he had about seven
or eight patches all over his body. He was hooked up to four or
five different machines and had a very thick tubes going down his
throat with more going up his nose. Not knowing what to do or
what to say, I began to cry. I cried so loud and so hard, the nurse
had to come over and asked me to leave. "Dad, wake up. Wake
up, Dad! NOW! You can't go now. Please wake up. We need you.
I love you. NO!" I was forced to leave the room because of my

behavior, and when I did I was taken to a different room, full of chairs, with two huge glass windows. I saw these windows and started to charge at them. If my dad was going to die, why should I stay alive? My life meant nothing without my dad.

My dad had a long, rugged recovery. Coming in and out of the hospital was very scary and frightening for all of us. To this very day my dad has trouble speaking. He is having seizures and doesn't remember things too well, but he is in much better condition than he was in before. The bullet is still in his head simply because it couldn't be removed, which makes me fear that something could go wrong at any time.

I sympathize with people who have lost a parent, or both, for that matter. I understand the fear that overcomes someone when a loved one is lost. He isn't the only one living with the scar, because I am also. Even though I am living with his scar, I sit back every day and remember that it is only a scar, and count my blessings that my dad is still alive.

Diary 113

Dear Diary,

Nothing hurts more than celebrating your mother's birthday on Christmas Eve when she's not around. It's been eight days since my mother passed away. Today, she would have been forty-eight. The holiday season is supposed to be a time of happiness that you can spend with your family, but this year turned out to be tragic. Normally, since Christmas Eve is my mother's birthday, she would get twice as many presents. I told her that this year would be different because she wouldn't have to do anything on her birthday. I was wrong. When she went to the doctor for an appointment, a month earlier, the doctor told her that she had a serious illness and that she had about three months to live, if not less. It turned out to be three weeks.

My mother died from terminal cancer. I knew this was going to happen after I found out she was sick; I just didn't think it would happen so soon. I was hoping she could spend Christmas with the family one last time. Just like last year, we were going to open up a couple of gifts on Christmas Eve and then the rest on Christmas morning. That was our tradition every year. Now all this has changed. This year, we didn't get a tree, there might not be a Christmas dinner, and I don't know what to do with my mother's gifts. What should I do with them? Should I keep them, get rid of them, or give them to my sister? I don't know. I know that while other people are opening their gifts, I'll be packing up my mother's things in boxes.

With my mother dying so suddenly and unexpectedly, I didn't get the chance to talk to her. It's the worse thing that could ever happen because I never had the chance to say good-bye. I have no closure; no "I love you!" Ms. Gruwell once said that "Timing is everything!" and her death couldn't have come at a worse possible time: during my senior year, a week before Christmas, and a few months before graduation.

My mother died on December 16th. That day, I knew something was going to happen because when I got to school, something inside me didn't feel right. When I came home, I noticed something new. She was on a respirator, but for some reason, I thought nothing of it. I thought it was just another piece of her medical equipment she got from the hospital because each week, she got something new. So I went to my room to prepare for our Freedom Writer holiday party that was taking place later that evening. As I was about to leave, my neighbor (who was visiting my mother at the time) yelled my name frantically from the other room. She told me that my mother had just passed away. I couldn't believe her. I had to see for myself. As I walked toward her room, I could hear my sister crying. Then I saw my mother and I froze for a moment. I couldn't do anything but stare. She was lying lifelessly in her bed. I knew deep down that if I had cried at that moment, I would have lost my mind.

Now I have unanswered questions and a lack of resolve. I am instantly an adult. Who's going to be there for me when I need help? I am alone; I don't have a parent living with me, I have no guidance.

Ms. Gruwell and the Freedom Writers want to help me get through my difficult time, but I keep pushing them away. I always tell them "I'm OK!" and "I'm fine . . . don't worry about me!" But the truth is, I'm not okay and I'm nowhere near being fine. I don't know why I won't let anyone in my life. I don't know why I won't ask for help. I was always taught that people don't give without receiving.

Now I need to make the choice to open up and not push people away. Being a Freedom Writer has taught me that people do so much without asking people for anything in return. Maybe they could help me get through my loss, and in return, I could open up to them and accept them as my second family. Then I won't be so alone.

Here's what the newspapers said about us. Some of the headlines:

Cathartic writing course chronicles students' pain

Teens honored for rising above background to become advocates for tolerance

Literature transforms student toughs

Writing to heal

Teen-age 'Freedom Writers' explore their problems through writing.

Teaching tolerance

Escape: Visitor tells students how she eluded Nazis by posing as another family's daughter.

Woman who hid Anne Frank is guest of Wilson High students

Honoring Anne Frank

Holocaust: Woman who hid the girl from Nazis brings her own story to Long Beach.

Truth Stronger Than Friction

Troubled Teens Find Hope Amid Holocaust

Bosnia's "Anne Frank" Zlata tells experiences to Wilson High

Teen Bosnian diarist brings history to life

Visit: Girl sits in on classes at Wilson High School in Long Beach. Students say they can identify with her war-torn childhood.

She Opened Their Eyes and They Opened Up Their Lives

■ **Education:** Erin Gruwell used the Holocaust to teach students about tolerance. Then they filled a book about horrors of their own.

Inspiring the students

Freedom Writers: Teens talk about hard work, goals, pursuing dreams now.

Civil Writers

Teacher, Student Authors Pitch Tolerance, Book in N.Y.

Senior Year
Spring 1998

Entry 8 · Ms. Gruwell

Dear Diary,

We just returned from Christmas vacation, and I just got a call congratulating the Freedom Writers for winning the Spirit of Anne Frank Award. The Anne Frank Center USA honors "those who have followed the courage of their convictions to step forward and actively confront anti-Semitism, racism, prejudice, and bias-related violence in their community." But there's a catch: We have to accept the award in person—next Thursday in New York!

During my college craze in October, I encouraged the students to apply for scholarships. I saw an advertisement in Scholastic's *Scope* magazine promoting the Spirit of Anne Frank scholarship for students who "combat discrimination in their own communities." It sounded too perfect to pass up, so I entered all 150 students as one entity. As I was filling out the application, my competitive side kicked in and I was convinced that my students *had* to win!

The day the Anne Frank Center received our application, a woman named Beatrice called and said she'd been "crying in her coffee all morning" because our application was so amazing. She went on to explain that the application was totally unorthodox because the Center only picks individuals, not groups. She wanted to know if I would resubmit my application and pick only one student as a representative of the group. I said no, we're a package deal. It's all or nothing.

In November, I went to New York and met with people from the center. We were clearly the front-runners to win the award, but the center was in a precarious position—how would we get the Freedom Writers to New York? I said, "Hey if we win, somehow, some way, I'll find a way to get the kids here."

Coincidentally, while I was in New York, the *L.A. Times* article about the Freedom Writers reran in a New York paper. When I got home on Sunday, my answering machine was filled with messages. I don't know how they tracked me down, but all these TV shows, magazines, and newspapers called, wanting to do a story on us. It was all very surreal, since we've lived in virtual anonymity for three years and in one weekend we suddenly had the opportunity to win an award—and now perhaps to appear on a TV show.

I tried to keep all the TV shows at bay until I could process everything. But when Connie Chung called during my third-period class, I knew in my heart that she would be the best person to tell our story for ABC's *Prime Time Live.*

I've got less than ten days to figure out how to get my students to Manhattan, meet Connie Chung, and maintain a sense of normalcy. The more attention we're getting, the more protective I've become. I feel like a mockingbird, dive-bombing anyone who wants to disrupt the dynamics of Room 203. If I feel they have ulterior motives or are the slightest bit disingenuous, I try to shelter the kids from them.

Even though we don't have hotel or plane reservations yet, something tells me that we'll find a way to be on a plane next week. The clothing company GUESS? actually called me after the article ran in the L.A. *Times,* offering to help our cause. Maybe I'll start with them to see if they can help me get some students to New York to accept this prestigious award in person.

Diary 114

Dear Diary,

I just got home from the GUESS? headquarters in L.A. Earlier in the week Ms. G told us that they had decided to sponsor the Freedom Writers and fly forty-five of us to New York City to accept the Spirit of Anne Frank Award in person. I was fortunate enough to be one of the students picked to go.

As soon as I got home, I was so excited. I told my mother that we met the GUESS? staff, and how they surprised us with gifts and gave us a brief history of the company. We also found out why they wanted to sponsor our trip to New York. I learned that the Marciano brothers (who are the founders) are Jewish and their father was a rabbi. During the Holocaust their family had to flee Europe.

I was very enthused and ready for the trip, so I decided to call my father and explain that I was leaving tomorrow. He didn't ask me if I was prepared for New York. He didn't offer to take me shopping or even to give me any money for the trip. Nothing!

After a disappointing conversation with him, I started to think. It's a shame how a company that does not even know me personally is willing to help me me so much. Yet I have a father who knows who I am, where I live, my telephone number, and he acts like I don't exist.

For eighteen years, his off-and-on actions have made an impact in my life. My father always promises me things and never comes through, which has made it hard for Mom at times since she's a single mother. During the holidays, he does bring me gifts, but when I really needed him to provide for me, he would act like he couldn't help me. I only ask him to help me when I have no other choice.

When I do, he procrastinates or tells me to ask my grandmother. It's not that I always want money from him. I want a supportive father figure in my life. Someone to be there in my corner. I always wondered why he never took time out to spend with me.

Receiving GUESS? clothes for our trip reminded me of my childhood and how I needed designer clothes to make me feel accepted by others in school. While everyone was wearing Nike and Cross Colors, I was wearing Pro Wings and swap-meet specials. Wearing them made me feel that I wasn't accepted by anyone. Not even myself! I didn't accept myself because I didn't have the right clothes. Sad, isn't it? Don't get me wrong, I was grateful for the clothes that I had on my back, but I just wanted to have designer clothes as well. Since my father wasn't making me feel wanted at home, I really needed to feel accepted by my peers at school. But in order for me to feel accepted by them I felt like I had to have the same things they did.

Now that I am a part of something like the Freedom Writers, I don't have to try to fit in or to buy my way into acceptance. Material things are no longer a top priority in my life. Of course I want nice things, but I don't feel as if I have to have them to feel complete. It's funny how material things mean so much to adoloescents. The problem is people grow up thinking that material things are what makes them worthwhile. Which is very untrue and causes them to be very shallow. Now as a young adult I've realized that love is more important than material things. Material things can't love you like a father can!

Diary 115

Dear Diary,

It's always been a dream of mine . . . to go to New York, one of those dreams that is always nice to think about, but that you know deep down inside will never come true. New York is where the action is; busy people rushing around on the sidewalk in a hurry to get to work, taxis speeding and honking as they zoom by, the huge billboards and booming lights in Times Square, and famous monuments like the Statue of Liberty and the Empire State Building.

I just got a phone call from Ms. Gruwell saying that I should plan on packing my bags because I was one of the Freedom Writers chosen to represent the group at the Spirit of Anne Frank Award in New York City. In order to be eligible to accept the award, we had to write an essay explaining why we would be good ambassadors for the occasion. We only had one day to write the essay, so it was difficult for me to pinpoint what I wanted to say in so little time.

I tried to act so calm when Ms. Gruwell called me; I didn't want to sound too eager. But the second that I hung up the phone, everything clicked and I realized what she had told me. Her words echoed over and over in my mind: "Pack your bags . . . pack your bags . . . pack your bags!" Wow! I actually get to go to New York! I've got to pack! I need more time! Agh, I need to go to the mall! There are so many things I need to get! I need a heavy jacket! I heard it's really cold in New York now; it's been snowing there a lot lately.

I'm so surprised that I'm one of the forty-five Freedom Writers that was chosen to go to New York. At the beginning of the year, I wasn't too sure if I would even be able to get into the class. The demand was so intense that only a handful of people were selected to join the class senior year; the majority of the students have had Ms. Gruwell since they were freshmen.

Since some of my friends had been in the class for their entire high school career; each week, they had something new to say about the class and about Ms. Gruwell. They only had awesome things to say . . . never anything negative. My friends would tell me that they would meet a famous author one week and, the next, they would be read a really interesting book.

They could tell Ms. Gruwell anything and everything, almost like she was one of the kids. She understood them. Most teachers aren't like that; they give you your homework and then send you on your way, never getting to know you. Some of my former teachers have had four or five favorite students in the class and overlooked the rest entirely. Ms. Gruwell is so much different. She gets to know you . . . she wants to get to know you.

Despite all the positive stuff, I had mixed feelings about getting into the class. I was totally ecstatic about being a part of something that I'd heard so many wonderful things about. But I was completely terrified. For some reason, I thought that everyone in her class would hate me because I joined the group after they'd been together for three years. I didn't want to be an outsider.

I soon learned that there was nothing to worry about. As the year progressed, I have figured out that the others accepted me as one of their own. It's almost as if they've adopted me into their "family" . . . a family that knows no color lines and only sees what lies deep within your heart.

Diary 116

Dear Diary,

The first night in New York was exciting. We arrived and all I could think about was bumping into somebody famous. Our stay was going to last four days. Everyone was anxious to get started with our schedule. The ride from the airport to the Marriott Hotel was absolutely breathtaking. I tried to contain my excitement, but was not able to. "Oh my God!" I said. All of us could not believe how beautiful the skyline looked. New York seems like a magical place where anything can happen.

Ms. Gruwell has been working for Marriott International for many years to support our outings. I thought the New York Marriott Marquis was so luxurious. The view was magnificent; we were right in the middle of Times Square. Taxicabs roamed the streets of New York and lights covered every inch of the city. The Marriott staff made us feel right at home.

When we went to Washington, D.C., Ms. Gruwell let everybody choose his or her own roommates. In Washington, D.C., it was obvious to Ms. Gruwell that everybody chose the people they felt more comfortable with. "New York is going to be different," she explained. This time around, she was going to chose our roommates for us. Ms. Gruwell can never do things the simple way. She always has some big teaching scheme even when we are nowhere near a classroom. The room situation ended up being one of the best lessons of my life.

The first night in our rooms scared me because there were four girls—three being of different races. The only reason I felt uncomfortable was because I have never experienced sharing a room, a bed, or a bathroom with people outside of my race. When I was a little girl I had three best friends who happened to be Chinese, African American, and Caucasian. They had sleepovers all the time, but I never attended any of them because my father did not allow it. He always told me that he had provided a house for me to sleep in, and that I had no business sleeping in someone else's house. I soon began to wonder whether my father was old-fashioned or prejudiced.

I did not know about my father's true feelings until I was fifteen years old. My older sister had a boyfriend who was African American. One night my sister and father had an argument. I heard him say that if she ever married her boyfriend, he would never give her his blessing. It was depressing to hear, but the truth finally came out about him. He was prejudiced, and it hurt.

Now, all of the sudden in New York City, my roommates were ironically African American, Caucasian, and Asian, just like my best friends back in elementary school. I felt very uncomfortable changing in front of them at first, especially sleeping in the same bed with an Asian girl. All I could think about was my father. I woke up the next day tired and restless. We all took showers in the morning and walked down to breakfast on time. There was hardly any communication between us the first evening, but the second night would be different.

After a long day in the city, we finally returned to our hotel rooms. We were hungry and decided to order room service, but we didn't have any idea what we were getting ourselves into. Three hamburgers, two fries, one chicken sandwich, and drinks ended up costing us $43.11! New York was expensive and we could not stop laughing at the cost. After we ate, we starting talking, and before we knew it, it was four o'clock in the morning. The next day we began to share clothes, shoes, toothpaste, and even deodorant.

My experience made me realize my father's beliefs were wrong. I felt a strong bond grow between me and my roommates. I believe that I will never again feel uncomfortable with a person of a different race. When I have my own children someday, the custom I was taught as a child will be broken, because I know it's not right. My children will learn how special it is to bond with another person who looks different but is actually just like them. All these years I knew something was missing in my life, and I am glad that I finally found it—

Diary 117

Days like this create memories worth living for. My day began with tears of happiness after receiving the Spirit of Anne Frank Award, and ended with tears of sadness after watching the play of *The Diary of Anne Frank* on Broadway. The Freedom Writers also had the privilege to meet and bond with prestigious people and some New York City high school students.

At breakfast, the Freedom Writers were exhausted from staying up late the night before, but we were looking forward to receiving the award. Later that day, when we arrived at the ceremony, all eyes were set upon us. The award had never been presented to so many people at one time, and this showed the true symbolism of our cause.

We were the last ones on the program to receive the award. One of the recipients of the award was Gerald Levin, CEO of Time Warner, and we were honored to win an award with a powerful millionaire like Mr. Levin. When it was our turn, a majority of us were already crying. Linda Lavin, the actress who plays Ms. Van Daan in the play, made us cry even more when she said we "made her feel proud to be part of the human race." She read a list of our accomplishments so that the audience could understand what we were all about. When she said "how proud I am standing here looking at you," the rest of the Freedom Writers lost it. We were bawling.

Later in the evening we walked from our hotel rooms to the theater to watch *The Diary of Anne Frank* starring Natalie Portman and Linda Lavin on Broadway. Everyone dressed up with nice dresses, slacks, and ties. The guys looked so handsome, and the girls beautiful as always. After the play Linda Lavin invited us to stay to meet all of the cast members, which made it even more meaningful.

Winning the spirit of Anne Frank Award and seeing the Broadway play made me realize what Anne meant when she wrote in her diary: "I want to go on living even after my death."

Diary 118

Dear Diary,

Tomorrow, we are leaving New York to head home. In the last three days, I have seen places I never dreamed I'd see, and I have met people I never thought I would meet. A month ago I had no idea I would visit New York City! And now, here I am, staying in a *huge* Marriott, right in the middle of Times Square!

I've lost count of all of the places I have been. We have been all over the city, riding the subway and walking. We went to Rockefeller Center for the Spirit of Anne Frank Award ceremony, we toured Scholastic, Inc. We met the CEO, vice president, and some of the editors. We visited the Doubleday publishers. We saw a lot of the famous buildings, like the Chrysler Building, the World Trade Center, the Empire State Building, St. Patrick's Cathedral, Radio City Music Hall, Carnegie Hall . . . Tomorrow, we're going to see the Statue of Liberty!

And the people we've met! Connie Chung, Linda Lavin, Gerald Levin, Peter Maass! I didn't have a lot of experience with famous people before this trip and I didn't know what to expect. These people don't "need" anything from us. Still they took the time to speak to us, sit down and spend time getting to know us, letting us get to know them. They ate with us, laughed with us, cried with us. They gave us memories to last a lifetime.

Lots of people in powerful positions take advantage of those who aren't. Unfortunately, my dad is one of them.

My father is an attorney who's an expert at using the Big Lie to milk the system. When my parents were getting divorced my father decided he wanted my brother, sister, and me to live with him. None of us wanted to be around our father, let alone to live with him. The court appointed a group of psychologists to decide who we should live with. The chief psychologist had a limp handshake, and a weak laugh. This was the stranger who was to determine our fate. He claimed that my mother had brainwashed me into hating my father. The simple truth was that I hated him because he had a ruthless temper.

One weekend when my siblings and I were visiting my father, he flew into a treacherous rage. My father locked my brother in the backyard and left him there without food or water. Finally, at the end of the weekend, the time came for us to go home. My brother was incoherent with fear and hunger. He just wanted my mom to hug him close, while he wept. I told Mom that Dad had not fed him all weekend. I couldn't find the courage to tell her the rest of the story.

Tragically, none of the psychologists understood the pain my father put us through. My brother and sister were ultimately forced to live with him. The court couldn't see my father, with his "Good Old Boy" mask, as the evil person he was. He was willing to do anything to get what he wanted. He even bribed the psychologists for a recommendation in his favor.

My dad hasn't changed over the years. He continues to say hurtful things to me. And even though I don't live with him, he still is verbally abusive, constantly telling me I won't graduate and that I don't deserve to be a Freedom Writer. But *I am* a Freedom Writer and being one is an escape from the rest of my life. This trip and being a Freedom Writer are the most wonderful experiences of my life. Despite everything, I am still graduating in

June and entering college in August. I know that my father will try to stop me. I also know that when I become powerful, I will break the cycle of abuse my father started by doing everything in my power to help, not hurt others.

Diary 119

Dear Diary,

Tonight I met my idol, an ordinary man with an extraordinary gift. In my opinion Peter Maass is more than just a journalist, he's a hero, and living proof of what can be accomplished when good people do something. I remember the first time I read an article by Peter Maass, during my sophomore year right before we met Zlata. The article was in *Vanity Fair*, and it was titled "Ground Zero," based on his encounters in Bosnia. His words were very blunt and vivid. He told tales of hate crimes and atrocities so horrid that I couldn't stop reading. He wrote about men being forced at gun point to rape their daughters. It made me wonder what would have happened to Zlata if she would have stayed in Sarajevo.

I can't believe Ms. G tracked him down and invited him to come meet us at our hotel in New York. I mean, there he was, my idol, right before me. Meeting him was perhaps the most intense moment of my life. I couldn't believe I was in the same room with one of the only journalists who managed to get a one-on-one interview with Slobodan Milosevic.

There was something missing from this puzzle that was supposed to be picture-perfect, though. When he was done talking about his experience in Bosnia, I wanted to know something. Before I knew it I said, "I watch *National Geographic* on television and I don't understand how a journalist can just sit and watch an animal die? Is it the same when you're covering a war? Do you simply sit and watch people die?" The room became silent. Some of the Freedom Writers were shocked by my question, and others seemed to be offended on Peter's behalf. But I just had to know.

After the silence, Peter began to explain how he often has to push his personal views aside and not get involved. He told us that anything he did other than being a journalist could upset some wicked balance. If he got involved in a dangerous situation, he would not only jeopardize the lives of the people he was trying to help, but his life, and the life of his crew as well. If he were to be killed, his death would ensure that there would be more Bosnias. After he was done explaining his role as a war correspondent, I felt content. Now I have an even greater respect for his courage. He wasn't letting evil prevail by watching and doing nothing. By writing about the images he saw in Sarajevo, he was ensuring that no one would deny that ethnic cleansing was taking place, and that thousands of innocent men were being taken to their deaths.

Tonight I met my idol, Peter Maass . . . I can't believe it.

Diary 120

Dear Diary,

. . . And the Pimp of the Year Award goes to . . . our "agent," Carol. She has helped us set foot into a door filled with new opportunities. If not for Carol, we would have never thought that we could actually publish our classroom diary.

Carol got the name "Pimp" because the first time we met her someone asked what an agent's role was, and the answer was . . . she's like a pimp. Not to mention the fact that she was wearing a red jacket, a fedora, a cane, and had a French chauffeur. (Really.) I was somewhat confused when they said that she was like a pimp. My vision of a pimp is someone who is the complete opposite. To me, a pimp is a tall, smooth-talking middle-aged man who uses his slick ways to manipulate the minds of young women—not a five-foot-tall Jewish grandmother!

Carol is smart, witty, and she knows how to play the game. From what Ms. G has told us, she will not take any money from us, and she is helping us out of the kindness of her heart. From what I saw of her today, I trust her, and believe she'll look out for us.

Diary 121

Dear Diary,

The Freedom Writers are finally being published! I am overjoyed the publisher will be Doubleday, since they also published *Anne Frank: The Diary of a Young Girl*, the second most read book in the *world*—topped only by the Bible.

All of this is like a dream come true. I have loved writing since I could remember. When I read my first V. C. Andrews book, *Dawn*, I tried to write my own book. I was impressed with her story. Mine was almost exactly like hers, except for the names of the characters. I got to the thirteenth chapter and decided that I needed to develop my own writing style.

The poet in me evolved from attending political meetings with my stepfather and his comrades. My first poem was titled "The American Dream," a tale of a woman immigrating to this country—"the land of unlimited opportunity"—and barely being able to feed her family. My stepfather was proud of me; he did everything but laminate the poem. I continued to write. Each year my poems became more and more mature. I wonder if it was the same for Toni Morrison and Louise Erdrich—two of my favorite writers.

When I told my stepfather about Doubleday publishing *The Freedom Writers' Diary*, you can imagine his response. "Doubleday!" he said. "They are one of the biggest publishing houses." His friends (all of whom he told as soon as I told him) are thrilled because I will be added to the short, but ever growing list of African American female writers.

It is scary to be launched into the publishing world. I hope this will be the beginning of a new me, after years of simply writing to purge myself of pain. I look forward to sharing my writing, and no longer imagining myself as the "starving artist."

Diary 122

Dear Diary,

As we stood around the room in a group waiting to take a picture with Connie Chung, Ms. Gruwell announced something to us that would change our lives—we had a book deal with one of the most prestigious publishing companies in the world. At that moment, I realized that if we want to be successful, we'll have to work as a team.

I know from my own personal experience working as a team can bring a lot of pressure, especially when you are a star athlete. Which brings me back to my junior year, when we went to the second-round basketball playoffs, and were expected to make it to the championship.

Before the game, I went into my coach's office to talk to her. She said that she knew we could beat the other team—it was just a matter of our going out and doing it. But she warned us not to get too cocky. I guess I was feeling pretty cocky, because her words didn't faze me. After all, we were the league champs, the papers loved us, and college scouts were sending me letters like crazy. As the team captain, things always came easy for me, so I just assumed it came easy for everyone else. I was wrong.

I was getting dressed for the game; I started feeling more pressure than usual. This was just a game, wasn't it? Why was I so nervous? I felt like all the pressure was on *me*—not the team. My hands started to sweat and my stomach felt like it had a million knots in it.

When we arrived at the other school, I felt like my insides were ready to explode! As I talked to my teammates, I looked into their eyes and saw the fear bottled up inside them. As we warmed up, all I kept saying to myself was "We have to win, we came too far and worked too hard not to."

During the jump-ball, my stomach erupted, I tapped the ball, and the crowd went ballistic. At first, we looked liked the mini "Dream Team," but our dream only lasted for about ten minutes—a quick ten minutes! That's when all the pressure came back on me. I felt like it was me against the other team, but in reality, I had four other players on the court with me. In my coach's eyes, I could see her agony—we were losing! It seemed as though she wanted to be on the court with us. At that point in time, I knew it was all up to me, since nobody else wanted to do the job. I felt like I had to save the game. It was all on me.

There were only four minutes left in the fourth quarter, and we were down by five points. All I could see was my team falling apart. It looked like there was no hope. I tried to help my team win the game, but they'd given up. How could they give up? This was the "big game"! We were supposed to win! I was not about to lose!

With two minutes remaining, my coach called a time-out. During the time-out, the looks on my teammate's faces were astonishing. The cocky faces I'd seen earlier were now of despair. I thought to myself, "Is there really hope?" Yes, I had to pull this off. I hate losing. And in front of all these people, especially our fans! I had so much tension and pressure resting on my shoulders. Time was running out—could I save it?

The time ran out. The game was over. And I didn't save it! Even though I scored 24 of our 37 points, I felt like I let my team, my coach, and my fans down. I felt like it was all my fault. I started to cry.

After the game, as, I got dressed, I realized it wasn't my fault—or any one person's, for that matter. It was the whole team's fault. We went into the game thinking it was already ours—and when it wasn't, we fell apart.

This year we are in the play-offs, and we are not going to fall apart. We've put too much into it and now we were playing our best basketball, and we are working as a team. It doesn't all rest on my shoulders.

For our book to work, we have to work as a team. It can't be one star athlete and 149 benchwarmers. Ms. G can coach us, but she can't play for us. Just like the saying "You can lead a horse to water, but you can't make it drink."

Diary 123

Dear Diary,

Today Ms. Gruwell was in New York to meet with our book publisher, and we had a substitute. Whenever a class has a substitute, chaos is imminent. When someone took my chair, I exploded. Maybe it was pent-up frustration, or could it be that not all Freedom Writers are carrying their workload? This can't be possible . . . or could it be?

I am reminded of a story Ms. Gruwell read in her sophomore class, and I recently saw on video. The title was *Animal Farm*. This story revolved around the premise of creating a utopia where everyone is treated fairly and is completely equal. The reality of this is that just like in the book, not everybody works the same or cares the same. It is not an equal environment.

We can safely refer to the Freedom Writers as a Freedom Writer Farm, entirely consisting of what we like to call Boxers and

Mollys. A Boxer is a hardworking person, and a Molly would be the opposite. Molly is the name of one horse in the book *Animal Farm*. She was a white horse who wore ribbons in her hair, and felt as though she didn't have to contribute to the cause. Boxer is the name of another horse in *Animal Farm*. He was a plain horse who was born strong and sturdy. He put his all into everything he did. He worked so hard that he became as stubborn as glue. The reward for being involved with the creation of a book, and being part of something that can change one's life, is right in front of the Mollys, and yet they do not take advantage of it. They expect others to carry the workload for them. The Mollys of the world have to realize one thing, that a Boxer can only do so much.

Our lawyer, our teacher, and Carol are all here to make our book "an all for one, one for all" type of operation. However, the irony is that humans, like the animals in *Animal Farm*, do not work equally. If this is the attitude, then everything is destined for failure.

Ms. Gruwell says that the only way the Freedom Writers could be destroyed is from someone on the inside. That is just it, plain and simple! These people (the Mollys) need to get their act together, or get the hell out!

Diary 124

Dear Diary,

I never thought I would be kicked off the basketball team, especially my senior year! I have devoted four years of hard work to my coach and my team. Four years of early-morning practices, late-night practices, summer league practices, and winter break practices. Who knows how many laps I had to run, how many side aches I've endured? Not to mention all the verbal abuse I've encountered. To sit and watch my teammates win CIF championship from the stands? I don't think so!

I have always been a key player on the team. My teammates worked hard with the help of my attitude and motivation. I knew what it took to get them pumped up. So why was my coach kicking me off the basketball team? On one hand, my attitude was beneficial to fellow teammates. I would whisper things to girls on the team to make them mad, and also to make them play harder. That same attitude was the one my coach didn't like.

Yeah, I have an attitude. Yeah, I'm sarcastic and mouthy; I will be the first to admit it. But what seventeen-year-old isn't? I am me, and I am not about to change my attitude for coach or anyone else. Coach didn't like the looks I made. She always thought I was trying to upset her. She always thought I was talking about her when she turned around. She would say stupid things, and all the time the team started laughing. Coach thought I was making them laugh, but it was her. I should be a bodybuilder, with all the push-ups and suicides she made me do.

I know I have talent, and I have always wanted to play basketball in college, but who is going to notice me sitting in the stands?

All I could think about was, "Why was she doing this to me?" I just can't be a conformist like most of the girls on the team.

For three weeks straight I swallowed my pride and walked into my coach's office to discuss my removal from the team. At times I thought she understood where I was coming from, and would give me another chance.

I never did get back on the team. She gave up on me, and I felt as though life had as well. Basketball was the only consistent thing I had in my life. It was how I relieved the stress of everyday life. I could go to practice and forget everything outside the gym. Basketball was everything to me. I loved it. It was my life.

Though I didn't play for my high school, I went to every game. I watched them win the league championship. I watched them go to CIF, and I watched them go to the championship game I dealt with the pain of not playing and sat in the stands. I wanted my coach to know that she may have given up on me, but I would never give up on my team. My self-esteem and my confidence are low at this point, but I haven't given up. Especially not with my old teammates coming and telling me how the coach would use me as an example. When the girls would practice lazy or not play with intensity she would say "Girls, you should work hard. Joan would work very hard to get back on the team."

The fact that I was not playing basketball anymore opened up the door to another opportunity for me. I was able to become more involved in the activities that I was only giving a quarter of myself to. One of those activities was the Freedom Writers. When I was kicked off the team, the Freedom Writers were asked to come to New York to receive the Spirit of Anne Frank Award and also to tape a segment for *Prime Time Live*. There were only a few of us that were allowed to go. We had an option: either write a paper on why you should go to represent the Freedom Writers, or we didn't have to go. I chose to write. I knew that some of the girls on the basketball team really wanted to go, but due to the fact that there was a game in a couple days they were not permitted to go. That decision was not made by Ms. G but by the coach.

I always believed that for every bad thing comes a good thing. My attitude is better these days. I bite my tongue a lot. I now know that "Attitude is everything!" I'm not perfect, no one is, but I'm trying.

Like Ralph Waldo Emerson said, "To improve is to change, to be perfect is to change often." I am far from perfection, but I'm changing.

Diary 125

Dear Diary,

What the heck just happened? Out of a hundred and fifty Freedom Writers, I have been chosen to speak in front of Barbara Boxer, our senator! Why me? Why would the Freedom Writers want the most outrageous student in the whole group to represent them in front of someone who could change their lives forever? The thing that really trips me out is that it wasn't just Ms. Gruwell who decided that I should be the keynote speaker, it was also the other 149 Freedom Writers who, for some strange reason, believed in me . . .

From the beginning of my freshman year up until this very day, I have had to be the center of attention. My freshman year I had the whole Gothic image going on and thought I was a vampire. I pierced my nipple and my mother nearly had a heart attack. I was on restriction for a month. My sophomore year I told everyone that I was a fairy and with fairy characteristics, I fluttered out of the house without parental consent. I got locks put on my windows and was restricted for a month. My junior year I was totally out of control! I wanted to rebel in any way that I could. I cut class almost every day, I shaved my long blond hair off and dyed the little bit that was left jet black. Unfortunately, I forgot to put Vaseline around my face and I ended up with black dye stains dripping down my face for about two weeks. That took ten years off my mom and I got restricted for another month. If that wasn't enough, I later pierced my tongue and had the very blasé "I don't care about life" attitude. At sixteen and a half my mom found out I was cutting classes with my twenty-one-year-old boyfriend. She threatened to put him in jail and I was on restriction twenty-four hours a day, seven days a week—possibly forever. It didn't matter, those restrictions were getting quite old. I snuck out of the house anyway and almost went to jail myself when I got caught outside past curfew by the cops. What made me realize that I should slow down on my wild streak is when Ms. Gruwell threatened to kick me out of the Freedom Writers. That got my attention—fast! I depended on the Freedom Writers to always be there, and I was tongue-tied when Ms. G got fed up with my crazy antics. I was putting everything else before my education and she would not put up with it.

I still can't see why they chose me to speak to a senator, instead of a Freedom Writer who deserved it. Well, I'm not going to let down the Freedom Writers, Ms. G, and especially not myself.

Diary 126

Dear Diary,

I yelled, "Viva los Freedom Writers!" in front of an audience of university professors at UC–Irvine's "Pursuit of Peace" conference today. I can still hear that "writers" part echoing in my head. I was hoping to hear laughter from the Freedom Writers in the audience because usually they're the only people who laugh at my antics. But the entire crowd burst into laughter. Hysterics, actually. I even got a standing ovation! How odd! This has never happened before. People usually laugh *at* me—never *with* me.

Ironically, the last time I was at UCI, I was in their Child Development Center being treated for ADD when I was eight years old. At the time, I was trying to understand what ADD meant. I had no idea what it was. All I knew was that it was controllable and wouldn't affect my work habits . . . if I take the prescribed drugs. I didn't pay much attention to ADD when I was young. Now I have learned that it could stay with me until I die.

Because of my ADD, I have done some wacky stuff in the past—where unfortunately, there were no standing ovations! I remember a time when I was young and I charged full steam ahead into a Coke machine. "Look out! Here comes the RAGING BULL!" Everyone was looking at me. I was out of control and on a rampage! *Bang! Bang! Clank! Bang!* The banging and the clanking was my head crashing against the soda machine. Next thing I knew, I was lying on the floor while everyone was getting free Cokes. This is not the sanest way to gain popularity! Most people would use quarters to get soda, but I used my head. Not the "normal" thing to do, huh?

The Coke fiasco was a result of not taking my medication. I take Ritalin to control my disorder. It's small, but it packs a punch. It has the power to control me, like a lasso on a horse. The medicine goes into effect thirty minutes after consumption, but if I forget to take it, the effects afterward are unpredictable. For instance, one time I went to my garage and started to hit the punching bag with my head, then my fists. I had no anger or frustration that needed to be released from my body. There was no reason for me to be out there. You could say that I was just killing time.

When I was younger, I was constantly the butt of everybody's jokes. I had to get attention because nobody liked me or tried to be my friend. Now that I'm grown up, I don't have to try so hard, because friends come naturally.

I'm surprised that I could make a highly intelligent audience laugh. A bit of comic relief, so to speak. What's good is that the professors didn't try to alienate me from the rest of the Freedom Writers. Maybe they saw something special in me that my other teachers had never seen before.

Now I can't wait to start college because there are all types of people who are just like me—different and weird. It's good to know that I don't need to change for others but to search for people who will take me as I am—without any strings attached!

Diary 127

Dear Diary,

For the past four years we have been learning about tolerance and how you should accept everyone no matter what. Well, acceptance isn't something that comes naturally for people who have to deal with me. Many people don't accept me when they find out I'm a lesbian.

I realized I was a lesbian just recently, when my best friend told me that she loved me and I returned her love. It's funny to think about how dramatically your life can change in a matter of minutes. After coming to terms with who I am, I had so many questions. I was confused and scared and didn't know what to do. What if people found out about us, would they still accept us or would they turn their backs on us? What would our close friends think when they found out? How would they treat us? Would we still be welcomed in our little social group?

What will our families do when they find out? Will they stick by us? And what if the college we will be going to found out? Would we be kicked out of school because of who we choose to be with? After all, it is a religious school and the by-laws say that homosexuality will not be tolerated.

After all these questions ran through my mind I was even more scared and confused. I couldn't answer half of them, and the other half I already knew the answers to but didn't want to face them. This experience has led me to believe that the people who always tell you that they are your friends, no matter what, are really the first ones to go. When I told a few of my friends that I thought I could trust, they were the ones that had the biggest problem with me. They told me I was going to hell and that they didn't want anything to do with me. The few family members we told had no problem with our sexuality. The hard part will be when the time comes to tell our parents. My mom has told me she would love me no matter what, but when it comes down to it, will she, or will she be like some of my friends and leave?

Diary 128

Dear Diary,

Me? Prom queen? I can't believe this. This has been the best night of my life! I feel like Cinderella. Everyone was so excited for me, but all I could think about doing was calling my mom. For some reason, I knew it would mean more to her than it did to me. It wasn't so much that I wanted to tell her that I had won, but instead I wanted to thank her and dedicate the whole night to her.

"You look so beautiful with that crown on," my mom said. She stayed up all night waiting for me just to see me with my crown, sash and flowers. "You are like a trophy to me." When I saw my mom's tears, it made me realize how much she had sacrificed for me to be here. I never really understood the struggle she went through, but now it all makes sense to me.

My family was very wealthy in my country. Because my parents were so high up in the government, my brothers attended one of the best private schools, and my younger brother and I had our own baby-sitters. My mother owned one of the best beauty salons at the time. She had very important clients who were involved with the government and the entertainment business. My parents were always working, and we were left most of the time with our baby-sitters. Getting good grades was always expected from us, due to the schools that we attended. We had everything there was, except the family bonding.

I was born in Nicaragua, a country where a communist regime was implanted, after Somoza lost his presidency. When communism spread, my family was in danger because their political status changed.

My father, being the accountant of the Somoza family, was automatically considered an enemy. My two older brothers were at a higher risk of being forced to join the army because of their ages. Young boys were taken away from their families to be brainwashed in a communist doctrine and trained for war. We were living a life of darkness and without hope. Something had to be done quickly.

My mother was six months' pregnant when she decided that she would have to be the one to immigrate to the United States with my brothers because my dad was constantly being watched. My mother had to leave everything behind. She gave up her money, her business, the good life that she had, but most important she had to risk leaving her three-year-old daughter and her six-year-old son behind. My mother had to decide whether to risk her life for her two older sons, or stay and watch her sons and husband die in a war. She couldn't take us all with her. First of all it was a lot of money, and second it would have been too obvious if we all had left. My innocent mind couldn't understand what was going on at the time, though. I didn't understand why she was leaving me behind.

My father, brother, and I waited about a year before we reunited with my mother, my two older brothers, and my new baby sister. That was one of the best feelings that I had ever felt in my entire life. Both of my parents knew that coming to the U.S. was going to be really hard. Not only was out lifestyle going to change dramatically, but they also knew they would have to start from scratch. Indeed, when we came to the U.S. we were practically just another number added to America. Although we hadn't been a "real" family before, in that moment it felt as if we could never be apart.

From that time on, we have had several difficulties trying to adapt to a culture that wasn't ours. My parents have worked very hard to still give us the good life that we once had. We don't have all of the materialistic riches we once had, but now we have something much more valuable than we had before.

I never quite knew about my heritage, or the positions that my parents had in the government, until we started talking about my culture in Ms. Gruwell's class. Everything was actually a shock to me when I found out the reason why we had to leave Nicaragua. It was as if it had happened in a past life. Ms. Gruwell encouraged me to talk with my mom about what had happened. When my mom was fixing my hair before I left for the prom, I kept thinking that those two hands that were touching my hair were the very same hands that made her very successful in our country.

I never really appreciated her sacrifice until tonight. I didn't realize that I had a very important person right before my eyes. Not only did this the person risk her life for me and my brothers, but it is also the person who has supported every decision and every accomplishment that I've succeeded at. I would have never had the opportunity to be prom queen if my mom didn't risk her life to bring us here. Now when my mom calls me her "trophy," she means that I am her most valuable possession. That's why I feel that this crown is really for her. She is the real queen.

Diary 129

Dear Diary,

We just won an award from the American Jewish Committee, called the Micah Award, for fighting injustice in our society. On the cover of the invitation, it said, "Whoever saves one life saves the world entire." This statement is, without a doubt, one of the most powerful things I've ever read. Because of silence, the

Nazis tormented six million innocent souls to death. Because of silence, over one million people perished during the reign of terror by the Khmer Rouge. Because of my silence, two innocent little girls were sexually abused. Silence ensures that history repeats itself.

Winning the Micah Award inspired me to make a drastic change in my life and not be silent anymore. After nine years of suffering, I finally decided to take the step I feared most—speaking out. With all the fear stored in my heart, I finally built up the courage to tell my mother that I had been raped. I was only nine years old when I was molested, but it took me another nine years to talk about it. The saddest part of it all is that a person my parents trusted—the baby-sitter—victimized me in my own home. After meeting many survivors of the Holocaust who felt ashamed of what had happened to them and even felt guilty, I can now relate to how painful it must have been to tell their stories. I always felt that what had happened to me was my fault, but I now know that I was just an innocent victim. I'm absolutely not the one who should feel guilty.

Recently, I was at a party with my cousin, when out of nowhere, I asked her if she had ever been sexually abused. I couldn't believe I had asked her that, but the way she allowed her boyfriend to treat her reminded me of how I allowed my boyfriend to treat me. I was afraid of her answer because I didn't want anyone else to go through what I had gone through. When she confessed that her uncle had molested her, I was shocked. That was the same person who had raped me!

Later that night, I couldn't get that quote, "Whoever saves one life saves the world entire," out of my mind. This was my chance to break the silence. If I could save at least one little girl from my ex–baby-sitter, I would be satisfied. I felt sad, but I also felt relieved because I knew that I wasn't the only one. I guess that gave me more confidence to speak out. I decided that I was

going to report him so that he would no longer be able to scar anyone else the way he scarred the lives of my cousin and me.

When I told my cousin that I had decided to report him she
confided that a younger friend of ours had also been molested.
Three young lives were affected forever. I know that there are
probably more. I know that there will be more if I don't do something.

So I have come to the conclusion that I will report him. I
don't want to report him just to get revenge. I just want to stop
this injustice once and for all. Ms. G taught us that "Evil prevails
when good people do nothing." I am a good person. And I refuse
to be a bystander any longer. So I'll kill the problem at the root.
I'll save a life, and in the process, I'll save the world entire.

Diary 130

Dear Diary,

We only have a few weeks before graduation. I sit here looking back at my four years of high school. I've been thinking about
the quote "History repeats itself" that Ms. Gruwell talked about
in class. Over the last four years, she's shown us many situations
of how the past is similar to the present. We've learned how the
Germans tried to eliminate all of the Jews during World War II
and how just recently the Serbians tried to eliminate all of the
Croatians and Muslims in Bosnia during the 1990s. We also have
seen how two diaries written during different time frames, one
being Anne Frank's and the other Zlata Filipovic's, were both
screaming out the hardships of a war. History seemed to repeat itself when Zlata became the modern Anne Frank.

Today, I carry the quote about history with me 24 hours a
day. Nobody in my family has ever gone to college. I thought I
was going to be the first to break this chain in my family. For a
brief moment, this was a reality. I was accepted into a prestigious

technical school. I had also received notification of my financial aid. I saw myself living the college life, all I needed was to graduate from high school.

Then, the unthinkable happened. My dad was diagnosed with a serious health problem and my life had to immediately change. Following this unpredicted situation, I had to decline acceptance to the college I was going to attend. All of the financial aid I once received I had to give back. I'm very sad, disappointed and, at certain times, frustrated by this decision. But, I have no other choice—my family must come first.

Since my dad was the only source of income before he got sick, I've had to become the man of the house. Being the man of the house means no more school for me and certainly more working hours. I also have to cheer up my mom and my younger brother. This is very hard for me because half the time I feel like crying, but I want them to think I'm strong. So most of the time, I hide behind a mask.

Since there is no money coming into our family, my mom had to give up the apartment we rented. She sold my dad's car and most of our furniture to pay the bills my dad left behind when he went back to Mexico. Since he's got a U.S. citizen, he had to go back to Mexico to get a kidney transplant.

Today, I look back and realize how amazing, precious, and powerful both time and life can be. In one second, you can be on top and have everything going your way. The next second, everything goes wrong and you find yourself at the bottom. Weeks before what is supposed to be the happiest time in my life, I find myself struggling just to pay for my graduation cap and gown. I'm not worried about being poor, though. After all, I've been there before. I come from a poor background, so it's nothing new for me. (History does repeat itself, I guess.) I see it as going back to my roots. But, it was nice being on top for a bit.

At this point in my life, I feel like a dry leaf dropping from a branch of a tree, uncertain of its destiny. I'm just here waiting to see where the road of life takes me, and hopefully I'll make the best out of it.

Diary 131

Dear Diary,

Wow! I'm an all-American! Me? I can't believe it! I just got home from signing my letter of intent to play football at a PAC-10 school. A full-ride scholarship to college! Four years ago, I would have never pictured this. Football was just something I did along with drinking, smoking, and drugs. School was something I tried not to do. As I look at my life now, football is one of my top priorities, but just four years ago when I was a freshman, getting high was the only thing that mattered.

Since I was very young, maybe six or seven, I have wanted to be a football player. I played park league and Pop Warner football into junior high. But when new friends introduced me to drugs, I began to lose interest in football. I started drinking and smoking moderately in the summer after sixth grade. I was twelve years old.

My drug experimentation soon spun out of control. I started ditching school, stopped going to football practice, and dropped all my old friends. My new friends were all into drugs, too, so it made it easier to get high. This transformation took two years before full-on addiction. By the time I had reached my freshman year in high school, I was smoking pot three to five times a day. Besides smoking, I was drinking around the clock.

Soon drinking and smoking wasn't good enough. I needed a bigger and better high. I tried everything that I could. I would try or do anything to get high. I had shroomed, tried many uppers and downers. I had tried acid (LSD) time and again.

The worst for me was nitrous. It was the most addictive drug

I did. It was different than anything I had done. When I could not get it, it absolutely took control of me. Nothing else mattered. I had a nitrous oxide tank in my closet so I could get my daily high. I remembered one time when I had run out and it would take a day to get it filled up, but that was too long. I needed to get high right away, so I tried a whip cream bottle, but it did nothing for me. I remembered watching a news special that talked about how people get high with household cleaners. So that's what I decided to do. I went into my closet and found some computer cleaner and it did the trick.

My mom and dad kept after me about my grades and stuff. They wouldn't just let me go my own way. They didn't know how bad my drug and alcohol use had gotten. My mom found out about Ms. Gruwell, who was doing all these cool things with her English class. Since my mom is big on reading, she got me into the class my junior year in hopes that I would "catch" some of Ms. G's excitement.

Ms. G's class, a camp experience with my church, and my parents' continued encouragement helped me to see the mess I was making of my life.

I cannot believe that just a couple of years ago that was my life. Not only was I screwing up my brain but also my relationship with my friends and family. My mind-set was unbelievable. Now getting high is something I don't even think about. I would much rather be with my friends or working out. I am so pumped that people who care about me saw my potential and never gave up.

I have been working hard in school and in the gym to be ready for football at the college level. I went from an F to the second-highest A in all the chemistry classes my senior year. I know I have what it takes and I am going to do what it takes to make my next goal, a college degree and an NFL career!

Diary 132

Dear Diary,

It's amazing how life works in mysterious ways. My day started out with incredible news, but ended in tragic defeat. It went from a huge high to a huge low. In the morning, a major league team picked me in the first round to play professional baseball, and in the evening, my baseball team had to play in the semifinal round of the championship. This game would be my last chance to show how hard our team had worked all year. But it was hard to concentrate on the game because people from the stands were congratulating me about getting drafted. All this attention shoved unwanted pressure in my direction.

Unfortunately, the game ended in disappointment. My team lost, and just like that, my high school baseball career is over. It's hard to take because I've played with these guys since I was in Little League. We've gone through a lot together, including two Little League World Series.

Still, the question of my baseball future is undecided. I have so much pressure to deal with. I can't believe that at seventeen years old I have to make a decision that will dramatically affect the rest of my life. I recently signed a letter of intent to play baseball at a prestigious college. They're offering me a full-ride scholarship. On the one hand, I know college could be one of the greatest times of my life, but on the other, starting my professional baseball career early could help me reach my goals sooner. I understand the demanding schedule of minor league baseball, but I also realize that I might not get a second chance to sign if I go to college.

Ms. Gruwell's been really understanding with this whole process, because her dad played baseball and she understands the game. She said my choice is almost Shakespearean. So the question remains: To sign or not to sign?

Diary 133

Dear Diary,

Last night I got the greatest news of my life! I found out I got accepted to UCLA, the only school I ever wanted to go to. Yet my joy about the situation seemed to upset a few people at school today. When I told people in my AP Government class, a class that is predominantly white, with one black person besides myself and two Latinos, instead of congratulating me, they immediately asked "What's your GPA? What did you get on your SATs?" As if to imply that I didn't deserve my acceptance. One girl simply lost her mind. She began to yell about how unfair it was that I got in and she didn't. It didn't stop there. She began telling other people that I didn't deserve it, and that I only got in because of my race. Which made her look more stupid than she was trying to make me out to be, because everyone knows that Prop 209 went into effect this year and our class was the first to be affected by "anti–Affirmative Action" laws. This I heard from a friend of mine who is not a Freedom Writer.

She told me about many of the other people who were upset because I got in and they didn't, people who don't even know me. She also told me not to worry about those people. I earned my acceptance, and if they don't like it, too bad. I thanked her for comforting me and went on to Ms. G's class. On my way there I ran into one of my former teachers and told her my great news. With a blank face she said, "That's amazing, because you know there's no more Affirmative Action." I thought to myself, "If I were white I would have been congratulated, because getting into college is what I'm supposed to do. If I were Asian her reaction would have been 'Well, of course you got in. You're super smart.' Yet because I'm black or even if I were Latino it's 'amazing' for me to have gotten into a school like UCLA." I couldn't believe she was saying this to me. I may have understood, and even joined her in amazement, if I'd done poorly in her class, but I'd always done really well.

When I got to class and told Ms. G about my acceptance she made this huge announcement in front of the whole class. All the Freedom Writers started cheering and rushed over to hug me. They were so happy I thought they were the ones that got in. My best friend, also a Freedom Writer, wrote it on the chalkboard, so all the Freedom Writers would know. So all throughout the day Freedom Writers were hugging me and saying how proud of me they were. It was crazy, but I loved it. Like any family, the Freedom Writers shared in my joy. My accomplishment was now our accomplishment.

Diary 134

Dear Diary.

Graduation is just around the corner and I feel like this fake smile has molded into my skin. I am torn between happiness and sadness, like something has got a hold of my heart and is pulling it in two different directions. No matter which way I go, it seems like the other side is tugging harder.

My heart stops beating every time I hear someone mention where they are going to school, or how excited they are because they have just been accepted to their first choice in universities. I feel like my heart is tied in a knot that won't let it beat freely. I am enormously happy to see so many Freedom Writers excited and anxious to go off to college, but don't they realize what leaving means? Am I the only one who is afraid of what is about to happen?

I feel so selfish. I wish I could rewind the clock, but I know that's impossible. I can't seem to wash away this feeling of déjà vu as I think of my Freedom Writer family leaving me; this family that has always made me feel at home. I feel like it's almost gone, and I pray that it's not for good.

When I think of the Freedom Writers separating to start their new college life, my heart starts beating fast. Faster and faster, so that I have to put my arms across my chest because it feels like it's going to burst out of my rib cage. As I have my arms across my chest and I feel my heart going a thousand miles an hour inside of me, I start drifting into a memory that I have tried to forget.

I start remembering that night in my horribly ugly pink room. I heard arguing in my parents' bedroom. The sound was unfamiliar to me, since my parents never argued. Maybe they did argue, but not in my presence. Then I heard heavy footsteps. Afraid, I ran out of my room, just in time to crash into my father, who would later only be known as "that man." "What's wrong? What is happening?" I asked. Hoping I would understand if he answered me. "Nothing," he said. "I'm just going to the bathroom. Go back to bed—it's late!"

As I sat in my room, I heard a door slam, the front door. I ran to the bathroom and found it empty. At the tender age of four, I knew my father was gone from my life for good. I don't know why, but I just had a feeling that I'd never see him again. And I haven't.

As I sit here hugging myself, I find myself with the same exact feeling as when I was four. I am dreading the day I will have to let the Freedom Writers go. I don't want to look back one day and think of the Freedom Writers as "them" or "that group." I don't want us to part. As my heartbeat decreases and that knot that encloses my heart loosens, I think that maybe, just maybe, everything will be all right. After all, the Freedom Writers are nothing compared to "that man."

Diary 135

Dear Diary,

It is terrifying to feel your breath slip away and no matter how hard you fight no air can reach your lungs. And worse is the false sense of security you get when you come up, only to be pushed right back under. My grades were at an all-time high, my mother and I were getting along better than we had in years, water polo season had just ended, and I was going to be on varsity swim, I had a job as a lifeguard for the summer, I was to start college in the fall, I was graduating in a couple months, and I had a boyfriend who was good to me. I was gasping for air, waiting for the tidal wave to push my head underwater again, only to let me up for my next gasp of precious air.

Not even four months after James and I started dating, I started feeling an increasing nausea, I knew without a doubt that I was pregnant. I kept hoping I was wrong, but when I went to the doctor, she confirmed what I already knew. Where had I gone wrong? I had been careful not to have unprotected sex; I had learned my lesson last time I had become pregnant. Then I remembered the night the condom broke.

When I had become pregnant at fourteen, it was because of my own irresponsibility. I felt that I had no choice but to have an abortion. Afterward, though, I felt like I had killed part of myself—I began to drown. It took almost three years to recover from the depression that engulfed me after the abortion of my first child. I wanted to take my chances having this baby.

I told James my decision and though he was obviously apprehensive, he was willing to go along with what I wanted to do. He understood what I went through previously, but I was worried that we were not ready. Of course, I was right, but what could I do? I needed to take this risk; hopefully James would stick it out with me.

When I told my mother of my pregnancy, she said that she had guessed as much, because (1) I had not had my period in a month, and (2) when you live in a house full of women, all cycles seem to be the same. She warned me that my decision to have the baby would change my life. There were going to be things I had planned for that would not be possible. My grandmother told me, "You know you can't start college in the fall, and they won't let you be a lifeguard while you're pregnant." At school, I told my swim coach about my pregnancy. She, in turn, told me that she could not let me compete, it was too dangerous for the baby and me. A giant tidal wave of fear washed over me. I would have to put all of my plans on hold. No job as a lifeguard this summer, no starting college in the fall, no more swimming. Instead, I was drowning again.

After feeling sorry for myself for a couple of days, I decided that I had no reason not to fight for air and freedom. True, things were not going exactly as planned, but do they ever? Breathing again, I began to rearrange my future plans: college would start in the spring, and I would take summer classes. I might find a job that paid more than being lifeguard, and I was one of two people picked, out of 150, to represent the Freedom Writers at an award banquet.

As I breathed, truly released from the grasp of all that inhibited me, I began to see how blessed I was. I was graduating with straight As and I still had the support of my friends and family. No longer was I choked with fear. Instead, I breathed deep, exhilarating breaths.

Diary 136

Dear Diary,

"I know why the caged bird sings." For many people this might sound like a normal poem, but to me it's an analogy of my life. I sometimes feel as if I am a bird without wings and the door on my cage is not open. A bird doesn't sing because it's happy, it sings because it's not free. It is the same for me, but instead of singing, I write. I write quotes, poems, and journal stories almost every day so that I can escape reality, because sometimes it's unbearable.

Reality is difficult for me because of where I live. I live in a neighborhood where the sounds of gunshots are my lullaby. The smell of weed lingers in the air and most of the people around drink 40s like it's going out of style. The crime in the area is horrific. People have either been locked up or are on the streets dealing drugs. I live in an area where Asians, Latinos, and African Americans are the majority. But in my neighborhood, I'm the minority. The people here usually refer to me as "White Boy," or "WB," if you will, because I'm the only one in the area.

For as long as I can remember, I have always been the minority. After school, I ran home rather then walking with a friend. Why would I run? Well, I'm sure you'd run too if you were always threatened or beat up because you were different. And walking with friends? I never made any friends because I never got along with anyone. Actually, they didn't get along with me. I would usually get in a fight because I walked in their territory.

It is ironic to see the same people in my neighborhood fight each other all the time. Yet in the classroom, we all get along. Due to our diversity, we were featured on *Prime Time Live* with Connie Chung. In fact, we just heard that Southwest Airlines is going to honor us with the Freedom Fighter Award because they believe in our cause. They're also going to give us a huge scholarship donation to help all of us with our college tuition. Southwest Airlines contacted us a couple days after they watched us on the *Prime Time Live* special.

I hope to become a pilot so I can escape the pressures of my life and rise above all the tension that surrounds me. The irony is I have a fear of heights, which prevented me from flying to Washington, D.C., and New York with the Freedom Writers. Ms. Gruwell is setting up another trip this fall. This trip is to San Antonio, Texas, and Southwest Airlines is going to sponsor this event as well. I hear a couple of Freedom Writers might get to go. I hope I go. If I go, this trip will help me break free from my cage.

Diary 137

Dear Diary,

Ever since Ms. Gruwell announced that the Freedom Writers with the top thirty-five grade point averages would win computers when we graduated, I started getting As and Bs on my report card. I even raised my attendance from mediocre to perfect.

Our senior year finally came and Ms. Gruwell was announcing at the Freedom Writers' "Open-Mic Night" who the lucky recipients of the computers were. "Last but not least the thirty-fifth computer goes to . . ." and Ms. Gruwell turned to me and said my name. I got butterflies in my stomach; I could not believe that out of 150. Freedom Writers I was one of the ones chosen to get a computer. I had hoped to receive a computer, but truthfully, I didn't believe that I would raise my grade point average high enough to win.

In my neighborhood gang violence and drug trafficking play a big role and kids have no one to look up to as an example of hope. Like most of the kids in my neighborhood, I had no one to look up to or emulate until I meet John Tu. He has inspired me to become an entrepreneur and start my own computer company. I want to eradicate the violence that is going on in my neighborhood and give back to my community the way John Tu has given back to me. I want to become the role model that kids in my neighborhood lack and to someday have kids in my neighborhood look up to me the way that I look up to John Tu.

Besides donating computers, John Tu has given a couple of Freedom Writers jobs at his company with benefits and Christmas bonuses. Handouts are like putting a Band-Aid on a bullet wound, but John Tu does not give people handouts, he gives people hope. Not even in my wildest dreams did I think that I would meet a millionaire, especially a millionaire that cared about my well-being. John Tu helps people through education, financial support, and high moral standards. I thank God for sending him into my life. He has given so much to me, and because of his actions I want to give to others, and hopefully someone will follow after me and the cycle of hope will continue.

Diary 138

Dear Diary,

Oh my God, it's gone! I can't believe that my "Someone Special" gold charm is gone. I knew I was wearing it when I went to sleep. At first I panicked. Then I frantically searched through my covers and looked under the bed. Finally I realized that "they" took it. How could they just take it off my body like that? They promised me that they wouldn't steal from me again. I forgave them for pawning my Nintendo, TV, and VCR. But how can I forgive them for stealing the most precious gift that they ever bought me? How could they steal something that meant so much to me? How could they steal from their own child?

Nothing has been the same since my parents started smoking crack. The house is always filled with the smell of stale, burnt cocaine. The odor is left behind in the pores of their skin. So, when I go to give them a hug, the smell still lingers. I hate seeing their eyes all big and bulging, their bodies twitching like a fish out of water.

After watching them hit the pipe like there is no tomorrow, I know that they have a serious problem. Getting high is their daily routine. It is like they don't care if they have children or not. All they really care about is feeding their urge for drugs. Because of their behavior, I sometimes starve. There is never enough food. I try to study and do my homework to keep my mind off of the food shortage, but the sound of my stomach growling doesn't help. I'll go to watch TV and all of a sudden the lights will cut off. I'll go to find the power switch, but it's not the power, it's because my parents didn't pay the utility bill. We are always behind on our car payments and rent, too. I once brought a friend home after school and there was an eviction notice on the door. I was the laughing-stock of the neighborhood.

When I was younger, they would lock me up in the closet because they wanted to get high and beat up on each other. One day it got so bad that my father smashed my mother's head in be-tween the couch and the wall. I became so used to being in the closet that I put snacks in there and a mini TV to watch. All I could hear on the other side was screaming and yelling. I felt as if there were some type of war between my parents and the drugs. Of course the drugs were winning. Being in the closet was my only escape. I felt like Anne Frank in her attic, except the Nazis were roaming outside her attic and my parents were outside the closet door. Even though the closet was my safe haven, I never felt completely comfortable inside it. I always wanted to be set free. I felt as if they were going to forget that I was in there.

I can't believe it's a few days before my graduation and they're still taking! They don't get it. When is it going to stop?

My parents took more than they ever gave. It's like they had no conscience. Unfortunately, there are people who are like my parents, who shamelessly take from others with no remorse, but I will break that cycle and be a giver. I realize that I am like Shel Silverstein's *The Giving Tree* and my parents are stealing all my apples. Soon there will be nothing left for me to give. I know that tomorrow they will be doing it again. They will be getting high from my gold charm. Now I see what is really special to them . . . the drugs instead of me.

Diary 139

Dear Diary,

I can't believe it! I'm actually going to be the first person in my family to graduate!!! I have so much excitement to share with my relatives that I can hardly contain myself. I wish that each one of them would stand in that crowd in six days and scream my name as I cross the stage, switching my tassel from left to right with a diploma in my hand.

But it hurts to say that I don't have their support. In my relatives' eyes, my destiny is like the rest of my cousins'. My parents and I fight to prove to them that I can make it, that I *will* make it. But often I feel like they just want me to fail.

The only true family that God has given me is my loving parents and the supportive Freedom Writers. They have all motivated me to go above and beyond everyone's expectations. They saw potential in me that no one else saw, including myself. Recognizing my potential is what gave me the courage to enter a contest to be Graduation Class Speaker.

While I wrote and revised my speech, the Freedom Writers gave me constructive criticism. While I rehearsed, my parents listened patiently. They gave me hope that I could make it. But deep inside I knew I wasn't going to win. I was terrified when the list that announced the graduation speaker was posted. I couldn't bring myself to look at it. Reading the list would mean finding out whether my dream had come true, or whether it would just be another triumph for those who had no faith in me. I closed my eyes, folded my hands, squeezed them tight, took a deep breath, turned, counted to three, and opened my eyes. I wanted to scream and cry at the same time, but all I could think about was running to the Freedom Writers, and calling my parents because I had won the contest to be Graduation Class Speaker.

It won't be until June 11, 1998, when I can proudly say, "Now my dream of being the first person in my family to graduate is coming true!" I have learned that it doesn't matter if your inspiration in life comes from negative or positive events. The most important thing is to learn and go on. Twenty or thirty years from now, when we have accomplished world peace, when we have succeeded in ending racism and intolerance, the world will remember that the Freedom Writers kept their promise.

Diary 140

Dear Diary,

I can't sleep. Funny though, it's for different reasons than it used to be when I was just a kid strung out on speed. Sleeping under cars. Skin and bones. Well, a lot has happened since then. I'll take you back to freshman year.

"You butt heads with me and you're going to lose."

"Well, we'll just see about that."

Those were the last words spoken between my mom and me before I took off. I was obsessed with independence, but I was yet to realize I was trying to reap the benefits of being in charge of my life without taking any of the responsibilities that came along with that. But can you tell that to a fifteen-year-old boy trying to find his niche in the world? Not me, anyway. So I had enough.

"Learning the hard way" is a nice way to describe the next few years after I walked out that door.

I don't need to go into all of my war stories of the streets. There are too many of those. But here's one moment at the end of ninth grade. It was the last week before summer and I was making the transition from weeks away from home to a month. And not a day could pass without the help of that white powder. I didn't even need it to get high anymore. Now it was just vital to function. My body needed it the same way it needed air. Well, just when I thought I couldn't take another night out there, someone else decided it for me. I wanted to take some sugar cubes laced with LSD and I flipped out. The police ended up taking me into custody for assault under the influence. In one heartbeat things would never be the same.

"I'm going to take your ass, white boy."

The first words spoken to me in jail. Words I will never forget. This was a whole new world, and I didn't have a clue how I got there. By the grace of God, the courts sentenced me to spend the next year in rehab. As much as I hated the system at that time, looking back I realized that they saved me from myself, and saved my life. I was no longer capable of functioning in the outside world. So I went to spend the next year in an adolescent rehab facility.

Rehab was a long, hard road. It was full of laughter, crying, and everything in between. But in those long twelve months I found out some things. I found out who I was. The real me. I didn't need to use drugs to be a happy person. I was worthwhile and special. I realized my family loved me very much and this world could be such a great place to live if you just realized the structure for coexisting with the other five billion inhabitants. I took summer school for two years and actually got a semester ahead. Finally it was time for the real test. To rejoin society as a new and improved person. I left in mid-1996 on outpatient status.

Not an easy feat. The majority of my friends in there didn't last, and out of the few that were still with me when I left even fewer survived as outpatients. Only the strong survived.

I graduated from outpatient after ten months. They sent me off two months early because I worked my program so well. Things were a lot different when I came home. Therapy brought me back together with my family, and we were getting along great. I had my freedom now, and it was because I earned it this time. There was new sense of appreciation for the outside world now. It was such a great feeling to pick what I wanted to eat instead of eating what was put in front of me, but to sit here and say it was easy being back home would be a bold-faced lie. We moved to a new house to give me a fresh start. I went to a new high school, too. I saw a lot of my old friends, but I found we had just grown into different people. That wasn't the life I wanted. There was a lot of pressure at school, so I had to surround myself with good people. And I went to support groups. And that brings us up to now.

Like I said, I can't sleep tonight. Don't get the wrong idea—Kleenex is about the only thing I put near my nose these days. It's because I'm graduating tomorrow. I never thought I would make it, but I did. I'm not just graduating, though. I'm going to get some awards, too. I kept up my overall GPA above a 3.5 all four years. I even got a 4.0 one semester. I also made the honor roll and got an award for taking extra classes. In twelve hours I'll be in my cap and gown getting ready to walk, and the minutes can't go any slower.

Not only is school great, but a lot of other things have taken a turn for the better. I got a job soon after leaving rehab and have been working real hard. Two months ago I got an even better one and I have been working full-time. Just last week I got a brand new truck for graduation. I'm making the payments on it myself. I'm going to need it, because I'm starting college in the fall. Oh yeah, I put a little meat on my bones, got some color in my skin, and those pimples even went away. Yes, I'd definitely say things are looking up. It has been a bumpy ride these last four years, but I found out that there is something better to live for than drugs . . . me.

Diary 141

Dear Diary,

Tomorrow is the big day. I am graduating from high school. I have proven to everyone that I would graduate on time with everyone else in my class. Very few people believed that I would graduate. I proved to the nonbelievers that they were wrong.

From the day I was born I have lived with hardships that most people couldn't even bear. At birth I was not expected to survive past my first birthday. It took four months before doctors diagnosed me with cystic fibrosis. Most CF patients succumb to death before the age of thirty. Here I am eighteen years later knowing that I will graduate tomorrow. I just can't wait to see the look on my mom's face as I walk down the aisle and receive my diploma. My mom is the person who's supported me every step of the way.

The last few years have been truly tough on me and my family. Knowing that my health was deteriorating every day took its toll on my mother. My sophomore year was the first time I had actually struggled in school. I had two sinus surgeries and missed ten of the first twelve weeks of school. I would try to keep up by going to school once a week to pick up work. Some of the Freedom Writers would take time to help me if Ms. G couldn't. They always seem concerned about me. I continued to fall behind in school, so that left only one option: I had to enroll in home school. I thought that would help me and lessen the stress in my life, but it didn't. The tutor that was assigned to me was very intelligent, but not very reliable. I became my own teacher for the next two years. Even though I was in home school, I would still try to participate in Freedom Writer events. I met Zlata and went to the Museum of Tolerance. Due to my fragile health, I couldn't go to Washington, D.C. One thing that was good is that I was always welcomed at school even though I no longer had classes there.

On June 10, 1997, I received my gift of life, a double lung transplant that I have waited over two years for. I was so happy and excited, but not scared that it might be a failure. I have learned to deal with the fact that I might not make it through the transplant. I knew deep down that it would be a piece of cake and I was right. I did not lose any weight and I actually stood an inch taller. I didn't look pale anymore; my skin had turned a healthy pink because of the oxygen flowing through my body. I felt great. In October of that same year I returned to school with my doctor's permission. In April 1998, I received the Most Inspiring Student Award, given to those who have overcome great obstacles and succeeded in life. I also received a $1500 scholarship for college. I was proud of myself for not giving up and proving everyone wrong.

Once I finish telling you this, I plan on trying on my cap and gown and pretending I am walking down the aisle like I will be tomorrow. Yeeessssss!!!!

Diary 142

Dear Diary,

If four years ago someone would have told me that Ms. G was going to last more than a month, I would have laughed straight in their face. She wasn't supposed to make it; *we* weren't supposed to make it. But look at us now, the sure-to-drop-out kids are sure to reach higher education. No one would have thought of the "bad-asses" as high school graduates—as any kind of graduates. Yet, in four years we will be college graduates. Our names will be on the alumni lists of Columbia, Princeton, Stanford, and even Harvard.

Who would have thought of the "at risk" kids making it this far? But we did, even though the educational system desperately tried to hold us down. By labeling us at an early age, they were almost able to affect our school record for life. It wasn't until someone realized that "tracking" is wrong that the stereotyped "at risk" urban high school kids were given their chance. These urban kids, however, were never truly given the chance to prove that if only given the opportunity, we could rise to the occasion; and rise to the occasion we have.

Four years ago, it would have been unimaginable for us, a group of diverse kids, to work together in class discussions, and today, we learn together, we laugh together, we cry together, and we wouldn't have it any other way. We managed to make it past all the superficial labels like "at risk," or "below average"; even the ones that were put on Ms. Gruwell, like "too young and too white." Not only did we make it past all these small obstacles, but also through a wide range of triumphs and tragedies.

I remember back in our freshman year, people still didn't understand the importance of a pen instead of a gun. They were always either getting shot or jumped, sometimes they were even the jumper. We've come a long way since our days of race riots and Proposition 187 walkouts, though. I look back and I can't believe the way we used to be with Ms. G. We used to do anything and everything to try to break her, and just when we thought she was broken, she would prove us wrong.

Then came sophomore year, and everything started to become a little more focused, all the blurry faces became a little clearer, and we all got a little closer. East Siders, Bloods, and Crips turned into Oskar Schindlers. Then came what we still view as our salvation, the "Toast for Change." We took fake champagne and plastic cups, and toasted to a clean slate, a second chance. A second chance to prove everyone's assumptions wrong and a second chance to prove to ourselves that we could make it.

Our junior year was when we truly started to discredit all of the stereotypes. We decided to make a promise to ourselves that education and tolerance were going to be first. We tore into books that were designated for advanced placement classes. Holden's thoughts in *The Catcher in the Rye* were becoming clearer as we were going through the same things in our own lives, and Celie's pain in *The Color Purple* became very familiar. The most important thing that happened that year was during our second semester. It was when we were baptized the Freedom Writers; a name that will forever stay with us, as individuals, and as a movement.

There's only one way to describe this insane, chaotic, crazy, fun, happy senior year: the time of my life. Thanks to the media, our message exploded. We were in the *L.A. Times*, on *Prime Time Live*, and won *a lot* of awards, and every other minute there was a phone call. The message that we had been trying to build for four years affected everyone in its path, like a huge wave.

Looking back, I can't believe that those same unteachable kids who refused to speak to each other are today's Freedom Writers . . . the same Freedom Writers who became a family. I wonder how we're going to follow up on this one. How can you top off four years of the greatest experiences a teenager could have? I don't know, but I'm sure Ms. G has something up her sleeve, she always does. I can't believe we actually made it, we actually have a diploma that says that we can get out of high school. Four years ago that's all we wanted to do, we wanted to get the hell out. If we would have, though, what would have become of that guy that used to carry a gun, or that other white kid that actually turned out to be my friend? I bet if it wasn't for this second family, a lot of people wouldn't even be with their first. Like that girl that ran away with her boyfriend, or that other guy who used to be all into drugs and ended up back with his family. I guess we have more than just great experiences to be thankful for. I'm going to miss all of those things, but what I'm definitely going to miss most is our classroom, Room 203.

That room wasn't only a room, though, it was our attic, our basement, and our "kick-it spot," like Ms. G used to call it. I wonder what it's going to be like turning the lights off for the last time. The room is definitely never going to be the same. It's never going to be witness to brilliant ideas at eleven o'clock at night, or police escorts because someone set off the alarm. It'll probably never see a group of kids who went from little bad-asses to role models, proving everyone, even themselves, wrong. Our lives were shaped in this room and now it will never again be the place of people crying, hugging, hating, commiserating, or tolerating, but who knows? It's always been said that "All good things come to an end," but I'm learning that they don't have to.

Epilogue

I have a dream that . . . little black boys and black girls will be able to join hands with little white boys and white girls and walk together as sisters and brothers.
—MARTIN LUTHER KING, Jr.

While the Freedom Writers were standing on the steps of the Lincoln Memorial in Washington, D.C., in the spring of 1997, something magical occurred. As if on cue, all 150 of them joined hands and began to slowly retrace the same steps Martin Luther King, Jr., walked down over thirty years ago. Many were reciting lines from his "I Have a Dream" speech when someone began to chant, "Freedom Writers have a dream!" Soon everyone joined in, and their voices became one. I watched them in awe, knowing this was the "dream" Martin Luther King had envisioned. I was so proud of them! I felt like they were my kids, and for the first time I understood why moms cry at school plays and graduations.

When they got to the bottom of the steps, someone said, "Ms. G., now that we've followed in the footsteps of the Freedom Riders by coming to Washington, D.C., our next field trip should be Anne Frank's attic. After all, that's where our journey began." Upon hearing this suggestion, several people started to cheer. Unfortunately, I was not one of them. I was still in "mom" mode and I had to deal with the practical matters of our trip, such as making sure no one got lost or got on the wrong Metro. So planning another trip, especially one to Amsterdam, was totally out of the question. I thought if I just ignore them and their allusions of grandeur, then they'll eventually forget about it.

But, the seed was already planted. There was no chance of them "forgetting" about our future field trip. Instead, the idea began to gestate. What began as a simple trip to Anne's secret annex expanded into a tour across the entire European continent. So days after graduation, with diplomas in hand, the wheels were set in motion for our journey abroad. With the same tenacity they used to bring Zlata and the rest of the world to Room 203, they devised a plan that would take us to Europe the following summer.

Since Europe was over a year away, the kids' education took precedence. The Freedom Writers began college in the fall of 1998. Some attended community colleges, while others went to major universities in states that stretched all the way from Massachusetts to Hawaii. Though their college plans led them in different directions, their common goal remained the same. As to be expected, the first semester was overwhelming for some and liberating for others. The Freedom Writers had to learn how to adapt to dorm life, avoid the "freshman fifteen," and perfect the art of cramming. Between juggling part-time jobs and studying for midterms, they could barely keep afloat.

Without the comfort of Room 203, they had to adjust to new environments and their newfound freedom. Initially the transition was difficult. Room 203 wasn't just a classroom, it was home, a safe haven. I realized that in order for them to grow, they had to branch out and explore new ground. Some took off from the gate running, yet others took baby steps through uncharted territory. Regardless of how fast or slow the pace, each Freedom Writer was moving forward in his or her own way.

Not only are they still moving forward, they're pulling others along too. Mothers, fathers, relatives who went astray, and friends who lost their way. The Freedom Writers also hold sacred the memories of those robbed of of a long life. One of those is Anne Frank. So whenever the pressure seemed too intense and it seemed that they were about to fall, they remembered Anne's words.

> . . we have the opportunity to get an education and make something of ourselves. We have many reasons to hope for great happiness, but we have to earn it. And that is something you can't achieve by taking the easy ways out. Earning happiness means doing good and working, not speculating and being lazy.
> —ANNE FRANK, July 6, 1944

Anne's words also inspired me because I too left the safety of Room 203 and said goodbye to Wilson High. I became a "freshman" professor at California State University, Long Beach (CSULB) as a "Distinguished Teacher in Residence." My new position entailed sharing the lessons of the Freedom Writers with future teachers. Ensuring that there will be other 203's and extended families like the Freedom Writers so that our experience will not be the exception but the norm. Being new to CSULB made me emphathetic to the Freedom Writers' insecurities and what they were going through at colleges. But I was committed to be there for them whether they stumbled or succeeded.

As in the past, others joined our journey along the way. Days before the second college semester began, we met the civil rights' activist Harry Belafonte, who was motivated to meet us after seeing the Freedom Writers on television. His tales about Rosa Parks, Martin Luther King, and the Freedom Riders encouraged us to be more than just tourists on our impending trip to Europe. He told us about the training and preparation the Freedom Riders took before they headed across America in a bus. He made us realize that if we were planning to embark on a symbolic trip, that we too must be prepared. Suddenly, our trip took on a new tone. Since Mr. Belafonte was a dedicated supporter of the Freedom Riders, he challenged us not to talk the talk, but to walk the walk.

Mr. Belafonte's words were like a starter gun. We realized that the Freedom Writers was more than just a name. The Freedom Riders, Mr. Belafonte explained, risked their lives to benefit the civil rights of human kind. If we were truly going to emulate the Freedom Riders, then our writing must transcend the walls of Room 203 and our individual plights and become a universal message. Our passion for writing and changing the world was rejuvenated.

With the help of Long Beach City College and Barnes & Noble, we created a college course that would allow us to hone our craft. We found other ways of expression, explored other genres, and shared the podium with other voices. In our writing symposium, entitled "Fighting Intolerance," we solicited help from some of our literary idols. Authors like the incredible journalist Peter Maass and famed Latino poet Jimmy Santiago Baca inspired the students to continue to use writing as a form of empowerment rather than violence. Both Maass and Baca used written expression to embrace their identities and the Freedom Writers followed suit.

The students continued to write and began to forge stronger identities and to create a sense of community and an outlet for expression. The Columbine High School tragedy made the Freedom Writers realize how fortunate they were. But unlike the majority of the country, the Freedom Writers were not quick to vilify Klebold and Harris. Instead, they were empathetic because many of the Freedom Writers felt just as alienated and misunderstood as Klebold and Harris before they found their voices. Before my students found the safety of Room 203, many saw violence as a solution. It wasn't until the students learned about the pain of Anne Frank, Zlata Filipovic, and others—and saw themselves—were we able to come together as a "family" and label ourselves the Freedom Writers. It wasn't until we established a supportive classroom environment in Room 203 and were allowed freedom of expression that the students realized violence is never the answer.

Although I'm not an expert on the subject, I've always felt that all kids yearn to rebel. Understanding this rebellious nature, I encouraged the Freedom Writers to use a pen as a means of revolution. Through their writing, they discovered they shared a common identity, which united them into a community that connected them, not separated them from the world. Unfortunately, the young men in Columbine didn't share a community like the Freedom Writers. Instead, they were alone and on the fringe. Their cries for help fell on deaf ears. And rather than picking up a pen and finding a solution, they turned to guns and bombs instead.

In the wake of the Columbine tragedy, the Freedom Writers felt even more committed to preach peace. They deliberately sought young kids who were slipping through the cracks and had been written off as their personal crusade. By doing so, they created a program called "Celebrating Diversity Through the Arts" geared toward teaching tolerance to kids who have been marginalized by society and don't feel like they fit in. With the help of Barnes & Noble and the Seamless Education partnership in Long Beach, the Freedom Writers began mentoring elementary, junior high, and high school students about the importance of picking up a pen, rather than a weapon, whenever there is a problem; the Freedom Writers have become Ambassadors of Tolerance.

To continue spreading our message, we've planned a trip to Europe that will bring our literary journey full circle. Tragically days before we planned to leave for Europe, one of our beloved Freedom Writers passed away on July 13, 1999. He was planning to be one of the Ambassadors of Tolerance—but due to complications from cystic fibrosis, his body rejected his lung transplant. At the funeral, his brave mother boldly told us that her son accomplished all three of his goals—to get his driver's license, to graduate from high school, and to go to college. (And he did it his way—he got to drive a Mustang, he graduated from high school with honors, and he received a scholarship for college.) The last thing he wanted to do was go to Europe with us. So his mother would know that her son was with us in spirit, the Freedom Writers pledged to light a candle in each city we visit and, upon our return, give her a diary of our trip.

We'll visit a number of symbolic sites such as Auschwitz, Sarajevo (where we'll be reunited with Zlata), and the War Tribunal at the Hague. Then we'll visit Anne's secret attic in Amsterdam to pay homage to the young woman who in the worst possible situation still believed that "in spite of it all, people are really good at heart."

Afterward, we'll return to America on the brink of a new school year and share our new diaries, forge new paths, and continue doing whatever we can to create a peaceful and tolerant world.

Maybe the end of our journey is really just the beginning . . .

The Freedom Writers see this book as the third leg of a relay race. Anne's story inspired Zlata, who has been hailed as the modern-day Anne Frank. Zlata then reciprocated by passing the baton to the Freedom Writers. We hope this book will inspire you to be the fourth leg of the race by encouraging you to pick up a pen and be a catalyst for change.

Acknowledgments

A young man walking down the beach observed an old man picking up starfish that had washed up on the shore. As he got closer, he saw the old man throwing them back into the ocean. He approached the man and asked, "What are you doing?" The old man replied, "If I don't throw the starfish back in the water, they're going to die." "But there must be thousands of beaches and millions of starfish. You can't save them all. Don't you know you'll never make a difference!" The old man reached down and picked up a starfish and simply replied, "I'll make a difference to this one."

As John Tu told us this story, the Freedom Writers felt like the starfish who washed up on the beach. But luckily, people recognized that they needed help. So Erin Gruwell and the Freedom Writers would like to thank all the unsung heroes who were willing to make a difference . . .

STEVE and KAREN GRUWELL—who inspired us to have the courage to follow our convictions and fight the good fight!

CHRIS GRUWELL—who gave so much of himself, so we could give to others

JOHN TU—who is our guardian angel and the epitome of *The Giving Tree*

DON PARRIS—who is our friend, confidant, and a true miracle maker

CAROL SCHILD—who believed our voice should be shared with the world

MARVIN LEVY—who recognized the magnitude of our message

SHARAUD MOORE—who is the original catalyst for change

The Dream Team Moms—who provided us with unconditional love and support (Debbie Mayfield, Mary Rozier, Fran Sandei, Marilyn Tyo, and all the other precious parents and guardians)

ANTHONY SANZIO—who honed our voices into a harmonious choir

GERDA SEIFER, RENEE FIRESTONE, MEL MERLESTEIN, and the many Holocaust survivors who shared their story with us—we promise we'll never forget!

Dr. COHN and KARIN POLACHECK—who gave us the freedom to dream

Wilson High supporters—who were an integral part of our "village" (the names are too numerous to list here, but you know who you are and we'll never forget you)

NANCY WRIDE—who was the first to tell our story to the world

PETER MAASS—who inspired us to fight intolerance through writing

U.S. Secretary of Education RICHARD RILEY—who believes that everyone deserves the right to an education

The Marriott Hotel, International (especially Ms. G's concierge family)—who allowed us to be a classroom without walls at home and abroad!

United Airlines—who gave many of the Freedom Writers "wings" for the first time

Barnes & Noble (especially AMY TERRELL and CARRIE FISHER)—who helped bring literature to life and shared the love of books with our community

GUESS?—who shared the Big Apple and big dreams with us

Southwest Airlines—who gave us the "freedom to fly"

University of California, Irvine—for celebrating diversity

National University—who originated "Freedom Writer Magic"

California State University, Long Beach—who expanded our horizons

Long Beach City College—who replaced Room 203 as our second home (especially Robert Hill, Rick Perez, Frank Gaspar, and Betty Martin)

Scholastic, Inc.—who helped make reading fun

The Museum of Tolerance—who opened our hearts and minds

The Anne Frank Center, U.S.A.—who keep Anne's spirit alive

LINDA LAVIN—who made us "proud to be part of the human race" too

CONNIE CHUNG, TRACY DURNING, and ROBERT CAMPOS—who shared our story with millions

MARLY RUSOFF—who believed in us

JANET HILL—who has become an honorary Freedom Writer

And to all our family members, friends, loyal chaperones, colleagues, college and graduate students, and avid supporters who have helped us along the way.

And also to you, *the reader*—we now pass the baton to you . . .

The Tolerance Education Foundation

In 1997, Erin Gruwell founded The Tolerance Education Foundation in order to obtain tax-deductible contributions to help pay for the college education of The Freedom Writers and to achieve their goal of promoting tolerance. The Foundation maintains the copyright of this book, and 100 percent of all royalties from the sale of *The Freedom Writers Diary* will be used for The Freedom Writers' college tuition.

If you wish to support the work and programs of The Freedom Writers and The Tolerance Education Foundation, please forward your contributions to:

The Tolerance Education Foundation
2029 Century Park East, Suite 4000
Los Angeles, California 90067-3026
Attention: Don Parris

In addition to supporting the Freedom Writers, the Foundation is currently promoting tolerance education to the public and encouraging academic achievement and the pursuit of higher education in disadvantaged communities through mentoring programs in inner-city primary schools, publishing tolerance-themed materials, and advocating tolerance and education through speaking engagements before various civic, education, and conflict-resolution organizations. The Foundation is also developing a tolerance education curriculum for secondary schools which it hopes to complete next year.

The Tolerance Education Foundation is a tax-exempt, nonprofit, public-benefit foundation, organized under the laws of the State of California and tax-exempt under section 501(c)(3) of the Internal Revenue Code.